other titles in the

series

Frommer's

irreverent
guide to
San Francisco

4th Edition

By
Liz Barrett

HUNGRY MINDS, INC.

a disclaimer

Please note that prices fluctuate in the course of time, and travel information changes under the impact of the many factors that influence the travel industry. We therefore suggest that you write or call ahead for confirmation when making your travel plans. Every effort has been made to ensure the accuracy of information throughout this book and the contents of this publication are believed correct at the time of printing. Nevertheless, the publishers cannot accept responsibility for errors or omissions or for changes in details given in this guide or for the consequences of any reliance on the information provided by the same. Assessments of attractions and so forth are based upon the author's own experience and therefore, descriptions given in this guide necessarily contain an element of subjective opinion, which may not reflect the publisher's opinion or dictate a reader's own experience on another occasion. Readers are invited to write to the publisher with ideas, comments, and suggestions for future editions.

Your safety is important to us, however, so we encourage you to stay alert and be aware of your surroundings. Keep a close eye on cameras, purses, and wallets, all favorite targets of thieves and pickpockets.

Published by HUNGRY MINDS, INC.

909 Third Avenue
New York, NY 10022

Copyright © 2002 by Hungry Minds, Inc.

ISBN 0-7645-6565-6
ISSN 1085-4835

Interior design contributed to by Tsang Seymour Design Studio

special sales

For general information on Hungry Minds' products and services please contact our Customer Care Department within the U.S. at 800-762-2974, outside the U.S. at 317-572-3993 or fax 317-572-4002.

For sales inquiries and reseller information, including discounts, premium and bulk quantity sales, and foreign-language translations, please contact our Customer Care Department at 800-434-3422 or fax 317-572-4002.

Manufactured in the United States of America

what's so irreverent?

It's up to you.

You can buy a traditional guidebook with its fluff, its promotional hype, its let's-find-something-nice-to-say-about-everything point of view. Or you can buy an Irreverent guide.

What the Irreverents give you is the lowdown, the inside story. They have nothing to sell but the truth, which includes a balance of good and bad. They praise, they trash, they weigh, and leave the final decisions up to you. No tourist board, no chamber of commerce will ever recommend them.

Our writers are insiders, who feel passionate about the cities they live in, and have strong opinions they want to share with you. They take a special pleasure leading you where other guides fear to tread.

How irreverent are they? One of our authors insisted on writing under a pseudonym. "I couldn't show my face in town again if I used my own name," she told me. "My friends would never speak to me." Such is the price of honesty. She, like you, should know she'll always have a friend at Frommer's.

Warm regards,

Michael Spring

Michael Spring
Publisher

contents

Introduction

San Francisco, so Rudyard Kipling said, "is a mad city inhabited by perfectly insane people whose women are of remarkable beauty." What he didn't say was that half of those women are men.

It is no secret that San Francisco is the gay capital of the world, but that certainly is not the city's only personality. This place thrives on a collective case of multiple personality disorder, which it considers as harmless and amusing as a game of musical chairs. You can nosh Cal-Asian food served by "gender illusionists" (waiters in major drag) at South of Market restaurants, but don't forget that the same neighborhood also bred the city's latest social-ladder casualties: Internet start-ups. The invasion of dot-com Internet nerds and their Marketing Barbie accomplices in the Financial District helped critics keep alive one of San Francisco's favorite traditions—proclaiming the end of the world as we know it. The journalists and the people they complain about are curious and inseparable bedfellows.

That intractable counterpoise is precisely what makes San Francisco such a great city. You can go to the opera in blue jeans or have a hamburger in a tuxedo. Let a snooty doorman in white gloves carry your Louis Vuitton luggage into the Fairmont Hotel on S. Nob Hill or toss it into a rental car and check into the

Phoenix, a funky Tenderloin motel where the late John F. Kennedy Jr. once got double-booked into a room with Blondie star Debbie Harry. Dress in black from head to toe and squish belly-to-butt with the South of Market hordes at Slim's, a nightclub started by musician Boz Scaggs, or dust off your gold sequins and sip champagne at Bimbo's 365, a swank time-warp supper club where you almost expect to see Lucy and Ricky Ricardo at the next table.

Do anything you want, any way you want, and you'll fit right in. Visitors, in fact, tend to feel so simpatico with San Francisco that they can't resist comparing it to their own hometowns. New Yorkers justify their fondness for the city by saying it's not like the rest of the West, that it is the only city with any real culture west of the Mississippi (or west of the Hudson River, for that matter). Europeans insist that San Francisco is much more like Europe than America. Even expatriates of cozy heartland locales have found parts of the city wonderfully familiar.

In truth, San Francisco is not New York at all, nor would it want to be. Aside from the get-rich-quick temptation of the fleeting Internet boom (re-run of the Gold Rush), it is still true that most people don't come here to make the Big Time—they come to have a *good* time. When you sit down at a bar, fellow drinkers may well strike up a conversation with you, but you probably won't be asked where you went to school or who your daddy is. Frankly, nobody gives a damn. It's not that San Franciscans are indifferent or without ambition; it's just that they are focused more on a cordial lifestyle than on an impeccable pedigree. Besides, it wouldn't be polite to ask, and San Franciscans are nothing if not polite. (If you've ever attempted to negotiate the streets of New York in an automobile, you'll be relieved to know that Bay Area drivers do not cruise the city with their horns permanently engaged in the honk mode.)

There are also a few flaws in the whole San-Francisco-is-so-much-like-Europe idea. Being considered the "Paris of the West" is a compliment, one supposes, though it is highly doubtful that all those chain-smoking French existentialists would ever put up with San Francisco's tough no-smoking laws. Nor would the city's vigorous entrepreneurial mentality be likely to appeal to that crowd. It was suggested to one young French waiter, for example, that he was lucky to work at one of the finest restaurants in the city.

"Lucky?" he asked incredulously. "Lucky to have a job?"

"Ah, you are French," the customer replied.

The waiter smiled proudly. "To the bone," he said. Voilà.

North Beach is supposedly the most European-style neighborhood in the city. It's true that you can drop by Figone Hardware for a set of imported bocce balls, but just down the block in Washington Square, Asian senior citizens gather on Sunday mornings for group tai chi across the street from Mario's Bohemian Cigar Store, the cafe where Francis Ford Coppola is rumored to have scribbled the first *Godfather* script.

Half-Italian, half-Asian, North Beach is also the very womb from which thoroughly American beatniks originally sprang. It still houses Lawrence Ferlinghetti's City Lights Bookstore and Vesuvio on opposite sides of Jack Kerouac Street. Farther down the Columbus Avenue umbilical cord, psychedelic shops staffed by the progeny of sixties hippies sell original Fillmore concert posters for a small fortune and blast Richie Havens' albums at decibel levels that left their predecessors among the hearing-impaired. Lyle Tuttle, whose tattoo client list included Janis Joplin, has his own mini-museum in celebration of painted flesh. It's a fitting bookend to a neighborhood bordered on the other extreme by strip joints and peep parlors. You make the call—is this Europe?

It's easy to see how exiles from midwestern college towns find the Haight and the Mission District so familiar and yet still exotic enough to entice them. Both neighborhoods are constantly reinventing themselves, and each new incarnation includes remnants of past lives, like apartments that have collected eccentric odds and ends left behind by a succession of short-term tenants. The corner of Haight and Ashbury now houses a GAP and a Ben & Jerry's ice cream store, but the sidewalk is still a loitering ground for restless, purple-haired teenagers in tie-dyed T-shirts and leather jackets. The smell of illegal smoking materials is so thick, you can take a single deep breath as you walk by and get happy for the rest of the day. Within one 3-block stretch is the Piedmont Boutique, a glamorous gewgaw shop that caters to drag queens and strippers; Cha Cha Cha, a trendy, crowded tapas bar; and Aub Zam Zam, home to a bartender who's known as the martini-making equivalent to Seinfeld's Soup Nazi.

The Mission District is itself another planet, or so it seems. Part Latin Quarter and part New Bohemia, it mixes traditional Mexican and Central American culture with lesbians, beatniks, poets, musicians, hipsters, and assorted pretenders of virtually every urban persuasion. Vivid murals dress the neighborhood like a Diego Rivera fantasy, and virtually every corner taqueria is worth a taste-stop. The sidewalks on Mission Street are trimmed in bright orange-and-blue tiles, and the center of the barrio is lined with palm trees. Yet a block away, cafes, bookstores, restaurants, bars, nightclubs, and a vibrator museum have turned Valencia Street into "the hippest hood in the city," according to Chip Conley, whose lively hotels have lodged everyone from Brenda Lee to Nirvana. Valencia Street has been officially discovered by the upscale restaurant trade and is now referred to as "the Valencia Corridor" by foodies and club-hoppers who leave their cars in guarded lots while they suck down gourmet dinners and signature cocktails. The corridor includes a few tame blocks of Guerrero Street as well, but few big-spenders venture over to Mission Street, where they might be subject to close encounters of the street kind. Happily, however, many of the older bars and cafes still retain a funky, bohemian feel and a solid respect for the Latin culture that has always anchored the neighborhood. While retro-punk cha-cha bands play at the Latin American Club, mariachis stroll a few doors down to play a few tunes and pass the hat at La Rondalla. And by big-city standards, it's still relatively inexpensive. If you skip the hype and take in the entire neighborhood—the wonderful Latin mélange of Mission Street with all its alleys and side streets as well as the Valencia scene—you'll feel like you are taking a vacation to two completely different and equally festive countries at the same time.

Nor is there any place like San Francisco itself—much to the relief of conservative talk-show hosts and other petulant patriots, who often liken the place to Sodom and Gomorrah. Face it, the city has always been a haven for those who are a tad on the weird side by Presbyterian standards. That's why people came out here in the first place—to escape from the oppressive conventions of an East Coast dominated by Old World principles. If San Francisco had a Statue of Liberty, she would beckon, "Send us your odd, your bizarre masses, your tired beatniks, ancient hippies, drag queens, poets, and artists, your temperamental opera singers and recalcitrant pastry chefs, your feminist firebugs and immortal quarterbacks, your transsexual tennis players yearning to breathe free."

Lest you get the idea that the entire city is an alternative universe populated strictly by the cast of *La Cage Aux Folles*, it should be clearly stated for the record that scads of utterly "normal" people reside in San Francisco's many diverse districts, from the breezy bayside Marina to the steep cliffs that bounce crashing waves back out to the Pacific Ocean. The Sunset District seems like a middle-class suburb, cut off from the city's clamor by Twin Peaks and Golden Gate Park. The Marina has a Safeway where singles congregate to squeeze more than the melons, but the neighborhood also houses little old ladies and upwardly mobile lawyers alongside millionaire ballplayers and stately yachtsmen. St. Francis Woods is a hidden, fairy-tale neighborhood with private drives and storybook houses. Pacific Heights—renamed Specific Whites by *Betty and Pansy's Severe Queer Review*—is a beautifully manicured enclave for San Francisco's richest and most powerful elite. (There is a pit bull inside one of those gigantic Victorian mansions, but the discreet sign merely warns: "Chien bizarre." Apparently they expect their burglars to speak French.) The modern apartment complexes in Diamond Heights could be in Pocatello, Idaho, and no one would know the difference, at least not from an architectural standpoint.

The irresistible beauty of San Francisco lies in its innate refusal to fit into any mold, beginning with the very ground upon which it is built—steep hills and wide valleys dropping off suddenly at the edge of the continent. It's cold in the summer and warm in the winter, with sudden and notable exceptions, of course. It has been struck by earthquakes that would have destroyed other cities, but merely brought out the best in San Francisco. During the earthquake that interrupted the 1989 World Series, ordinary citizens jumped out of their cars and directed traffic on the streets. Plumbers, truck drivers, and major-league ballplayers climbed into the rubble with rescue workers to try to save people trapped in the collapsed freeway. There was virtually no violent crime on record for nearly three days—no looting, no rioting, not even any hoarding of supplies. When the World Series resumed three weeks later, 64,000 people—some wearing hard hats just in case—joined hands and sang out with homegrown rock icons Jefferson Starship: "We built this city on rock and roll."

This is it. This is why Tony Bennett left his heart here. This is why no invasion of gold diggers, real estate developers, corporate raiders, marketing bimbos, or Internet entrepreneurs has ever been able to keep San Francisco from shaking things up. Betty and Pansy offer visitors the following advice: "Give yourself one year, and then if you don't like San Francisco, you can leave.... San Francisco is a wonderful place to change your mind. Nobody holds you to yesterday's decision."

San Francisco Neighborhoods

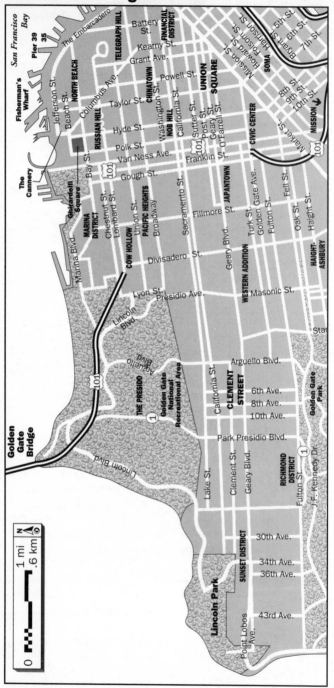

you probably didn't know

Why can't I call it Frisco?... Most locals would sooner hear fingernails scratching across a chalkboard. "Frisco" sounds too much like "Vegas" or some other honky-tonk town. And it certainly doesn't suggest a place where you'd leave your heart. In any case, it's best to skip the indelicate nickname unless you're willing to accept dirty looks, slow service, and tables by the ladies' room.

Where are the best "vertigo views" of the city?... Standing at the top of some of San Francisco's steeper hills, you may feel a tad trembly and nauseous, like Jimmy Stewart in the Hitchcock film *Vertigo*. To heighten this sensation, take a glass-elevator ride, available for free in several of San Francisco's elegant hotels. The Westin Saint Francis (Union Square) has the fastest elevator in the city, ascending at 1,000 feet per minute. If you can keep your eyelids up and your stomach down, you'll catch panoramic views of downtown, Coit Tower, and the bay. Around the corner from the Saint Francis, the Pan-Pacific Hotel has a 17-story ride, but the cars face the inside of the building, looking onto an atrium that's one of the most elegant in the city. Five blocks away, at the Fairmont Hotel, take the skylift, which zips up at about 100 feet per minute to the Fairmont Crown, 24 floors up, for a leisurely view of Chinatown, Nob Hill, the Financial District, Coit Tower, and the South Bay Peninsula. Beware of small weddings in the elevators—they can seriously cramp your view. Down at the Embarcadero Center, the Hyatt Regency's glass lifts take you to a revolving restaurant/cocktail lounge that offers a great 360-degree view and ridiculously overpriced drinks that invariably include the requisite hardware—paper umbrellas, swizzle sticks, pineapple chunks, you name it. Mel Brooks panicked on the way up here in *High Anxiety*.

Where's the best place to hop on a cable car?... When you catch a ride on a cable car—yes, they do look like the ones in the Rice-A-Roni commercials and, yes, they do ring those bells—don't wait in line with all the tourists at the turnaround stops at the beginning and end of the lines. Walk a few blocks up the line (follow the tracks) and do as the locals do: Hop on when the car stops, hang on to a pole, and have your $2 ready to hand to the driver. He'll take coins or bills, and can even make change. Warning: Don't stand too close behind the gripman or his elbow might smash into your chest when he yanks the brake to stop the car. And whatever you do, don't call them "trolleys"—you'll be branded instantly as a tourist.

How does one dress for fog al fresco?... From June through August—summertime in the rest of the Western world—fog tends to engulf San Francisco from late afternoon until noon the next day. If you're a baseball fan, you'll soon discover one of the main reasons the Giants built a new ballpark: The old Candlestick Park was so chilly at night that it was equipped with one of the bay's 26 foghorns. Locals don't mind the mist, though. They dress in layers and immerse themselves in it. To make the most of a glorious foggy morning, sip a frothy cappuccino in a cozy neighborhood cafe until around noon, when the fog burns off and you can tie your sweater around your waist, roll up your shirtsleeves, and soak up the sun for a few hours. And no matter what the weather seems like during the day, always bring a coat or jacket along at night.

What is meant by "basic black and perils?"... If you're going to wear black, stay out of the ocean. Sure, thousands of local surfers have worn black wetsuits and survived, but others have found Pacific sharks to be most unreasonable—their vision isn't all that great and they have a fierce appetite for sea lions, a hazardous combination for unidentified black-coated mammals floating around at suppertime. Fortunately wetsuits come in a variety of bright colors. (While you're out catching a few waves, be on the lookout for rock star Chris Isaak. He loves to surf near his home at Ocean Beach.)

Where is the best place to park?... That's a question that baffles even the meter maids. A quick survey of the neighborhoods will reveal cars parked and double-parked on sidewalks, in front of fire hydrants, in towaway zones, on corners, in crosswalks and, in the Mission District, right down the middle of the street. The math is fairly simple: There are around 800,000 cars in the city on any given day, and fewer than 600,000 parking spaces. That adds up to 2.3 million parking tickets a year and unknown numbers of drivers still circling the city in a frenzy. There are a number of downtown, city-run garages that won't require you to mortgage your house in order to park for a few hours, but in most private garages you can pay up to $22.50 for a Friday night in popular areas like North Beach. Avoid the whole mess by using public transportation or cabs.

What's the best way to avoid getting mugged?... Muggers aren't a huge problem in San Francisco, but the city does have its share of pickpockets and other assorted scam artists who tend to prey on tourists. Standard rules of urban behavior apply: Don't keep your wallet in your rear pants pocket, and leave your purse at home or keep your hand on it all the time, especially when you're riding a bus (a favorite haunt of pickpockets). The favorite crime in San Francisco, actually, seems to be car vandalism, especially in the Mission District, where a car parked on the street for more than an hour has at least a 50/50 chance of getting its mirrors smashed. Solution: Take a cab.

What do you say to San Francisco cabbies?... The most-often-asked cabbie question in San Francisco is, "How often do you have to change your brakes?" Believe me, you don't want to know. One driver estimates that the hills are so treacherous he has to change his brakes once a week, while another casually replies, "Oh, a couple times a year, maybe." Either way, most drivers would rather avoid the topic, especially if you're headed down a grade that would rival K–2. Best advice: Forget the slope; look out the side windows instead.

What's the best-kept secret about the symphony?... If you're a morning person who loves classical music, the San Francisco Symphony's open rehearsals have a seat with your name written on it. Before most major concerts, the symphony allows the public to attend open rehearsals at Davies Hall ($15 for unreserved seats, $25 for reserved). Aside from the bargain-basement price, many afficionados prefer these rehearsals over the concerts because the music is equally exquisite and you get to see and hear the performers and conductors in a relaxed, intimate circumstance. Most open rehearsals take place on Wednesday mornings, 9am to noon. They sell out quickly for popular international performers, so call the Symphony box office (tel 415/864–6000) for a schedule while you are still planning your trip, and order tickets in advance if possible.

Who was the last emperor?... Around the time of the Gold Rush, San Francisco was home to California's first monarch—not a butterfly or a drag queen, but a self-coronated royal who called himself Emperor Norton. (He also claimed to be Protector of Mexico.) Still commemorated 150 years later by a town that cherishes its oddballs, the emperor was a real, live person who got invited to all the society affairs, whether or not the city fathers believed his claims to sovereignty. The old codger had a lot of influence on local customs and was apparently quite an impressive figurehead. A century later he gained further immortality, portrayed as a close friend who visited Ben Cartwright at the Ponderosa on the television show *Bonanza*. Even Hoss tipped his hat to His Majesty. If that's not proof of authenticity, what is?

How long has San Francisco been a gay capital?... During the Gold Rush, "real" women were so scarce that desperate prospectors gladly paid them 3 ounces of gold for a single kiss. No one knows how many enterprising impostors whipped out the Max Factor and painted their lips red to pick up a few extra nuggets back then, but mascara and falsies have rarely seen a sales slump since. According to Trevor Hailey, the city's premier gay historian, the city became an established haven for the gay lifestyle with the Gold Rush; then the opening of the Panama Canal led countless gay sailors to this port, followed by an influx of gay artists and entertainers during the Bohemian era of the twenties and thirties. World War II brought thousands of Pacific-bound military men—yes, queers in the armed forces, whether General Eisenhower knew it or not—many of whom returned after the war to live where their forbidden lifestyle was accepted. By the time the Beat movement bongoed to the cultural forefront in the fifties, there was no question that North Beach was the place for gay "angry young men" to proclaim their sexuality to the world. Every major city has a gay subculture, but there's nothing "sub" about San Francisco's gay culture—it is definitely a predominant and celebrated part of life here.

What does the future hold?... A *Chronicle* poll once estimated that 37 percent of Bay Area residents believe in astrology; virtually every newspaper in the city features a horoscope. The most eccentric is definitely Rob Brezsny's "Free Will Astrology" in *SF Weekly*. He might tell you that you are "the pothole in the road to ruin" or suggest that you "stroll on over to the oldest tree you know and pour a bottle of mountain spring water over your head while confessing all your sins."

What hotel actually launders money?... For years, every coin tendered at the Westin Saint Francis Hotel was put through a sort of tumbler that sterilized all those copper pennies and buffalo nickels so that no customer ever received a coin in change unless it could pass the white-glove test. The famous money-laundering service was temporarily suspended in 1994 when the career coin washer retired, but the hotel's human resources department was finally able, after a search that lasted more than two years, to find a suitable replacement. The rich and famous can rest easy once again, knowing that the Saint Francis is no longer handing off dirty money.

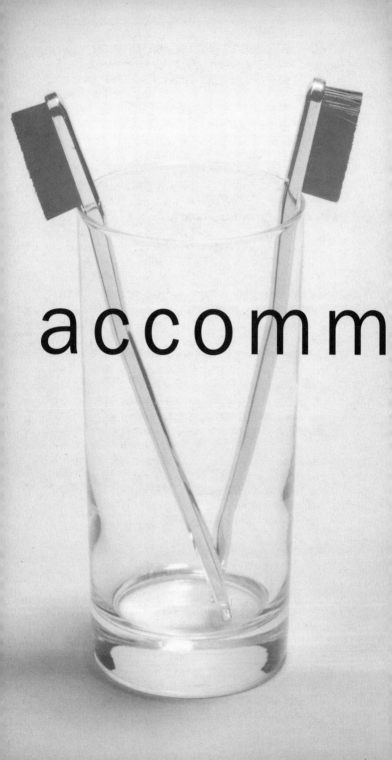

accomm

1
odations

San Francisco's
famous palace
hotels—which are
as extravagantly
grand as grande
dames get—are
finally getting a

run for their money. Sure, the conventional rich may still lust after a night in the **Fairmont Hotel**'s $8,000-a-night penthouse suite: a three-bedroom, four-bath mini-mansion with a grand piano, two-story circular library with 4,000 volumes, dining room that seats 50, 24-karat gold fixtures, lapis lazuli fireplace, secret passages, and its own vault. If that price tag's too high, the Fairmont's standard rooms, at $189 and up, are still less expensive than equivalent accommodations in New York, London, Paris, or Tokyo. But these days, stylish celebrities—who can afford any room in the city—are shying away from the huge luxury hotels in favor of more chic, intimate boutique hotels that cater to a younger, more hip crowd.

San Francisco's thriving boutique hotel scene is no longer dominated by one or two hospitality czars—dozens of lavish, quirky, extravagant, cozy, and eccentric little hotels dot the entire city—but always near the center of that universe is Chip Conley, whose Joie de Vivre hotels set the "fun" standard in the city. Conley, an anarchistic entrepreneur who is a cross between Conrad Hilton and the Mad Hatter, got his start by following the example of Bill Kimpton, a reclamation genius who started the trend of buying fading older properties and transforming them into chic, contemporary cash cows. The Kimpton Group includes the **Hotel Triton**, an abstract expressionist's dream come true; the **Hotel Monaco**, a renovated 1910 Beaux Arts jewel; the four-star **Prescott Hotel**, where guests get preferred seating at Wolfgang Puck's famous Postrio restaurant; and more than a dozen others. Kimpton hotels tend to be a bit more traditional (and occasionally more expensive) than Joie de Vivre's lodgings, but both focus on creature comforts and meticulously designed interiors. Conley's lodgings usually focus on a theme, from the film-freak **Hotel Bijou** and the literary **Hotel Rex** to the **Phoenix**, a psychedelic-tropical inner-city motel full of urban artistes, and the understated but ultra-luxurious **Nob Hill Lambourne**, a spa for health-conscious business travelers. One of the newer groups is Personality Hotels on Union Square, a quintet of downtown boutique hotels that includes the **Hotel Metropolis,** a modernistic beauty that invites guests to "indulge yourself in the wilder side of the color wheel," and **Hotel Diva,** a high-style tribute to stainless steel that was voted Best Hotel Design by *Interiors* magazine.

Do you see a pattern here? Cutting-edge interiors and A-list celebrities? Maybe. But there's a difference between a celebrity and a legend, and many of the latter prefer the city's more traditional charms: quiet Victorian elegance and the assurance of privacy, if not anonymity. When Luciano Pavarotti is in town, he stays at the elegant **Inn at the Opera**, a tiny, 25-foot-wide Victorian hotel where services include complimentary clothes-pressing upon arrival. Before his death in 1996, legendary poet Allen Ginsberg chose North Beach's **Hotel Bohème**, a hip, cozy, and surprisingly quiet haven on Columbus Avenue, just footsteps away from Lawrence Ferlinghetti's City Lights Bookstore.

If you're not particularly impressed with the notion of sleeping in the same digs as the rich and famous—or the in-debt and infamous—try one of the city's scores of neighborhood inns. Europeans love the **San Remo Hotel**, a three-story Italianate Victorian hidden away on a quiet residential block of North Beach; rooms start at $55 and the funky little rooftop cottage/penthouse with its own sundeck and panoramic view is one of the best deals in San Francisco at $150 a night.

If your budget is tighter than Dwight Yoakam's jeans, you'll be happy to know that for $30 to $45 a night, you can stay in a private single room at the fully staffed **Central YMCA**, where you'll get free continental breakfast in the morning along with the use of the health club and pool. Or go super-cheap ($22.50 a night) and dorm up at the **San Francisco International Hostel (AYH)** in Fort Mason, at the edge of the posh bayfront Marina District with close-up views of the Golden Gate Bridge.

Finally, in the "Too Weird to Leave Out" category, there once was an RV Park out by China Basin, in the heart of what had become the city's Multimedia Gulch (Internet start-up heaven). But the site of a hundred Winnebagos lined up in neat little rows is now an ordinary parking lot for the Giants' new ballpark. Sayonara, canasta games. Happy trails, car caravans. The search for a new RV Park continues, though, and you can get the latest updates by leaving your e-mail address at the official website (www.sfrvpark.com).

Winning the Reservations Game

First of all, forget the major hotels if you're planning to visit in October. Some of them are almost fully booked 20 years in advance during the best-of-all-possible months in San Francisco. Don't let that discourage you, though—the most interesting places to stay, and the best deals, are rarely on the standard list of hotels that appears on travel agents' computer screens, so they don't get booked up so fast. San Francisco's tourist season is year-round, and hotel prices tend to remain fairly fixed throughout the year (a few increase between April and October). You're not likely to find an off-season bargain

ACCOMMODATIONS | INTRODUCTION

rate around town, but many hotels, especially in tourist areas, offer special rates for multiple-night stays, including meals or discounts on tours and attractions. The deals range from downright pathetic—a free bottle of cheap, plastic-corked champagne and a Gray Line tour through Fisherman's Wharf—to the sumptuous, whimsical "romance packages" offered by the Joie de Vivre hotels. Not all packages are advertised, so always ask the hotel or reservation agent if any are available. If you want to stick to the tourist-and-conventioneer circuit, last-minute vacancies and special discounts may be available through reservation services, most of which are computerized so they know exactly which rooms are available. Many of these services offer 50% to 75% discounts. The San Francisco Convention and Visitors Bureau offers booking services to the general public through **Leisure Reservation Services** (888/782–9673) or online, where you can look at maps of the city and choose your hotel by neighborhood, style, and price (www.sfvisitor.org). Or try **Hotel-Locators.com** (tel 800/576–0003; www.hotellocators.com), **San Francisco Reservations** (tel 800/677–1550; www.hotelres.com), **Central Reservations** (tel 800/950–0232), or **hoteldiscount.com** (tel 800/364-0801; www.180096hotel.com). **Bed and Breakfast California** (tel 800/872–4500; www.bbintl.com) can set you up in one of more than a hundred private homes, guest houses, and inns in San Francisco, starting at $70 a night (two-night minimum). The service's specialty is matching travelers' tastes and budgets to their ideal place to stay, including a few private sublets of entire homes or apartments. Owner and director Sharene Klein has moved to the Los Angeles area, but her San Francisco staff can still tell you every detail about the properties, often down to the kinds of flowers that bloom in the garden. Tell them what kind of vacation you hope to have, and they'll put you in a place that's likely to make it happen. **American Property Exchange** (tel 800/747–7784) rents luxury apartments, condos, houses, and flats at $95 to $330 (off-peak season) a night; **Best of Nob Hill–United Commercial Brokers** (tel 800/634–2567, 408/279–3747 outside California) handles five Queen Anne Victorian apartments with antique furniture, fireplaces, and laundry service at weekly or monthly rates of $125 to $200 per night (minimum two-night stay). Many other short-term options are outlined in a free visitors kit available through the San Francisco Convention and Visitors Bureau (tel 415/974–6900; www.sfvisitor.org). There are hundreds of travel reservation sites on the Internet. Here are just a few that offer secure reservations and online discounts: San Francisco Hotels advertises rates that start under $125 (www.hotelssf.com); Hotelreservations.com offers discounts on almost every hotel in the city (www.hotelreservation.com); San Francisco Hotel Reservations features discount rates and the ability to search by specific criteria (www.hotelres.com/sfr/); San Francisco RoomFinders has discounted rates at more than 200 hotels in the Bay Area and the ability to search by type of discount (www.stayinsanfrancisco.com).

Is There a Right Address?

Most of San Francisco's major hotels are located near the **Financial District**, **Union Square**, and **Fisherman's Wharf**. The prime spots for world-class luxury hotels are Union Square and **Nob Hill**. Many small boutique hotels and inns are mixed among the giant towers and palaces, so don't let the touristy neighborhoods scare you off completely—the location is extremely convenient for walking and for access to public transportation. But—and it's a big "but"—you can easily be sucked into paying much more money than is necessary for a room with about as much personality as a Holiday Inn in Elko, Nevada. The thing is, you can't tell from the outside of the building or from the lobby what the rooms will be like. Take the **Westin Saint Francis,** for instance. It's an absolute architectural gem, one of the loveliest hotel exteriors in the Western world, but the rooms in the tower are, well, ordinary. Sure, they're spacious and full of expensive furniture, but they still look like they were punched out of the Universal School of Semi-Fancy Hotel Room Design. The whole thing is just too pastel. The views are spectacular, but you can see those from the elevator, and that's free.

Neither **Chinatown** nor **Japantown** is loaded with hotels, but each is worth considering. Japantown isn't as interesting as it sounds—mostly a bunch of import shops and food stands in a bland mall—but it does have the most authentic Japanese hotel in the city, the **Radisson Miyako Hotel,** with Zen gardens, futon beds, and in-room Shiatsu massage. Chinatown is crammed with everything: Crammed with people, crammed with fish, crammed with aromas, exotic vegetables, cheap souvenirs, great little food joints—but it's not crammed with good places to spend the night. You can, however, find a bed in Chinatown for $30 to $40 if you don't mind sharing a bath. You can't beat the location—near downtown, Union Square, North Beach, and (perish the thought) Fisherman's Wharf.

The **Tenderloin**—usually called by other names to divert attention from its reputation as a seedy, whore- and drug-infested pit—is a block-by-block situation. One minute you can be strolling past a series of charming little shops and neighborhood taverns, and the next you're being accosted by panhandlers in front of a dilapidated homeless shelter or a shop that sells pornography. On the outer edges of the neighborhood are some of the trendiest and most fun lodgings and restaurants in town, but as a rule, the hotels there are either faded old beauties or transient houses best left to guests who rent them by the hour for "professional" purposes.

Van Ness Avenue is a long stretch of wide road that cuts through the city from the Mission District to the Marina. Inch for inch, it probably has more chain hotels and motels in its immediate vicinity than any other street in the city. It also has some beautifully restored old standards, like the **Hotel Richelieu**, that are close to entertainment and theater but mercifully removed from the constant stream of pickpockets and hustlers that usually hovers around theater districts. (The Great American Music Hall puts up most of its performing artists at the Richelieu.) The **Civic Center** area houses the ballet, the opera, the symphony, the main library, and City Hall, along with a number of wonderful boutique hotels such as the **Inn at the Opera** and the **Abigail Hotel**, and exquisite restaurants that are virtually empty after 8:30pm (San Franciscans tend to eat before performances). Right smack in the middle of it all is a plaza that has been a constant battle site for San Francisco's intractable homeless problem. Some people find that repugnant; others chalk it up as an integral part of urban life. Public transportation is a breeze in this centrally located neighborhood, and parking is very reasonable at the Civic Center garage. (Don't go to any of the private garages near the Opera House or you may have to call home for extra cash.) **Lombard Street**, in Cow Hollow, is Motel Row, dotted with low-profile, inexpensive places to stay. The area stretches from the Marina to the Presidio and there are plenty of scenic vistas and worthwhile seafood houses that are local favorites. Be warned, though: Some motels are a bit marginal and the neighborhood is far from the thick of the city's most interesting activities. The more residential neighborhoods—the Mission District, the Haight, the Castro, Noe Valley, the Sunset, Pacific Heights—have very few hotels, but many boast wonderful inns and bed-and-breakfast houses. The **Mission District** is a lot of fun, but has few places to stay; the **Castro**, the **Haight**, and **Pacific Heights** have several beautiful Victorian bed-and-breakfast options; **Noe Valley** is charming but primarily residential. Some of the inns in the outer reaches of the **Sunset District** offer the city's most gorgeous views of the Pacific Ocean.

The Lowdown

Irresistible deals... Europeans and seasoned travelers love the **San Remo Hotel**, an Italianate Victorian jewel hidden away in a residential area of North Beach. The owners haven't raised their rates for so long that single rooms start at $55 (not a misprint), but the San Remo would be a delight at twice that price. Rooms are small but very cozy, with antique beds and armoires, old-fashioned ceiling fans, and lace-curtained windows that open wide to let in the cool bay breeze and the sounds of San Francisco's lively Italian neighborhood. The atmosphere is friendly, casual, and totally international; bathrooms are shared, and even the water faucets are European—cold on the left, hot on the right. The **Phoenix** is the exact opposite of the San Remo. It is New World all the way, as American as Velveeta and Andy Warhol. Of all the city's trendy lodgings, the Phoenix is still the favorite place for deviant minds to meet. Rock stars and other eccentric celebrities flock to this inner-city motel next door to **Backflip**, an aquatic cocktail lounge and restaurant that is a scene in its own right (see Dining and Cafes).

Grande dames worth considering... The **Fairmont Hotel** is synonymous with elegant San Francisco. It sits on top of Nob Hill as though it alone were holding court over the city (never mind that the Mark Hopkins is virtually across the street). The lobby is fancy, fancy, fancy and the velvet furniture is red, red, red, matching the bellhops' uniforms. The overall effect is about a half-degree shy of gaudy, but its history keeps it within the grande dame category.

The **Mark Hopkins International** is a traditional favorite of San Franciscans who appreciate elegance but don't have much of a stomach for gewgaw. It shares the top of the hill with the Fairmont but is notably less glitzy. It's a few dollars more expensive than its Nob Hill neighbor, too, but by the time you're paying that much, who's counting? The rooms themselves are plush but not extraordinary, unless you want to spring for a large suite with a Jacuzzi and a view. The best part about the hotel is probably the famous Top of the Mark cocktail lounge, still one of the most romantic spots in the city and worth a visit even if you have no intention of staying at the hotel. It has been the traditional spot to kiss a lover good-bye since World War II. (Rumor has it that gay sailors started the tradition, or at least spread it around.) The charm of the **Westin Saint Francis** in Union Square decreased considerably when the huge tower was added on, but it still has a few merits. The front entrance, used for the television series *Hotel*, remains magnificent, and stepping into the lobby will probably always make you feel like a million bucks (or at least like you might need a million bucks to stay there very long). Afternoon high tea (or a wee martini) in the Compass Rose is a civilized antidote to the shopping frenzy just outside the door. If you're intent on staying at the Saint Francis, get a room in the older part of the hotel—the tower rooms are big and boring, except for their views, and they cost more.

Petite dames worth more than they charge... For the elegance of a grand luxe hotel at as little as half the price, try the **Donatello Hotel** in Union Square or the **Hotel Monaco** at the edge of the Theater District. The lavish, French-inspired Donatello is worth a visit just to see the massive stained-glass dome above the valet parking area in front of the hotel. Inside, the rooms are all oversized, with tall ceilings and huge windows; many of the successful young corporate types who frequent the Donatello happily shell out an extra $100 for rooms that open onto private, landscaped terraces. The guests at the Monaco are less buttoned-down than at the Donatello, but they definitely have a few dollars to throw around. Inside this majestic Beaux Arts landmark, the interior design is more sensual than stately—perfect for the theater crowd. A huge staircase sweeps from the lobby to the living room, and the grand chimney piece in the "pre-function" room rises to a mural of floating hot-air balloons that recalls the Wizard of Oz. The bellmen in full wooden-soldier regalia outside the four-star **Prescott Hotel** in Union Square are your first clue that this is a scaled-down version of the Fairmont. Your second clue is that the room rates are about the same, give or take a few dollars. But at the Prescott, you get more personalized service, and the penthouse suite only costs $1,200 a night (a fifth of the cost of the Fairmont's penthouse).

In search of painted ladies... San Francisco has no shortage of painted ladies, be they the brazen drag queen variety or the architectural type (Victorian mansions with elaborate paint jobs). Both are found all over town, but the most famous Victorian painted ladies—the ones featured in tourism posters—are on Alamo Square, virtually across the street from the **Archbishop's Mansion**, built in 1904 and now a bed-and-breakfast inn. The huge rooms and ornate decor almost make you dizzy, but "Texans love it," says the owner. "It makes them feel like they're in their own castle for a few nights." Most of the rooms have massive canopy beds, working fireplaces, and deep, old-fashioned bathtubs, and all guests are served breakfast in bed.

The **Red Victorian Bed and Breakfast Inn** in Haight-Ashbury, known affectionately as the Red Vic, is much more eccentric and much less expensive than the Archbishop's Mansion. It's right on Haight Street, and fits in perfectly, if that gives you a clue. Group meditation is offered every morning in the back of the lobby, and owner Sami Sunchild has left her artistic thumbprint all over the inn with poem-paintings that make you want to run right out and stick a flower in your hair. Each room has its own theme, from a Persian-esque suite that looks like a good home for a hookah-smoking caterpillar to a quasi-psychedelic "LOVE" wall that certainly does not appear to be conducive to sleep. Most rooms have shared baths; be ready for aquariums and other surprises when you go to wash your face. The Red Vic is fun, it's clean, and it's definitely only in San Francisco.

In the same neighborhood but not at all in the same vein is the **Victorian Inn on the Park**, at Lyon and Fell streets, just across the Panhandle from the house where Janis Joplin once lived. The inn, a registered historic landmark, is a restored Queen Anne Victorian that caters to a more subdued clientele than the Red Vic, though it, too, had its heyday as a hippie crash pad. It's an outstanding example of Victorian architecture, and the antique furnishings are comfortable and elegant, despite signs of wear.

When money is no object... The Clift Hotel (formerly the Four Seasons Clift) is just about flawless—a sophisticated, elegant retreat for aristocrats and other travelers with plenty of credit. The large, high-ceilinged rooms have been meticulously restored to their prime 1915 state, with all the modern luxuries added for dessert. The topper is the wonderful Redwood Room, a lusciously romantic art-deco piano bar. The **Stouffer Renaissance Stanford Court Hotel,** called simply Stanford Court by residents and taxi drivers, is a historic landmark up on Nob Hill that once housed the founder of Stanford University. Many San Franciscans consider this the ultimate landmark hotel, but some people find it a bit difficult to feel at home in a lobby with a stained-glass dome— church pews and a confessional wouldn't seem out of place. The antiques-filled rooms are more welcoming, but if they seem too stuffy, you can always head for the bathroom, where you can flick on the television, pick up the telephone, and lather yourself into a froth with French-milled soap.

When money's too tight to mention... There are lots of safe and comfortable, sometimes even scenic, cheap lodgings in San Francisco, starting as low as $10 a day per person. The best bets for quality and location are the YMCA, hostels, budget Chinatown hotels, and Lombard Street motels. The **Central YMCA** offers private rooms with shared baths from $29 a night, including free coffee and muffins in the morning and use of the health-club facilities and pool. There are also rooms with private baths and a dormitory (for AYH and IYH members only). The hotel is staffed 24 hours a day and there are no curfews; men and women are welcome.

Chinatown's bargains include the **Grant Plaza**, a clean, comfortable hotel that many locals recommend to budget-minded visitors. All rooms have a private bath, and start at $65. Another Chinatown cheap sleep is the **Hotel Astoria**, where rooms with shared bath start at $56 (some rooms also have private bath). Hostels include the **AYH Hostel at Union Square**, a relatively new facility for AYH members only, starting at $22 per night; the **Green Tortoise Guest House**, a North Beach spot that offers a choice of a hostel with dorm facilities ($19 to $22) or private rooms with shared bath (starting at $48 to $56); the **Inter-Club/Globe Hostel**, South of Market, with dorm and private rooms, a cafe, bar, and sundeck, starting at $21 a night; and the **San Francisco International Hostel (AYH)** at Fort Mason, a dormitory with a view of the Golden Gate Bridge, starting at $22.50.

Lavender lodgings... Gay tourists are to San Francisco what Disney World pilgrims are to Orlando: big business. So surrender, Dorothy. If the idea of seeing men holding hands is a problem for you, you're in the wrong town, especially during Gay Pride festivities in June. Basically, all San Francisco hotels are gay-friendly; many mainstream hotels offer Gay Pride discounts (ask when you call for reservations), and some lodgings cater almost entirely to a gay clientele. Many others that are not gay per se are staffed by a predominantly gay workforce, which can turn an otherwise ordinary little spot into a really fun place for gay travelers to stay. For the inside word, one of the best and funniest sources is *Betty & Pansy's Severe Queer Review*, available from A Different Light Bookstore (tel 415/431-0891, 800/343–4002). Recommended gay-oriented lodgings include all the Joie de Vivre hotels; the European-style **Edwardian San Francisco Hotel** (Market and Gough streets); and two other converted Victorians—the **24 Henry Guesthouse** in the Castro District and the Italianate **Inn San Francisco** on South Van Ness Avenue. Lesbian options include tiny **Bock's Bed and Breakfast**, on Willard Street near Golden Gate Park, but the owners "took a break" for a few months near the end of 2001 (offering only monthly sublets), so be sure to call in advance.

Turning Japanese... Despite its corporate ownership, the **Radisson Miyako Hotel** is authentic Japanese, even when that means bowing to Americans by including Western-style beds and bathrooms in many rooms. It's so much like an elegant Tokyo hotel, in fact, that most Japanese tourists opt for other, more "American" hotels for their vacations in San Francisco. Here's what's best about the Miyako: The rates (much lower than Hotel Nikko in Union Square), the in-room Shiatsu massages, the deep Japanese soak tubs, the *tokonama* (alcoves for displaying Japanese art), the down comforters on the futon beds, the Zen gardens inside the traditional rooms, and the sunlight filtered through *Shoji* (rice paper) screens on every window. Don't confuse this hotel with the Best Western Miyako Inn nearby. The latter is just another cheesy chain motel that happens to be on the border of Japantown—don't waste your time or money there. One of the most Japanese things about **Hotel Nikko** (Union Square) is the astronomical fee it charges for a Japanese suite—$1,500 per night. If that doesn't make you feel like you're in Tokyo, nothing will. These suites are not that much better than the Miyako's, but they do feature a better view of the city and an in-room well for performing the traditional tea ceremony. For Asiaphiles on a budget, the hotel has special packages starting at $199 (few are available, so reserve well in advance).

For writers in search of a muse... New York has the Algonquin, and San Francisco has Union Square's **Hotel Rex**. Hang around the lobby or browse in the antiquarian bookstore and you're likely to rub shoulders with celebrated writers and artists gathered for roundtables, book signings, readings, or just socializing. Playwright Wallace Shawn is among the many regular guests here. The walls of the lobby and guest rooms are a gallery of local artists' work, which owner Chip Conley bought to infuse cash into the art community after the 1989 quake. Be sure to look at the ceramic lamps: Each one was individually thrown by a local potter and each shade is hand-painted. Even the most ardent literary historians haven't been able to establish with certainty the exact number or locations of all the places Allen Ginsberg is rumored to have slept in his beatnik heyday; in his last years, however, he is known to have stayed at **Hotel Bohème**, a tasty little North Beach hotel just a short walk from Lawrence Ferlinghetti's City Lights Bookstore. A small black awning on Columbus Avenue is the only clue to the hotel's whereabouts (next to Stella Bakery and Cafe); you have to push the doorbell to get buzzed in to the narrow staircase that leads up to the foyer and reception desk. Do it, even if you don't stay there, just to see the foyer's dozens of museum-quality photographs of North Beach in the forties and fifties, including many shots of legendary poets and musicians holding forth in local joints. It'll take a lot more money to spend a night at the **Sheraton Palace Hotel**, originally known as just the Palace, where only writers who had already become rich and famous could afford to stay. Oscar Wilde stayed here when he was 27 years old and apparently drank the entire town under the table; Rudyard Kipling arrived a few years later, but was rejected by both the *Chronicle* and Ambrose Bierce's *San Francisco Illustrated Wasp*. The Sheraton Palace is still lavish and elegant; modern conveniences have been installed, but the furnishings are restored antiques that will make you wonder if any of Oscar Wilde's molecules could still be floating around in the upholstery somewhere. Meanwhile, as long as you're spending some money, consider the **Huntington Hotel** on Nob Hill, where Eugene O'Neill and his wife moved from the Fairmont after they left Tao House in Danville, some 30 miles away in the country. Today the hotel is still a discreet lodging for the "old money" crowd that wants to be left alone, as far as possible from anything resembling flash or celebrity. The **York Hotel** is neither a fancy landmark nor a charming North Beach haven, but it was home for a while to Ron Kovic, who wrote *Born on the Fourth of July* and *Around the World in Eight Days*. While staying at the York, Kovic wrote eight novels in 38 days, according to Don Herron's *The Literary World of San Francisco* (City Lights Books). (It's also considered to be gay-friendly.)

For movie hounds... San Francisco is a favorite site of filmmakers, and hotels make perfect backdrops. The **Fairmont Hotel** played center stage in the movie *Bullitt*, Steve McQueen's classic suspense thriller that has one of the all-time best movie chase scenes. The **York Hotel** is a must-see for Alfred Hitchcock fans: The stairway scene in *Vertigo* was shot here. Many San Francisco hotels have been featured in movies, but only one was designed as a shrine to them. In the heart of the theater district, **Hotel Bijou** looks like a sumptuous movie palace from the 1930s, with Hollywood portraits on the walls and each guest room based on the theme of a movie that was shot in the Bay Area. (Those 65 movies are all available for check-out from the hotel's video library). Best of all, there is an ornate mini-theater that shows San Francisco movies daily.

Taking care of business... To the business traveler, voice mail and a reliable data port are musts, but sometimes e-mail isn't enough. You've got to have 24-hour access to a fax machine, and if you stay at **The Ritz-Carlton San**

Francisco, you'll have one right in your room. The luxurious hotel also offers a fully operational business center, complimentary transportation, and every other amenity a generous expense account can buy. The **Nob Hill Lambourne** is a model hotel for health-conscious business execs. Not only does the Lambourne feature a full-service spa on the premises, every room has its own exercise equipment as well as personal computer, fax set-up, and compact stereo unit. All this special treatment costs the same or less than a nondescript room at some of the major hotels in the area. A bit farther from the Financial District, in Japantown, the **Radisson Miyako Hotel** caters to a clientele of lots of Japanese business travelers, with fax machines and voice mail in the rooms, as well as translation services. Business travelers seeking offbeat accommodations could try the **Inn at the Opera** or the **Hotel Bohème**, both of which are equipped with in-room voice mail and fax/modem hook-ups, yet offer a European-style ambience quite different from the standard business-travel hotel.

Family values... Oh, to be a kid again. They get all the good stuff and don't ever even think of offering to pay. Even some high-end hotels make a point of catering to youngsters, possibly on the theory that rich children grow up to be rich adults. At **The Clift Hotel**, children are supplied, free of charge, with everything from toys and Nintendo to milk and cookies and smaller versions of the luxurious bathrobes Mom and Dad are wearing. Parents can be provided with a babysitter and, if by chance they left the baby bag at home, every item imaginable (bottles, diapers, clothes, etc.) needed for an infant. The **Westin Saint Francis'** Kids Club is another program geared toward pleasing guests 12 and under: Members receive a sports bottle or sippy cup with complimentary refills at the hotel's restaurant, along with free food from a special kids menu, while parents can request such necessities as strollers, cribs, bottle-warmers, and stepstools. The Westin Saint Francis' glass-enclosed elevators add an amusement-park thrill to the whole experience. The **Hotel Metropolis** is just a block from the Powell Street cable car line, and if that gets boring, the hotel's "rooms just for kids" are perfect for goofing off, with bunk beds, scaled-down furniture, and—the best part—Nintendo.

If there's a pet in your entourage... A number of San Francisco hotels make special provisions for pooches, ranging from simply tolerating their presence to greeting them in the lobby with a doggie biscuit. For the lowdown on off-leash parks and beaches, as well as restaurants and cafes that will allow you to bring Rover in with you, get *The Bay Area Dog Lover's Companion* by Lyle York and Marcia Goodavage (Foghorn Press, www.foghorn.com/ bayareadog.htm). Lodgings that accept pets include some lower-priced motel properties such as the **Best Western Civic Center Motor Inn**, the **Laurel Motor Inn** in Pacific Heights, and the **Travelodge By the Bay** on Lombard Street's motel row; big mass-market chain properties such as the immense **San Francisco Marriott** and even, surprisingly, a couple of top-end luxury hotels—the **Westin Saint Francis**, the **Campton Place Hotel** (no dogs over 25 pounds—leave the Rottweiler home), and **The Clift Hotel**, whose Very Important Pet program includes a greeting with a biscuit. The small but distinctive **Hotel Monaco** offers a "Bone A Petit" package that includes, among other things, Evian water and a liver biscotti at turndown. Always call in advance for pet policies and required deposits.

Euro-style lodgings.... San Francisco's abundance of European-inspired small hotels and guest houses are part of the ambience that has led people to call it "the Paris of the West." The **Andrews Hotel** (Union Square) is a prime example. The small, family-owned Victorian is rich in history, going back to its incarnation as the Sultan Turkish baths, a turn-of-the-century men's club. Owner Henry Andrews oversees every detail, from the fluffy down comforters and fresh flowers in each guest room to the gourmet continental breakfast set up on each floor every morning. Insider tip: Ask for a "sunny bay king" room—they have lovely bay windows and are larger than standard rooms but they cost only two or three dollars more. The small **Hotel Juliana**, near Nob Hill, is a cozy, secure-feeling three-star hotel that is particularly popular with women traveling alone. It is also a secret hideaway for celebrities—at least, it was a secret until it was featured on *Lifestyles of the Rich and Famous*. You never know who you might meet at the free wine reception each afternoon. The comfy **Abigail Hotel**, a modest hotel near the Opera House and Civic Center, draws a young international crowd that prefers down comforters to backpacks, and appreciates the superb on-site vegetarian restaurant (Millenium). The rooms are a bit small, which makes the atmosphere even more European, and the "antique" furniture is old but not precious. With just ten guest rooms, **Jackson Court** is not exactly a hotel, but staying in this historic mansion in Pacific Heights will make you feel like European royalty. (In fact, many of the residents of this exclusive neighborhood are probably richer than royals.) Just around the corner, the 43-room **El Drisco Hotel** makes you feel as though you're staying at the pied-à-terre of a friend—a very rich friend with fabulous taste and the thickest towels in town. If you can afford it ($325), stay in the city/bay suite on the fourth floor, where huge bay windows on both sides of the suite provide views of the Golden Gate and Bay bridges as well as a sweeping panorama of the city itself. Bonus: If you want to go into town to work, shop, or take in the nightlife, there's free round-trip limousine service.

Luscious love nests... *Town and Country* said a night at the **Archbishop's Mansion** is "like a night in a well-written romance novel," which is ideal if you like romance novels. It's probably the only hotel in the city where you'll find a huge bathroom with a working fireplace and a claw-footed bathtub right in the middle of the room, smelling of perfume and just waiting for a candlelit soak for two. (Do you hear that mood music yet?) The next morning you can keep the spark alive as long as nature allows—the mansion staff will serve you both breakfast in bed. If that whole Danielle Steel thing bores you, perhaps the passion of the opera will get your motor running. Couples have been known to hold intimate wedding dinners in front of the fire at the Ovation restaurant at **Inn at the Opera**, then walk across the street to pump up the volume with a fervent aria at the Opera House. The Inn at the Opera is the most sumptuous small hotel in the city, and we do mean small—the entire building is only 25 feet wide, which kind of makes you wonder how Luciano Pavarotti keeps from feeling cramped when he stays there. Still, the sense is one of airy coziness, partially because all of the windows open for real fresh air. If you've got that truly, madly, deeply kind of thing going on, and you're willing to prove it with some serious money, take your amour across the bay to the lush, 22-acre **Claremont Resort Hotel, Spa & Tennis Club** and book a telescope suite, where San Francisco's lights will twinkle just for you all night long. It's one of the best views of San Francisco you'll ever find. The picture window is as big as a movie screen and is fitted with a wide, wraparound window seat custommade for those spontaneous harmonic convergences.

Provident penthouses... You don't have to spend $8,000 a night at the Fairmont to stay in an enchanting penthouse. For $150 a night, you can have your own little cottage and sundeck at the **San Remo Hotel** in North Beach. True, it is perched on a tarpaper roof and is more like a goofy houseboat than a luxury apartment, but the location and the view are great. Unfortunately, this little gem is no longer a secret, so you may need to book about five or six months in advance. On the other hand, not many people know about the gorgeous terrace penthouses at the **Maxwell Hotel** near Union Square. If you ever want to impress your associates or entertain your friends, this is the place to splurge ($375 to $595). There is no cheesy gold-plated anything, no marble floors, no frou-frou at all—the decor is modern but luxurious, sort of high-end Pottery Barn. The view is to die for. Room service is from Gracie's, the hotel's stylish American brasserie. Going up the scale, the **Prescott Hotel**, also in Union Square, has a more opulent penthouse: two fireplaces (including one in the bedroom), a baby grand piano, a state-of-the-art stereo system, and a dining room that seats eight for a private dinner catered by Wolfgang Puck's Postrio restaurant. If you charged your seven guests $175 a piece, you could cover the $1,200-anight fee. Just a thought.

I'm with the band... You don't have to be on assignment for the *National Enquirer* to be curious about rock stars, but you do have to know where they stay at night if you want to sneak a peek. We'll tell you some of the best spots, but you have to promise to follow the two cardinal rules of stargazing: (1) don't stare; and (2) don't ask. The **Phoenix** is the supreme hot spot for rock stars and other nonconformist celebrities. Originally a kind of futuristic, sleek motel in the fifties, then a hooker hall in the seventies and eighties, it was bought in 1987 by Chip Conley, who managed to snag his first celebrity guest, Brenda

Lee, when she stopped one day to ask for directions to another hotel. After that came Arlo Guthrie and a few others, and the celebrity guest register mushroomed. Sinead O'Connor, Wim Wenders, the Sex Pistols, Nirvana, the Red Hot Chili Peppers, M.C. Hammer, k.d. lang, R.E.M., John Waters, Dr. John, Etta James, River Phoenix, Keanu Reeves, Chubby Checker, David Bowie, Bonnie Raitt, Bo Diddley, and the Cowboy Junkies are just a few of the stars who have lounged by the infamous mural-bottomed swimming pool in the Tenderloin. Offbeat stargazing doesn't get any better, and the rooms start at $95, so reserve well in advance. The Hotel Richelieu, which once housed a lot of the bands that play at the nearby Great American Music Hall, has become a corporate hotel for United Airlines. The only way you'll spot a rock star there now is if they've come back from the airport with a flight attendant. Celebrity guests at the **Inn at the Opera** are more along the lines of opera stars, artists, and dancers—Mikhail Baryshnikov, Twyla Tharp, David Hockney, Placido Domingo, Oscar de la Renta, Robert Rauschenberg, Philip Glass, Herbie Hancock, the Tokyo String Quartet, and the principal dancers of the American Ballet Theatre—but there are a few surprises to round out the list, such as home-run king Hank Aaron, and Gaylord Perry, who holds the major-league record for spitballs. This superb hotel is very popular, so reserve well in advance.

It's modern art, dear... A number of hotels are worth visiting strictly for the interior design of the lobbies. **Hotel Triton** has an Alice in Wonderland on LSD feeling that doesn't go away when you walk out the door and face the huge, ornate dragon on the gate to Chinatown. Some of the desk clerks could use a little less attitude, but then again, they're used to acting unimpressed by guests like Lily Tomlin, Sharon Stone, and Courtney Love. According to their creative director, "Cher did Sonny Bono" there. **Hotel Diva** is a different kind of fantasy, namely stainless steel and cobalt. Sounds like a scary surgery room, but it's actually more like Zen sculpture—sleek, simple, and serene. If you'd like to spend the night at the Museum of Modern Art, this is your spot. The Diva's sister, **Hotel Metropolis,** did its designer lobby in acid green, tangerine, ice blue, and aluminum. The effect is spare and elemental, but the rooms are warmer, with lots of wood, color, and rich fabrics. The **Commodore** looks like a film set for a Picasso-meets-Popeye "Love Boat" episode. There are wavy aqua lines painted around imaginary portholes on the front doors, through which Keanu Reeves, Jon Bon Jovi, and other celebs have entered the lobby. While staying at the Commodore to film *Little City*, Bon Jovi loved hanging out in the attached Red Room cocktail lounge so much, he volunteered to bartend one night. A little less eccentric but equally popular is the new **Hotel Palomar** just footsteps away from the Museum of Modern Art.

We gotta get outta this place... Fog getting to you? Think you'll scream if you see one more panhandler on Market Street? Here's the cure: Get a car and drive across the Golden Gate Bridge, then another 12 miles to Mill Valley, one of those cozy little towns that forces you to use the word "quaint" to describe it. (It was, however, the setting for the '70s satire *Serial*, starring Martin Mull, Sally Kellerman, and a flotilla of hot tubs—luckily, most of the Marin County stereotypes that inspired this book and the 1980 movie have gone to spawn elsewhere.) Get a balcony room at the **Mill Valley Inn**, and mingle with the locals—half of them are screenwriters and you know how they love to talk. After that, calm down a bit at **Tea Garden Springs** (see Getting Outside) with a massage and an herbal elixir. If that still doesn't do it, get back in the car, head farther up the coast to Point Reyes National Seashore and check into **Manka's Inverness Lodge & Restaurant,** a hunting lodge built in 1917 and later transformed into a romantic inn; the extraordinary restaurant here serves game grilled in the fireplace and local line-caught fish. Try to get one of the private cabins, and whatever you do, don't miss dinner in the restaurant. If you have time, it's definitely worth driving another two hours to Mendocino, where a host of cozy seaside inns will soothe your spirit. Among the most unusual is **Stanford Inn by the Sea,** a working organic garden and farm on 10 acres between the Big River and the Pacific Ocean. A herd of animals, including 10 llamas, roams near the garden, which supplies produce for the inn's innovative vegetarian restaurant. And guests roam all around the river, beaches, and nearby village on mountain bikes provided free of charge by the inn. The rooms—each with a wood-burning fireplace—have all the amenities of a luxury hotel yet feel as snug as a family cabin. The inn's romance and comfort draw many celebrities looking for an escape; some, like San Francisco Giants' manager Dusty Baker, are regulars and have become family friends of innkeepers Joan and Jeff Stanford.

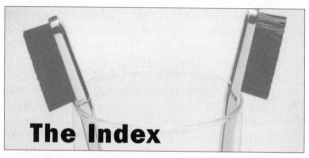

The Index

$$$$$	over $200
$$$$	$150–$200
$$$	$80–$150
$$	$50–$80
$	under $50

Abigail Hotel. This hotel is absolutely perfect for travelers who like charm, great food, international company, and an inexpensive bill when they check out (rooms start at $99).... *Tel 415/626-6500, 800/243–6510, fax 415/626-6580. 246 McAllister St., San Francisco, CA 94102, Civic Center BART/MUNI Metro station. 60 rooms. $$$* **(see p. 27)**

Andrews Hotel. This cozy family-run inn near Union Square preserves many Victorian details.... *Tel 415/563-6877, 800/926-3739, fax 415/928-6919. 624 Post St., San Francisco, CA 94109, Union Square, Powell-Mason cable car. 48 rooms. $$$* **(see p. 27)**

Archbishop's Mansion. This bed-and-breakfast inn has been hailed as the most spectacular place to stay in the city, and as the most elegant in-city hotel in the United States.... *Tel 415/563-7872, 800/543–5820, fax 415/885-3193. 1000 Fulton St., San Francisco, CA 94117, 5 MUNI bus. 10 rooms, 5 suites. $$$–$$$$$* **(see pp. 21, 28)**

AYH Hostel at Union Square. This hostel is in the heart of

Union Square and features several rooms with private baths for families, as well as the normal dormitory facilities.... *Tel 415/788-5604, fax 415/788-3023. 312 Mason St., San Francisco, CA 94102, Powell-Mason cable car; 7B or 38 MUNI bus. 260 beds, 30 with private bath. $* **(see p. 22)**

Best Western Civic Center Motor Inn. This budget chain motel is nondescript, but clean and convenient.... *Tel 415/621-2826, 800/444-5829. 364 Ninth St., San Francisco, CA 94103, Civic Center BART/MUNI Metro station. 57 rooms. $$$* **(see p. 27)**

Bock's Bed and Breakfast. This tiny, nonsmoking, lesbian-friendly bed-and-breakfast near Golden Gate Park has sundecks, laundry facilities, and fax service. Owners said they "took a break" for a few months, so call to check the current status.... *Tel 415/664-6842, fax 415/664-1109. 1448 Willard St., San Francisco, CA 94117, 5 MUNI bus. 3 rooms. $$–$$$* **(see p. 23)**

Campton Place Hotel. This small luxury hotel is noted for its elegance and comfortable intimacy. *Tel 415/781-5555, 800/235-4300, fax 415/955–5536. 340 Stockton St., San Francisco, CA 94108, Powell-Hyde and Powell-Mason cable car; 2, 3, 4, 30, or 45 MUNI bus. 100 rooms, 10 suites. $$$$–$$$$$* **(see p. 27)**

Central YMCA. This reliable old standard in cheap lodgings is an especially good deal when you consider that the rooms are private (some with private bath) and include use of the health club and pool. Dormitory accommodations are also available.... *Tel 415/885-0460. 220 Golden Gate Ave., San Francisco, CA 94109, Civic Center BART/MUNI Metro stop; 15 MUNI bus. 106 rooms, plus one 12-bed and two 4-bed dormitories. $* **(see p. 22)**

Claremont Resort Hotel, Spa & Tennis Club. The 22 acres of landscaped grounds are just the backdrop for the landmark Victorian hotel (1915), premier private tennis club, and a $6 million holistic health and beauty spa.... *Tel 510/843-3000, 800/551-7266, fax 510/549-8582. 41 Tunnel Rd., Berkeley, CA 94705, Rockridge BART station (plus a cab). 279 rooms. $$$$–$$$$$* **(see p. 29)**

The Clift Hotel. A haven for aristocrats and romantics on a

splurge, the Clift is the luxury hotel that other hotels want to be when they grow up.... *Tel 415/775-4700, 800/65-CLIFT, fax 415/441-4621. 495 Geary St., San Francisco, CA 94102, Powell-Hyde and Powell-Mason cable car; 2, 3, 4, 30, 38, or 45 bus. 326 rooms, including suites. $$$$$*
(see pp. 22, 26, 27)

Commodore. You have to go by this one just to check out the lobby. It's a goofball version of a cruise ship, with a lobby full of furniture that looks like it came out of a cartoon.... *Tel 415/923-6800, 800/338-6848, fax 415/923-6804. 825 Sutter St., San Francisco, CA 94109, California St. cable car. 110 rooms. $$$*   **(see p. 31)**

Donatello Hotel. The standard rooms may be the largest in the city, with 10-foot ceilings and huge windows; terrace suites open to lushly landscaped private decks.... *Tel 415/441-7100, 800/227-3184, fax 415/885-8842. 501 Post St., San Francisco, CA 94109, Union Square, Powell-Mason cable car. 94 rooms. $$$$*   **(see p. 20)**

The Edwardian San Francisco Hotel. A wide green awning welcomes you to this red-brick Victorian perched at the crossroads of the Mission District, the Hayes Valley, and Upper Market Street. You'll drool over the Gay paree/French Quarter motif: wrought-iron fire escapes on the front and ornate white wood railings surrounding the rooftop.... *Tel 415/864-1271, 888/864–8070, fax 415/861-8116. 1668 Market St., San Francisco, CA 94102, Van Ness Ave. MUNI Metro station; 7 MUNI bus. 36 rooms. $–$$*
(see p. 23)

El Drisco Hotel. Find out why the richest people in San Francisco choose to live in Pacific Heights by staying at this sumptuous, intimate hotel.... *Tel 415/346-2880, 800/634-7277, fax 415/567-5537. 2901 Pacific Ave., San Francisco CA 94115, Pacific Heights, 3 MUNI bus. 43 rooms, including 19 suites. $$$$$*   **(see p. 28)**

Fairmont Hotel. This is probably the most famous hotel in San Francisco, at the very tip-top of Nob Hill, yet it's not incredibly expensive, provided you stay out of the suites.... *Tel 415/772-5000, 800/527-4727, fax 415/391-4833. 950 Mason St., San Francisco, CA 94108, California St. cable car. 600 rooms, 62 suites. $$$$–$$$$$*   **(see p. 19)**

Grant Plaza. This bargain hotel in Chinatown is clean and comfortable. The rooms are kinda dreary, but the windows are large and let in plenty of light.... *Tel 415/434-3883, 800/472--6899, fax 415/434-3886. 465 Grant Ave., San Francisco, CA 94108, 15, 30, 45 MUNI bus. 72 rooms. $$–$$$* **(see p. 22)**

Green Tortoise Guest House. This nonsmoking facility attracts lots of young people, and has a sauna, laundry, free breakfast and Internet access, and organized tours.... *Tel 415/834-1000, 800/867-8647, fax 415/956-4900. 494 Broadway, San Francisco, CA 94133, 15, 30 MUNI bus. 100 beds, 17 rooms with shared bath. $* **(see p. 22)**

Hotel Astoria. This super-cheap Chinatown hotel has plain, but not shabby, rooms, some with shared bath. Airport pickup and some business services are provided.... *Tel 415/434-8889, 800/666-6696, fax 415/434-8919. 510 Bush St., San Francisco, CA 94108, 30, 45 MUNI bus. 90 rooms, 80 with private bath. $$* **(see p. 22)**

Hotel Bijou. A shrine to the silver screen, this small hotel in the heart of the theater district looks like an old-time movie palace and features movie-themed guest rooms.... *Tel 415/771-1200, 800/771-1022, fax 415/346-3196. 111 Mason St., San Francisco, CA 94102, Union Square, Powell-Mason cable car. 65 rooms. $$$* **(see p. 25)**

Hotel Bohème. This Parisian-style beatnik villa is both comfortable and chic at the same time. It's in the heart of North Beach, but the rooms are surprisingly quiet.... *Tel 415/433-9111, fax 415/362-6292. 444 Columbus Ave., San Francisco, CA 94133, 15, 30, 45 MUNI bus. 16 rooms. $–$$$* **(see pp. 24, 26)**

Hotel Diva. If you love the look of sleek stainless steel beds but crave the feel of luxuriant linens, join the artsy types who love this super-chic, ultramodern urban retreat.... *Tel 415/885-0200, 800/553-1900, fax 415/885-3268. 440 Geary St., San Francisco, CA 94102, Union Square, 38 MUNI bus. 111 rooms. $$$–$$$$* **(see p. 30)**

Hotel Juliana. A haven for celebrities and for solo women travelers, who love the cozy, safe feel of both the inn and the neighborhood.... *Tel 415/392-2540, 800/328-3880, fax*

ACCOMMODATIONS | THE INDEX

415/391-8447. 590 Bush St., San Francisco, CA 94108, Powell St. BART station; all cable car lines; 30 or 45 MUNI bus. $$$–$$$$ **(see p. 27)**

Hotel Metropolis. This 1930s landmark colonial revivalist building was renovated in 1998 with "vivid color and modern materials." Despite the inescapable artiness of the lobby, the rooms are down-to-earth and comfy. There is one special room just for kids (with bunk beds and Nintendo).... *Tel 415/775-4600, 800/553-1900, fax 415/775-4606. 25 Mason St., San Francisco, CA 94102, Union Square, Powell-Mason cable car; 38 MUNI bus. 105 rooms. $$$$* **(see pp. 26, 30)**

Hotel Monaco. This impeccably refurbished 1910 Beaux Arts landmark is now a four-star hotel with all the amenities that attract discriminating non-mainstream types.... *Tel 415/292-0100, 800/214-4220, fax 415/292-0111. 501 Geary St., San Francisco, CA 94102, Union Square; Powell-Mason cable car; 38 MUNI bus. 201 rooms, 32 suites. $$$$* **(see pp. 20, 27)**

Hotel Nikko. This Japanese hotel is perilously close to the Hilton and it has rubbed off. Most of the rooms are very Western, though the traditional Japanese suites are lovely.... *Tel 415/394-1111, 800/645-5687, fax 415/394-1106. 222 Mason St., San Francisco, CA 94102, Powell St. BART/MUNI Metro station; Powell-Mason or Powell-Hyde cable car; 38 MUNI bus. 500 rooms, 22 suites. $$$$–$$$$$* **(see p. 24)**

Hotel Palomar. Once you get past the typical San Francisco interior design fuss, there are several really good things about this hotel: cordless phones and 27-inch TVs in every room, Fuji spa tubs in all the suites, and package deals that include everything from a luscious spa to art tours.... *Tel 415/348-1111, 877/294-9711, fax 415/348-0302. 12 Fourth St., San Francisco, CA 94103, Market Street near Union Square, Powell St. BART station. 198 rooms, 16 suites. $$$$-$$$$$* **(see p. 31)**

Hotel Rex. This arts and literary salon/hotel draws artists and writers for book-signings, and conversation.... *Tel 415/433-4434, 800/433-4434, fax 415/433-3695. 562 Sutter St., San Francisco, CA 94102, Union Square,*

Powell-Mason or Powell-Hyde cable car. 94 rooms. $$$$
(see p. 24)

Hotel Richelieu. Just a few blocks from the Great American Music Hall all kinds of cool nightlife.... *Tel 415/673-4711, 800/295-7424, fax 415/673-9362. 1050 Van Ness Ave., San Francisco, CA 94109, 38 MUNI bus. 134 rooms, 23 suites. $$-$$$* **(see pp. 18, 30)**

Hotel Triton. Plush, upholstered chairs sit next to the modern, angular front desk; huge columns rise out of the royal-blue carpet. The guests look as arty as the decor.... *Tel 415/394-0500, 800/433-6611, fax 415/394-0555. 342 Grant Ave., San Francisco, CA 94108, 30, 45 MUNI bus. 140 rooms. $$$$–$$$$$* **(see p. 30)**

Huntington Hotel. Rooms are exquisitely—and individually—appointed, with museum-quality works of art and a blend of antique and custom-designed furniture.... *Tel 415/474-5400, 800/227-4683, fax 415/474-6227. 1075 California St., San Francisco, CA 94108, California St. cable car, 1 MUNI bus. 140 rooms. $$$$–$$$$$* **(see p. 25)**

Inn at the Opera. This tiny, 25-foot-wide Victorian jewel is the most distinguished small luxury hotel in the city and one of the most romantic.... *Tel 415/863-8400, 800/325-2708, fax 415/861-0821. 333 Fulton St., San Francisco, CA 94102, Civic Center BART/MUNI Metro station; 5, 21, 47, or 49 MUNI bus. 30 rooms, 18 suites. $$$$*
(see pp. 26, 28, 30)

Inn San Francisco. Once a private mansion, this gracious bed-and-breakfast offers a hot tub, sundeck, fireplaces, and complimentary buffet breakfast.... *Tel 415/641-0188, 800/359-0913, fax 415/641-1701. 943 South Van Ness Ave., San Francisco, CA 94110, 5 MUNI bus. 21 rooms. $$$–$$$$* **(see p. 23)**

Inter-Club/Globe Hostel. If you want to stay South of Market and bask on a sundeck, try this hostel. It has a dorm and private rooms, plus a pool table. Rates start at $21.... *Tel 415/431-0540, fax 415/431-3286. 10 Hallam Place (off Folsom St., between Seventh and Eighth Sts.), San Francisco, CA 94103, Civic Center BART/MUNI Metro station; 42 MUNI bus. 26 rooms. $* **(see p. 22)**

ACCOMMODATIONS | THE INDEX

Jackson Court. Reserve at least six weeks in advance for this 10-room brownstone mansion in elite Pacific Heights. Somewhat ornate in parts, it's also warm and homey, with exceptionally comfortable beds.... *Tel 415/929-7670, 800/738-7477, fax 415/929-1405. 2198 Jackson St., San Francisco, CA 94115, Pacific Heights; 12 MUNI bus.* $$$–$$$$ **(see p. 28)**

Laurel Motor Inn. This recently remodeled Pacific Heights motel has a great location plus kitchens, a complimentary continental breakfast, and free lemonade and cookies in the afternoon. Parking is free and pets are welcome.... *Tel 415/567-8467, 800/552-8735, fax 415/928-1866. 444 Presidio Ave., San Francisco, CA 94115, 3 MUNI bus. 49 rooms.* $$$ **(see p. 27)**

Manka's Inverness Lodge & Restaurant. Locals rave about this cheerful, rustic, little oceanside inn, with its remarkable restaurant, less than an hour from the city.... *Tel 415/669-1034. P. O. Box 1110, Inverness, CA 94937. On Point Reyes National Seashore. 14 units, 4 cabins with kitchens.* $$$–$$$$$ **(see p. 31)**

Mark Hopkins International. Sometimes overshadowed by its Nob Hill neighbor, the Fairmont, this classic 19-story luxury hotel should not be overlooked. Every room has a marvelous view.... *Tel 415/392-3434, 800/327-0200, fax 415/421-3302. 1 Nob Hill, San Francisco, CA 94108, California St. cable car. 380 rooms, 38 suites.* $$$$–$$$$$ **(see p. 19)**

Maxwell Hotel. You can't miss the sculpture of a shopper outside this restored 1908 art deco masterpiece, a tribute to the high-end shopping nearby in Union Square. The spacious guest rooms are done in deep, rich colors with plush fabrics and hand-painted lampshades.... *Tel 415/986-2000, 888/734-6299, fax 415/397-2447. 386 Geary St., San Francisco, CA 94102, Union Square; Powell-Mason cable car; 38 MUNI bus. 153 rooms.* $$$$–$$$$$ **(see p. 29)**

Mill Valley Inn. This three-story European-style *pensione* looks like a cross between an Italian villa and a California Colonial lodge, at the foot of Mount Tamalpais, alongside a redwood grove.... *Tel 415/389-6608, 800/595-2100, fax 415/*

389-5051. 165 Throckmorton Ave., Mill Valley, CA 94941. 25 rooms, 2 cottages, 1 executive suite. $$$$
(see p. 31)

Nob Hill Lambourne. This very sleek hotel looks like another ritzy, oh-so-spare hotel for the rich and private, but it's actually a reasonably priced lodging that attracts business travelers.... *Tel 415/433-2287, fax 415/433-0975. 725 Pine St., San Francisco, CA 94108, Powell St. BART station. 14 rooms, 6 suites. $$$$–$$$$$* **(see p. 26)**

Phoenix. One of the most wacked-out and popular lodgings in the city, this Tenderloin/Civic Center motel is best known for its famous guests. The decor is sort of psychedelic kitsch.... *Tel 415/776-1380, 800/248-9466, fax 415/885-3109. 601 Eddy St., San Francisco, CA 94109, 19, 31, or 38 MUNI bus. 44 rooms, 3 suites. $$–$$$* **(see pp. 19, 29)**

Prescott Hotel. This luxurious boutique hotel features massive cherry-wood furniture in the guest rooms. Guests get preferred seating at Wolfgang Puck's chic Postrio restaurant.... *Tel 415/563-0303, fax 415/563-6831. 545 Post St., San Francisco, CA 94102, Union Square, Powell St. BART station; Powell-Mason or Powell-Hyde cable car; 2, 3, 4, or 38 MUNI bus. 164 rooms, 36 suites. $$$$$* **(see pp. 20, 29)**

Radisson Miyako Hotel. One of the most tranquil, gracious hotels in the city. Opt for the luxurious traditional Japanese suites. Continental breakfast is included.... *Tel 415/922-3200, 800/533-4567, fax 415/921-0417. 1625 Post St. (near Geary Blvd. and Laguna St.), San Francisco, CA 94115, 38 MUNI bus. 218 rooms, 11 suites. $$$$$*
(see pp. 23, 26)

Red Victorian Bed and Breakfast Inn. There should be a sign in front of this lovely and eccentric Haight-Ashbury inn that reads: Welcome Back to 1967. Each room has its own theme.... *Tel 415/864--1978. 1665 Haight St., San Francisco, CA 94117, 7, 66, 71, or 73 MUNI bus. 18 rooms (5 with private bath), 1 suite. $$–$$$$* **(see p. 21)**

The Ritz-Carlton San Francisco. Handsome rooms, Italian-marble bathrooms, plush terry bathrobes, and twice-daily maid service are just some of the comforts here. Fully equipped fitness center, too.... *Tel 415/296-7465. 600*

ACCOMMODATIONS | THE INDEX

Stockton St., San Francisco, CA 94108, Stockton St. BART station. 336 rooms, 42 suites. $$$$$ **(see p. 25)**

San Francisco International Hostel (AYH). Fort Mason is the hub of the beautifully scenic Golden Gate National Recreation Area, and this dormitory hostel is right in the thick of it.... *Tel 415/771-7277, fax 415/771-1468. Building 240, Fort Mason, San Francisco, CA 94123, Powell-Hyde cable car; 30 or 42 MUNI bus. 160 beds. $*
(see p. 23)

San Francisco Marriott. You can't miss this gigantic building, looming like a huge jukebox over the Financial District. Decor is typical Chain Hotel Moderne. Unbelievable views of both the bay and the Golden Gate.... *Tel 415/896-1600, 800/228-9290, fax 415/777-2799. 55 Fourth St., San Francisco, CA 94103, Powell St. BART/MUNI Metro station; Powell St. cable-car turnaround. 1,500 rooms. $$$$$*
(see p. 27)

San Remo Hotel. The rooms at this delightful, clean, European-style hotel are furnished with antiques and have comfortable beds, big windows, and ceiling fans. The shared bathrooms on each floor are sparklingly clean and well kept.... *Tel 415/776-8688, 800/352-7366, fax 415/776-2811. 2237 Mason St., San Francisco, CA 94133, Powell-Mason cable car; 15 or 30 MUNI bus. 62 rooms, all shared bath. $–$$* **(see pp. 19, 29)**

Sheraton Palace Hotel. Once the Palace Hotel, this San Francisco landmark has now been restored to its turn-of-the-century distinction. With all the modern conveniences.... *Tel 415/512-1111, 800/325-3535, fax 415/543-0671. 2 New Montgomery St., San Francisco, CA 94105, Montgomery St. BART/MUNI Metro station; 7, 15, 30, or 45 MUNI bus. 550 rooms, 32 suites. $$$$$* **(see p. 24)**

Stanford Inn by the Sea. Movie and TV stars flock to this smoke-free, vegetarian, Mendocino hideaway to escape from the poisonous air and attitude of Hollywood. The tranquil seaside inn manages to remain totally unpretentious despite the splendid accommodations.... *Tel 707/937-5615, 800/331-8884, fax 707/937-0305. Coast Hwy. and Comptche Ukiah Rd., Mendocino, CA 94560. 41 rooms. $$$$$* **(see p. 31)**

Stouffer Renaissance Stanford Court Hotel. One of the most impressive hotels in the city, with a stained-glass dome in the lobby, antique furnishings in the rooms, and possibly the ghost of railroad baron Leland Stanford.... *Tel 415/989-3500, 800/677-1555, fax 415/391-0513. 905 California St., San Francisco, CA 94108, Powell-Hyde or Powell-Mason cable car; 1 MUNI bus. 393 rooms, 18 suites, 14 junior suites. $$$$$* **(see p. 22)**

Travelodge By the Bay. A bit more expensive than the other budget motels along Lombard Street, the Travelodge By the Bay offers a lounge, kitchens, and wheelchair accessibility. Pets are welcome.... *Tel 415/673-0691, 800/578-7878. 1450 Lombard St., San Francisco, CA 94123, 28 MUNI bus. 72 rooms. $$$–$$$$* **(see p. 27)**

24 Henry Guesthouse. Intimate little Victorian guesthouse in the Castro District.... *Tel 415/864-5686, 800/900-5686, fax 415/864-0406. 4080 18th St., San Francisco, CA 94114, J Church MUNI Metro. 5 rooms (3 with shared bath), 1 one-bedroom apartment. $$–$$$* **(see p. 23)**

Victorian Inn on the Park. A beautifully restored historic landmark with 12 rooms, some of which have working fireplaces and terraces overlooking the Panhandle.... *Tel 415/931-1830, 800/435-1967, fax 415/931-1830. 301 Lyon St., San Francisco, CA 94117, 7 MUNI bus. 12 rooms. $$$–$$$$* **(see p. 21)**

Westin Saint Francis. Perhaps the most venerable grande dame, the Saint Francis is located in the Union Square area. Rooms in the original old building are preferable to those in the bland modern tower.... *Tel 415/397-7000, 800/228-3000, fax 415/774-0124. 335 Powell St., San Francisco, CA 94102; Powell-Hyde or Powell-Mason cable car; 2, 3, 4, 30, 45, and 76 MUNI buses. 1,200 rooms, including 83 suites. $$$$–$$$$$* **(see pp. 20, 26, 27)**

York Hotel. The hotel's formal script logo, emblazoned on deep-green awnings, belies the relaxed atmosphere that prevails at the York.... *Tel 415/885-6800, 800/808-9675, fax 415/885-2115. 940 Sutter St., San Francisco, CA 94109, Powell-Mason or Powell-Hyde cable car; 38 MUNI bus. 96 rooms. $$$–$$$$* **(see p. 25)**

ACCOMMODATIONS | THE INDEX

San Francisco Accommodations

Abigail Hotel **13**

Archbishop's Mansion **19**

Best Western Civic
  Center Motor Inn **15**

Bock's Bed and Breakfast **23**

Central YMCA **11**

The Edwardian San Francisco Hotel **16**

El Drisco Hotel **7**

Green Tortoise Guest House **5**

Hotel Bohème **4**

Inn at the Opera **18**

Inn San Francisco **17**

Inter-Club/Globe Hostel **12**

Jackson Court **6**

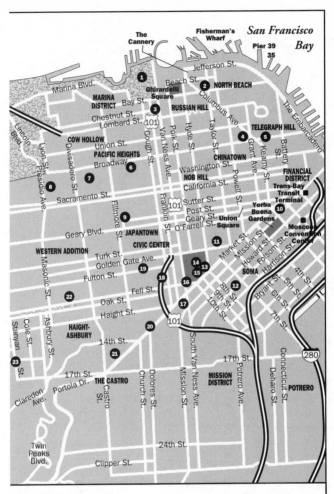

The Cannery

Fisherman's Wharf

Pier 39 35

San Francisco Bay

Jefferson St.

Beach St.

Marina Blvd.

MARINA DISTRICT

Ghirardelli Square

NORTH BEACH

Bay St.

Chestnut St.

Lombard St.

RUSSIAN HILL

Columbus Ave.

COW HOLLOW

Union St.

PACIFIC HEIGHTS

Broadway

Polk St.

Van Ness Ave.

Hyde St.

Taylor St.

Grant Ave.

Kearny St.

TELEGRAPH HILL

Battery St.

The Embarcadero

CHINATOWN

Washington St.

NOB HILL

California St.

Powell St.

FINANCIAL DISTRICT

Trans-Bay Transit

Lincoln Blvd.

Lyon St.

Divisadero St.

Presidio Ave.

Sacramento St.

Gough St.

Franklin St.

Fillmore St.

Sutter St.

Post St.

Geary St.

O'Farrell St.

Union Square

Yerba Buena Gardens

Moscone Convention Center

Geary Blvd.

JAPANTOWN

CIVIC CENTER

Market St.

Mission St.

Howard St.

Folsom St.

Harrison St.

WESTERN ADDITION

Turk St.

Golden Gate Ave.

Fulton St.

Oak St.

Fell St.

Haight St.

HAIGHT-ASHBURY

Masonic Ave.

Cole St.

Ashbury St.

Stanyan St.

14th St.

17th St.

THE CASTRO

Portola Dr.

Claredon Ave.

Twin Peaks Blvd.

Clipper St.

24th St.

Castro St.

Church St.

Dolores St.

Mission St.

South Van Ness Ave.

17th St.

MISSION DISTRICT

Potrero Ave.

Connecticut St.

Deharo St.

POTRERO

SOMA

8th St.

9th St.

10th St.

Bryant St.

5th St.

6th St.

7th St.

4th St.

280

101

Laurel Motor Inn **8**

Phoenix **14**

Radisson Miyako Hotel **9**

Red Victorian Bed and Breakfast Inn **20**

San Francisco International Hostel **1**

San Remo Hotel **2**

Sheraton Palace Hotel **10**

Travelodge By the Bay **3**

24 Henry Guesthouse **21**

Victorian Inn on the Park **22**

Union Square/Nob Hill Accommodations

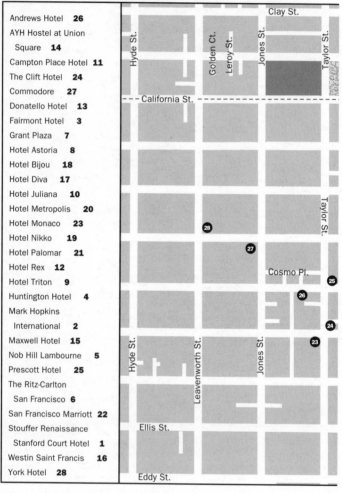

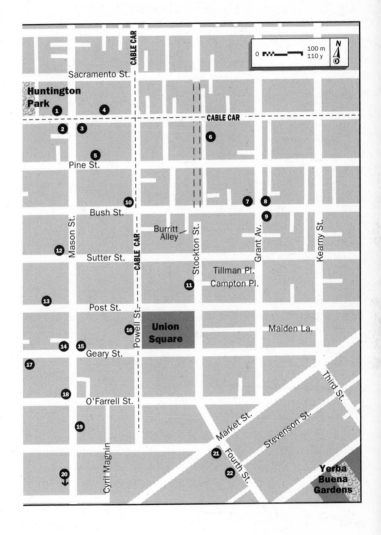

Sacramento St.

Huntington Park

CABLE CAR

CABLE CAR

❶ ❹

❷ ❸

❻

❺

Pine St.

❿

❼ ❽

Bush St.

❾

Mason St.

Burritt Alley

CABLE CAR

⓬

Stockton St.

Grant Av.

Kearny St.

Sutter St.

Tillman Pl.

Campton Pl.

⓫

⓭

Post St.

Powell St.

⓰

Union Square

Maiden La.

⓮ ⓯

Geary St.

⓱

⓲

O'Farrell St.

Third St.

⓳

Market St.

Stevenson St.

Cyril Magnin

⓴

㉑

Fourth St.

㉒

Yerba Buena Gardens

0 100 m
   110 y

N

dining a

2nd cafes

It's official:
San Francisco is
the best food town
in America. New
York had to accept
the backseat when
the City

by the Bay first won all of the top James Beard awards (the Oscars of the restaurant world) in 1997—and continued to dazzle food critics and draw the rising stars of the chef kingdom from all over the planet. And it's not just critics who love the food here. Readers of *Bon Appetit,* the world's largest-circulation epicurean magazine, have named San Francisco their favorite American city for dining out several years running. With more than 3,500 restaurants representing every cuisine on earth (and a few from outer space), the city that spawned California cuisine has become North America's ground zero for ingenious chefs. They are drawn not only to the creative freedom that has always defined San Francisco, but also to the year-round abundance of fresh fruits, vegetables, herbs, fish, and seafood that are Northern California's unique bounty. And the dot-com invasion—which had San Francisco teeming with rich Internet start-up companies and deep-pocket cyber-nerds—spawned even more restaurants that continue to thrive.

Oddly enough, it took local cooks until nearly the end of the twentieth century to figure out there was more to culinary life than steak and seafood, at which point they immediately went berserk with outlandish combinations of exotic ingredients and trickled raspberry vinegar on absolutely everything. Fortunately, most food fads—including that one—have the life span of a disposable razor, but there are some things you can always count on when you dine in San Francisco: a mélange of authentic ethnic eateries that is probably the most diverse in America; cafes, bistros, and formal dinner houses that serve extraordinary French food; a solid core of world-class restaurants inspired by California cuisine in all its transmutations; and, of course, the traditional grill fare that has been a staple since the Gold Rush. You could spend your entire vacation—and most of your money—eating at high-profile spots that have gotten more press than Jordan's comeback, but the best way to enjoy San Francisco's lavish feast is to explore the nation's most exotic variety of ethnic foods. Often the most interesting and delicious food is far less expensive than "see-and-be-seen" fare. There are far too many excellent restaurants to mention here, but the samples we offer will get you started on your own dining adventure.

Only in San Francisco

The sunny **Mission District** has long been famous for its Mexican restaurants and storefront taquerias, where locals take for granted lunchtime feasts of authentic barbecued pork *carnitas* and grilled steak (*carne asada*) for less than the price of a Big Mac. A steady stream of immigrants and refugees from Guatemala, El Salvador, Nicaragua, Chile, and Peru has brought dozens of new restaurants to the neighborhood, adding countless treats to the Latin American banquet table. While you're there, you'll notice an infusion of chic, upscale eateries along Valencia and Guerrero streets, an area that food critics have dubbed "the Valencia corridor" to distinguish it from the barrio that surrounds it. If you get past the snobby euphemism—and San Fran-cisco's interminable preoccu-pation with interior design—you can settle into food heaven without ever leaving the neighborhood. Chinese food is also synony-mous with San Francisco, but you can find that in almost every city. The true gems are the rarer **Asian/Pacific** cuisines such as Cambodia's complex mingling of coconut milk, lemongrass, lime, and classical French fish sauce; or Singapore's exotic seafood dishes that combine European, Indian, Chinese, and Malaysian influences.

Supper clubs are still the favored late-night haunts for gourmets, so swanky drinks like martinis are very chic, but San Francisco's own naturally fermented Anchor Steam beer and Gordon Biersch brews are high on the locals' list of favorite beverages (get it on tap, not bottled). Beer has been big in the city since the raucous Barbary Coast days, when the **San Francisco Brewing Company** pub (corner of Columbus and Pacific ave-nues) first opened its doors. After Prohibition, the 1907 establishment started legally producing its own beer (we love the Shanghai Pale Ale), which is available only at the pub or in extremely limited bottled batches at two neighborhood

Take a chef home

No one can visit all of the city's best restaurants during one vacation, but you can take more than 100 of the top chefs home with you, including all of the 1997 James Beard Foundation award-winners. The Concierge Recommends is a collection of signature recipes selected as favorites by San Francisco concierges —every-thing from "Assassinated Chicken" or "Tower of Foie Gras" to "Warm Chocolate Cake with Chocolate and Butterscotch Sauces." Pro-files of the chef, restaurant, and neighborhood are on the back of each recipe. This limited-edition cookbook is available at Bay Area book-stores, online from Amazon.com or Barnes & Noble (www.bn.com), or by mail order ($20 including tax and shipping) from Gala Pub-lishing, 555 Pierce St., Albany, CA 94706, tel 510/525-3861.

INTRODUCTION | DINING AND CAFES

liquor stores (the **Jug Shop**, 1576 Pacific Ave., and **Coit Liquors**, 585 Columbus Ave.). Don't try to take it home as a souvenir—the beer is not pasteurized, so it must be refrigerated to last even two weeks. Finally, though Irish coffee is far from a local invention, a visit to the **Buena Vista Cafe** (2765 Haight St.), a National Historic Landmark (see Diversions) for a cup of it—especially on a foggy late afternoon—is a time-honored tradition among locals and tourists alike.

How to Dress

Jackets and ties are rarely mandatory at San Francisco restaurants, but common sense should dictate the obvious: If you're going to a fancy place, dress up a bit. You'll probably need some sort of jacket, anyway, simply because it's so cool at night, even in summer. At casual establishments, anything goes. As long as you don't look like you just climbed out of a dumpster, you'll probably be acceptable no matter what you're wearing.

Getting the Right Table

Unless your major objective in going to a restaurant is to gawk at celebrities—or perhaps be mistaken for one—the right table isn't much of an issue in San Francisco. A few restaurants, such as the Ovation at the Inn at the Opera (see Accommodations), have one exceptional table (theirs is by a fireplace) worth booking in advance for a do-or-die romantic encounter, but the trendiest establishments tend to do the same thing as in every town: Pack in the hoi polloi wherever they fit. (The Index notes whether reservations are recommended.)

When to Eat

Unlike their New York night-owl counterparts, San Franciscans tend to dine *before* they go to the opera or ballet, not afterward. That means you need to reserve weeks in advance if you want to have dinner before 8 in any popular restaurant near a major theater or concert hall. After 8:30, however, you can get a table on the spot at Stars, the Hayes Street Grill, or other popular "opera ghetto" restaurants (those clustered near the performing arts mecca centering on City Hall and the War Memorial Opera House). Very few restaurants serve dinner after 10, so get your grazing over with before you go out on the town or you may be stuck with burgers or all-night coffee-shop food (see Eating with Insomniacs). Most breakfast places serve all day, with specials often ending at 11:30, and lunch tends to be whatever you feel like eating between then and mid-afternoon, when many restaurants begin to gear up for dinner. Mexican food seems to work for breakfast, lunch, and dinner, so you'll never have to go hungry if you can find your way to the Mission District.

Eating at the Bar

There is little doubt that dining out is the favorite pastime of San Franciscans, locals as well as visitors. Getting a table—or even a short-notice reservation—at a really popular spot can be frustrating if not impossible. So do what locals do: Skip that altogether and park yourself on a barstool. You can get in almost anywhere on the spur of the moment, and the service is often quicker and more relaxed than in the dining room. Occasionally there is a special bar menu, but typically the offerings are identical to the fare served at the tables. A bonus for travelers is that bar diners are usually quite sociable, so you'll get a rare chance to schmooze with the locals on equal footing. Try **Aqua, Backflip, Bruno's,** the **Cypress Club, Fringale, Harris', Moose's, Rose Pistola,** and all the hip spots on Valencia Street or anywhere else with a line to get in.

Chefs

The restaurant world is its own little soap opera. Every star chef was once some other star's sous chef, and the darling of one kitchen today is likely to be the hit of another restaurant tomorrow. **James Ormsby**, whose Italian-French soul

Getting wired

Need something to do with those twiddling thumbs after you've downed enough espresso to raise the dead? Try tapping your fingers on a computer keyboard to get linked to countless other cafe rats around the world. Since 1991, San Francisco cafes have offered coin-operated access to e-mail and community bulletin boards via SF Net, but no matter how many quarters spent, you still couldn't get onto the Net. Now a number of cafes have computers at the tables, with free access to the Internet and the World Wide Web. (See our section on the "The cafe superhighway.") To find Bay Area cafes that are hooked up to SF Net, check out www.sfnet. com. For links to cafes with their their own websites, type "internet cafes" at http://sfbay. yahoo.com or go to www.cyberiacafe.net/cyberia/guide for a guide to net-connected cafes around the world.

INTRODUCTION | DINING AND CAFES

food made the Financial District power-spot Aqua a huge
hit in its inaugural nine weeks, left in 1996 to open his own
Mission District supper club, Bruno's, and relinquished
Aqua to **Michael Mina**, who was named 1997's top "rising
star" chef by the James Beard Association. (Ormsby since
bounced all over town, from the Red Herring, to Roti's, back
to Bruno's, and to Plump Jack.) Meanwhile **Pat Loston**,
Aqua's adored dessert chef, moved on to North Beach's surrealistic Cypress Club. Before **Thomas Keller** took over
French Laundry in Yountville and was named the best chef
in the country by the James Beard Foundation, **Ron Siegel**
won national honors there. Siegel now presides at Masa's.
Timothy Au trained in the "opera ghetto" with Stars' **Jere-
miah Tower** before going to Washington Square Bar and
Grill in North Beach (both are now closed); Tower also
trained **Lynn Sheehan**, who worked in Union Square with
Julian Serrano at Masa's before she moved on to Mecca, an
Upper Market supper club now run by **Michael Fennelly**.
(Serrano took over Masa's after the death of founder **Masa-
taha Kobayashi** several years ago and has since moved on to
Las Vegas, leaving Masa's to his sous chef, Chad Callahan.)
Scott Warner left Restaurant Lulu (South of Market) for
North Beach's busy Rose Pistola, voted best new restaurant
in the country at the 1997 James Beard awards, then left
with owner **Reed Hearon** (Lulu) to get the Black Cat and
Blue Bar on its feet. **Anne** and **David Gringrass** opened
Postrio (Union Square) with **Wolfgang Puck** before the
debut of their own South of Market cafe, Hawthorne Lane.
The list goes on and on—and some of the city's best chefs
have commuted way farther than across town. **Alain Ron-
delli** came all the way from a three-star restaurant in Paris to
open his Clement Street bistro (now closed) at what used to
be Le St. Tropez, owned by **Gerald Hirigoyen**, who now
owns Fringale (South of Market) and Pastis (Financial District). **Fabrice Canelle** worked at Maxim's in Paris before
crossing the Atlantic—and the United States—to take over
Moose's, which was revamped by chef Brian Whitmer of
Carmel's acclaimed Highland Inn and is now run by **Jason
Miller,** who was **Bradley Ogden's** sous chef at Lark Creek
Inn in Marin County. And **Sylvain Portay** jolted all of New
York by abandoning Le Cirque in favor of San Francisco's
stylish Ritz Carlton dining room on Nob Hill. Portay, who
was named 1999 U.S. Hotel Chef of the Year, steered his
dining room to the number-one spot on *Gourmet* magazine's
"Rooms at the Top" readers' poll.

Cafe Society

When you hear people raving about the cafe scene in San Francisco, they're not referring to the posh bistros calling themselves cafes just to horn in on the French tradition of charging a small fortune for a dab of *je ne sais quoi*. They're talking about coffeehouses with names like **Jammin' Java Coffee House**, **Red Dora's Bearded Lady**, and **Muddy Waters Coffee House**— neighborhood caffeine dens that are often much more popular than bars as places to meet, hear music, listen to poetry, read, write, talk about art and politics, or just sit and watch the general buzz. The best cafes are basically ongoing block parties.

In recent years, Seattle has often been mislabeled by the media as America's gourmet-coffee center— primarily due to the success of the Starbucks coffee chain— but the problem with this whole Seattle blather is that coffee by itself is utterly insignificant. Seattle could sell enough coffee beans to fill up Mount St. Helens, yet it would still never be San Francisco. San Francisco's coffee-houses and cafes are the

The Real Poop on Starbucks

When every Denny's in America serves cappuccino with the breakfast special, blame it on Seattle. Not so long ago, a decent shot of espresso was a rare pleasure in that neck of the woods (and we do mean woods). Then suddenly, Seattle was hailed nationwide as the undisputed coffee heaven of the New World. They had discovered espresso sort of like Columbus discovered America—with little or no acknowledgment of those who had already cultivated it for generations. The most obvious player, Starbucks, is a publicly held company with a huge chain of coffee bars that are about as avant-garde as Mrs. Field's cookies. The company was started by a former San Franciscan who first imitated Berkeley's beloved family-owned Peet's coffee store, then bought Peet's, then sold Starbucks to venture capitalists (but kept Peet's), and now has to compete with Starbucks to try to stay alive. David created Goliath.

hearts and souls of their communities. Such small cafes have been the center of the city's vital bohemian scene since the turn of the century, and have enticed some of the world's most interesting artists and writers to not only visit, but stay. Chain coffee stores owned by giant corporations miss the point—and the social experience—entirely.

Navigating the Coffee Trail

In many of San Francisco's neighborhoods, there are at least two cafes per block—parts of the Mission District and the Haight average twice that many. The key to your own adventures in cafe-land is to get a feel for a neighborhood, remember that most cafes are defined by who goes there, and discover your own favorite spots as you go.

North Beach has been a bohemian stronghold for more than a century, known best for the Beat movement that originated there in the fifties, when Jack Kerouac and Allen Ginsberg were regulars at **Caffe Trieste** and **Enrico's Sidewalk Cafe**. Lawrence Ferlinghetti still hangs around—and displays his paintings—at Enrico's and **Caffe Puccini**. There are more than 20 cafes in one six-block area alone—bordered by Union Street and Broadway on the north and south, and Grant and Powell streets on the east and west. The coffee and pastries are very Italian, as is the opera music commonly heard on the jukeboxes, and the customers range from neighborhood residents having their afternoon coffee break to visitors from all over the world.

The **Mission District** cafe scene used to be totally funky, neighborhood-oriented, and the command post of Beatnik Central. Though the scene has become a tad less unorthodox, very few tourist types make it out to Valencia Street's coffeehouses. Still, locals come from all over the city to take in the live music and spoken-word performances—and to congregate with young, anti-fashion fashion-setters. Most of the cafes (and bars) are concentrated in the area bordered by 16th and 24th streets on the north and south, and by Mission and Valencia streets on the east and west.

The **Haight** is still a hippie haven of sorts, but the post-punk species is far better suited than its flower-child predecessors to hours of angst-ridden malingering at local coffee joints. The neighborhood isn't all nose rings, purple hair, and Jerry Garcia murals, though. You'll find cafes for every taste, from tranquil little pastry shops to ultra-hip hangouts virtually vibrating from the blare of loud music and the jolt of caffeine. Walk along Haight Street from Central to Stanyan streets, and don't neglect to venture a block or two up or down the side streets.

Other cafes we mention are located in three areas where you'd expect to find the city's cafe culture well represented: **Hayes Valley**, a small, sunny neighborhood perfect for strolling because it comprises only a few blocks along Hayes Street (between Franklin and Buchanan streets) with an occasional side-street detour; **South of Market (SoMa),** an industrial neighborhood where artists, architects, multimedia

gurus, filmmakers, and musicians live and work in warehouse
lofts (below Market Street, between Second and Tenth
streets); and the **Castro** district, San Francisco's infamous gay
mecca (mostly south of Market to about 20th Street, between
Castro and Sanchez streets).

Finally, there are the refuges—cafes that provide escapes
from neighborhoods that are often overrun by tourists or
other consumption-crazed breeds. The ones we mention are
located in the **Financial District** (Grant Avenue at Sutter
Street) and the gentrified section of **Fillmore Street** (near
Steiner Street).

The Lowdown

Grills in the mist... Long before there was California cuisine or nouvelle anything, mesquite-grilled seafood was
the most popular item at **Tadich Grill**, where mesquite
has been the charcoal of choice since the '20s. This turn-
of-the-century Financial District landmark still entices
the tourist trade and local traditionalists, but the surly
waiters are no longer charming to diners who prefer to
get their steaks before they're cold and their french fries
before they are soggy. As you'll learn if you go on any of
the Dashiell Hammett walking tours, **John's Grill** is the
place where Sam Spade ate his chops (actually rack of
lamb) while in pursuit of the Maltese Falcon. A replica of
the black bird, donated by Warner Brothers, sits in a display case outside John's small Hammett museum.
Founded in 1908, this downtown dinner house has
wood-paneled walls, period furnishings, and perfectly
grilled, tender steaks. South of Market's **Fly Trap
Restaurant** has moved a few blocks away from its original 1898 address, where flypaper was tacked to the tables
to keep the horses' pesky companions off the steaks, but
it still bases its menu on traditional San Francisco grill
fare. The decor is conventional but not stuffy—small
cloth-covered tables with cafe chairs and a variety of
maps and architectural drawings on the walls—and its
comfort-food specialties follow suit. Fish and seafood are
the mainstays of the **Hayes Street Grill** menu—which
changes daily—and they may be sautéed or mesquite-
grilled with a Mexican, American, French, Italian, or
Asian accent, depending on which accompanying vegetables are freshest that day. Grilled Alaskan king salmon

and pan-fried Hama-Hama oysters are typical favorites. Some purists bemoan the loss of the older, funkier decor—creaky floors and cafe chairs—to the carpeting and chic little banquettes of the new and improved Hayes Street Grill, but the food is just as good as ever.

For committed carnivores... The best pure-and-simple steak house in town is definitely **Harris'**, midway between Russian Hill and Pacific Heights on Van Ness Avenue, where luscious cuts of Midwestern corn-fed beef are dry-aged on the premises, killer martinis flow by the barrel, and the gigantic booths can swallow you whole. Everybody who's anybody carves flesh here; Robin Williams has been know to have steaks sent to him by taxi when he couldn't make it to the restaurant in person. For more exotic flesh feasts, try the Texas antelope, Wyoming Buffalo, or locally raised ostrich. **Izzy's Steaks and Chops** is also a meat-eater's dream, but its true glory is its status as a lively Marina watering hole. The steaks, though tender and delicious, may not be quite as luxurious as those at Harris', but they cost a lot less.

Seafood supremo... Many tourists leave San Francisco without ever discovering that there's more to its seafood restaurants than the fish joints around Fisherman's Wharf. Don't you make the same mistake. Swim on down to **Aqua**, the elegant, understated Financial District seafood house. Its biggest splash was a highly publicized "quiet dinner" for lovebirds Marcia Clark and Christopher Darden a few days after the O.J. Simpson trial ended, but many less notorious celebs, such as Sharon Stone, are frequent guests. Never mind that; Aqua is one of the finest restaurants in town, and chef Michael Mina was honored by the James Beard Foundation as the rising star chef of the year in 1997. The decor is sleek and simple, adorned only by lush exotic-flower arrangements. Mina's extraordinary menu follows suit: It's clearly focused with carefully chosen, stunning details. His alderwood-smoked salmon with roasted potato, crème fraîche, and caviar is exquisite, as is his signature tuna with foie gras.

See-and-be-scenes... Where you go to be seen depends largely on whom you hope to see—and how long it takes the trendies to get bored with the place. For years, Jeremiah Tower's Stars (near Civic Center) was the easiest place for commoners to rub shoulders with celebrities. But the place went belly-up, and namedroppers had to move on. One of the new prime spots is **MoMo's** (across from the Giants' new ballpark), where the bar is jammed with hard-working, hard-drinking Multimedia Gulch types and the crowded patio is known for Don Johnson—and other celebrity—sightings. It's also known for the terrific heaters that keep it warm and comfy even on the foggiest days. The food is mercifully unfussy, the martinis are legendary, and if you can't get a table (reservations are strongly recommended), you can eat at the bar. **Moose's** (North Beach) is a good place to go to stare at fashion models and young Republicans—if you don't mind eating in a room that feels big enough to host a national convention. The best people-watching is on crowded weekend nights, when the long wait for a table leaves people milling around in the foyer near the bar. **Enrico's Sidewalk Cafe** in North Beach has always been a great place to people-watch, and nightly jazz makes it even more fun. You can have a full dinner or just stop in for a drink (try the lip-puckering Mojito, a rum, mint, and lime-juice concoction).

The "Valencia corridor"... Depending on who you talk to, the recent infusion of upscale restaurants on Valencia Street is either the best thing that has happened to the food scene in years or just one more nail in the gentrification coffin that is burying San Francisco's funky neighborhood culture alive. Either way, the area's newest sleek, chic eateries are a wet dream for interior designers and food critics alike. See for yourself. Take BART or a cab to 16th Street and walk up Valencia to 24th, pop into alleys and side streets, and stop wherever the notion strikes you. It's tough to go wrong in this eight-block stretch, from an authentic Spanish-Basque tapas feast at **Ramblas Tapas Bar** to exquisite Vietnamese delicacies at the **Slanted Door** to an antidotal bite of Japanese fast-food at **We Be Sushi**. Ramblas is just one stop on the neighborhood's fantastic tapas tour (see "Tastiest tapas," below), but it was voted best in the Bay Area by the *Bay Guardian*. For the record, the building that houses Ramblas is a perfect example of the gentrification of the Mission District—it was formerly an appliance repair shop.

You'll probably have to wait a while to get into the Slanted Door, especially on weekend nights, but the food is so good that most people are happy to pass the time with a glass of Pinot Gris or some other delight from the superb wine list. Chef/owner Charles Pham, a former UC Berkeley architecture student, transformed a vacant, rundown building into a stylish two-level restaurant with intricate Vietnamese country cuisine that has had food critics raving—and customers lined up—since opening day. Flamboyant **Firecracker** is still a hot spot for northern Chinese cuisine (see "Some like it hot") and the extraordinary French-Asian hybrid, **Watergate,** is a culinary success though its classic approach—wood-paneled walls, white linen tablecloths, and Frank Sinatra in the background—may not weather the neighborhood's relentless trend storm.

Tastiest tapas... Cities everywhere have gone a bit mad for those little Spanish tidbits that are more than an appetizer but less than a main dish. They're so *ne plus* trendy in San Francisco that every chef in town has some little signature tidbit on the menu. It's just a matter of time before that nasty little Chihuahua is hawking them for Taco Bell. Until that happens, we're sticking with our tried-and-true favorites. The reincarnation of Pintxos, **Ramblas Tapas Bar** still serves the best Basque tapas in town. It's a good thing, as Martha Stewart would say, because the guy who opened it also owns the Thirsty Bear, a microbrewery with great beer but decidedly mediocre tapas and truly regrettable service. The service is iffy at Ramblas but nobody cares because the food is so good. Try the house-cured salmon, *patatas bravas,* and spinach Catalan, and wash it down with some microbrew or sangria. (Hint: If you feel like lingering a bit after dinner, avoid paying your bill until you're definitely ready to leave. Otherwise you'll risk getting the evil eye from your waiter and all the hungry diners waiting in line.) Just around the corner, **Esperpento,** a boisterous little spot decorated like somebody's surrealistic dream about a childhood piñata party, is always packed—for good reason. It wins the purist award for the most authentic Spanish tapas in town. And the paella—a steaming mountain of shellfish, pork, chicken, and saffron-flavored rice—is to die for. Order it with a variety of tapas and share it family-style. The noisy Caribbean-psychedelic-voodoo-queen atmosphere at **Cha Cha Cha** makes it the perennial favorite among tapas lovers who can't decide what they like more: the fiery food or the endless supply of potent sangria that flows from the bar. Fortunately for them, the place is so crowded they often have to sit at the bar for an hour or more before a table is available. Why not just eat at the bar? You'll save your taste buds, plus the bartenders are a major hoot. One of Danny Glover's favorite hangouts is **Timo's in the Zanzibar**, an eccentric, semi-Bohemian place that shares its Mission District home with a neighborhood bar called the Zanzibar. The tapas are just like the ones you get in Spain—treats such as roasted new potatoes in aioli, and potato cakes and fish with cilantro-mint salsa—and the crowd is interesting, artistic, and decidedly local. The best part about going to **Carta** is that its Upper Market cuisine map changes every month. They always serve both "small plates" and regular entrees, but one month might feature Peruvian *jalea de pescado* (batter-fried fish and seafood with pickled onions), and the next might be Turkish *manti* (dumplings with yogurt, garlic, and tomato sauce). One of the most popular months is January, which always features a "best-of" menu from all over the globe. Sit at any of the tables by the window and you can watch the refurbished cable cars from all over the world pass by on Market Street.

Hold the hype... No matter how endlessly food critics lavish praise on the super-restaurants, there are some sacred cows, like Berkeley's **Chez Panisse**, that aren't always worth the money and effort. To give credit where it's due, Chez Panisse has been the most important restaurant in the Bay Area's culinary development in the past two decades and chef/owner Alice Waters was honored as the 1997 Humanitarian of the Year by the James Beard Foundation. But sometimes students surpass their teachers, and these days there are plenty of other restaurants with more innovative chefs and less expensive tabs. The fact that you have to reserve a month in advance for a weekend dinner may be a testament to the restaurant's reputation, but it's also a pain in the neck, especially when you don't know if you'll be in the mood for the set menu when the day finally arrives.

Some like it hot... San Francisco's latest addition to the

DINING AND CAFES | THE LOWDOWN

four-alarm category is **Firecracker,** a stylish new Chinese restaurant that's right at home with its fiery hot Latin neighbors in the Mission District. Chef Phil Lee denies the California-fusion label that is often applied to his low-oil, low-sugar cooking: His cuisine is actually true to traditional Beijing cookery, in which the scarcity of oil was compensated by lots of garlic and spice. Firecracker's environment is also contemporary, yet faithful, to Chinese history, with old photographs on the walls and Chinese opera music mixed in with modern jazz. For authentic Thai food that's unbelievably delicious, and not watered down for uninitiated Western tongues, the Upper Haight's **Thep Phanom** can't be beat. The Thai wait staff, whose traditional garb suits the gracious, antique-laden dining room, usually tries to warn you when a dish is hot. Believe them. The super-hot delicacies include *larb ped* (duck salad with mint, hot chili peppers, red onion, and lemon); even the milder dishes, such as charbroiled catfish or deep-fried quail, are served with a variety of hot dipping sauces. For cooler options, try any of the mild curries, especially those made with coconut milk. **Cha Cha Cha** is still a Haight hot spot and now has a second location in the Mission District. It's an exhaustingly popular place, especially if you indulge in the house Sangria in the funky bar area during your inevitable wait for a table. (You may find yourself in line behind regulars like Chris Isaak.) And the Cajun/Caribbean food (mostly tapas) is absolutely fiery. That's saying something in San Francisco, where Mexican food has numbed most locals to anything cooler than a jalapeño. If the huge plates of flawless spicy ribs, beef, and chicken didn't already qualify **Flint's** of North Oakland as the undisputed barbecue-joint champion of the world, the fact that it serves as late as 4am would clinch the title. If you even *think* you like barbecue, hop on BART and ride over to North Oakland (Flint's is two blocks south of the Ashby stop)—there's nothing even close to this in San Francisco. It's all takeout, though, so if your craving comes at 3am, you may have to smuggle your greasy treasures into your hotel room.

Pass the dumplings, darling... The other little morsels that make tastebuds quiver in ecstasy are served from dim sum carts—tender shrimp wrapped in paper-thin dumplings, tiny crab cakes, octopus with hot peppers, and dozens of other Chinese delicacies. For exceptionally delicate dumplings, **Yank Sing** has long been the favorite of locals on the weekends—Financial District types tend to crowd into its modern, somewhat upscale dining room during the week—but nearby **Harbor Village** is a more serene and majestic alternative at lunchtime (11am–2:30pm). You won't find any unidentified steamed objects on their carts; instead you'll find dozens of authentic delicacies served by a meticulous wait staff. Every porcelain dish and carved chopstick reflects the Imperial aesthetic Harbor Village claims to have brought from Hong Kong, and the dim sum tradition allows you to enjoy all its refinement without the high tab of its exquisite dinners.

Best Chinese in Chinatown... R & G Lounge serves probably the best food in Chinatown. The dining room used to be in the basement of a commercial building, but a brighter upstairs room has opened to accommodate the burgeoning clientele drawn primarily by super-fresh seafood. If you think Maine has a corner on the lobster market, try a live one from R & G's tank. One huge plus is that the waiters will gladly translate the Chinese menu for Westerners, which expands the choices considerably.

Ultra-chic Chinoise... You usually don't think of donning a dinner jacket to chow down on Chinese food, but it's not a bad idea at **Tommy Toy's**, where elaborate meals are served by an army of tuxedoed waiters who will pick up your napkin before you realize you've dropped it on the floor. Unquestionably the most elegant Chinese restaurant in San Francisco, it's the top choice for both local and visiting celebrities, as the entryway gallery of Clint Eastwood memorabilia will attest. Whole, bright-red lobsters, trimmed and served tableside, are the house specialty.

South of the border in the Mission... The Mission District is crammed with Central and South American food that often outdoes native versions, thanks to the fabulous fresh ingredients that abound in San Francisco. Even the most ordinary taqueria beats a fast-food lunch by a mile. Start with our suggestions, then graze your own way through the neighborhood. **Los Jarritos** makes wonderful fresh tortillas and other home-cooked Mexican delights for a loyal following of locals, many of whom travel across the city—and sometimes the bridges—for its food and friendly ambience. Call in advance to find out when they'll be serving *posole* (a spicy chicken-and-pork stew that takes all day to prepare and is rarely available outside of home kitchens). If you want to get in a good mood fast, go to **La Rondalla**. It serves standard Mexican fare such as enchiladas, *chiles rellenos* (stuffed chili peppers baked in egg batter), and other recognizable dishes, but there's nothing standard about the atmosphere, from the year-round Christmas ornaments to the strolling mariachis who serenade on weekends. **La Taqueria** is an immaculate neighborhood favorite famous for its shredded pork *carnitas*, which fill soft, fluffy tortillas to make the perfect taco.

Chef/owner Gus Shinzato of **Fina Estampa**, another comfortable storefront establishment, is Japanese-Peruvian, and his menu relies heavily on Peru's spicy cross-cultural coastal cuisine, made with fresh local catches. Specialties include *parihuela*, a tomato and chili soup laced with the freshest seafood he can find, including mussels, clams, shrimp, squid, and other Pacific delicacies. Modest **El Nuevo Frutilandia** is one of the few places in the city to get home-cooked Puerto Rican and Cuban food (the fresh fruit shakes are wonderful, as are the Puerto Rican dumplings made of crushed plantain and yuca, filled with shredded pork). The odds of running into a horde of tourists here are extremely slim. Right next door you can get one of the best dinner deals in town at **El Trebol**, a Formica-table kind of place that serves Salvadoran/Nicaraguan treats like *pupusas* (handmade corn patties stuffed with cheese or meat or both) for less than a dollar and full meals (including rice and beans) for less than $4.

Seoul food... At do-it-yourself Korean barbecue joints the food is as much fun to cook as it is to eat. You barbecue marinated beef and pork on grills built into the tables, wrap the meat in a lettuce leaf and add whatever condiments you like—kind of a Korean burrito. **Brothers Restaurant,** one of many popular Korean eateries along Geary Boulevard (Richmond District), caters to a primarily Korean clientele—it's probably the most popular Geary Boulevard place with local Koreans, and the staff sometimes proves its own authenticity when you're making reservations in English. You can grill meats at your table's wood-fired hibachi or sample from the rest of the small menu. Brothers' kimchee (spicy pickled cabbage) is outstanding. A few blocks down the street, **Heavenly Hot** is a huge hit with families and big parties that love to play tabletop chef on the all-you-can-eat plan. The food is hardly gourmet, but you can choose from a staggering variety of hot pots (don't worry; there are pictures on the menu) and if you are under four feet tall, you eat for free. The Taiwanese hot pot food at nearby **Coriya Hot Pot City** (Clement Street) has been described as a cross between Japanese shabu-shabu and Korean barbecue. Each table has a hot pot and a grill, so you can steam or saute beef, pork, chicken, seafood, and vegetables to your heart's content. Again, you're the chef. The place is loud, crowded, festive, and does not serve parties of one.

A passage to India... Many of the best Indian eateries in the Bay Area are outside San Francisco in the Indian and Pakistani communities of the East and South Bay, but the best in the city, **Gaylord of India**, is in an unlikely spot—the middle of touristy Ghirardelli Square. Unfortunately, you'll pay rather dearly for the gourmet quality (about $35 per person, à la carte) and its wonderful view of the bay. One way to economize is to order the *thali* plates ($22 to $29 per person), which allow you to sample a wide variety of either vegetarian or tandoori dishes; then you can splurge on a luscious dessert, such as *kulfi* (homemade pistachio ice cream). A much less costly alternative is a multicourse meatless feast at **Ganges Vegetarian Restaurant**, a cozy refuge in a Victorian house near the Haight. There are low tables with floor cushions in back and Western-style tables and chairs in front. Owner Kukoo Singh plans to change the name soon, but the location and great food will stay the same. Classic specialties include stuffed baby potatoes, *alu-gobi* (cauliflower and potatoes), and stuffed bananas.

Asian delights... One of the first destinations on your San Francisco ethnic-food adventure tour should be **Angkor Borei**, the perfect place to sample Cambodia's intricate cuisine at the modest price tag locals have come to expect in the Mission District. The combination of spices in most any dish on the menu is intriguing—typically, sweet basil and tangy lemongrass are first to hit the tongue, then a short blast of hot chili pepper bursts through and, finally, soothing coconut milk brings the whole blend together. If the combination of tropical flavors and French culinary techniques makes you want to try even more sophisticated Cambodian cuisine (at a considerably higher price), try **Angkor Wat**, an elegant Richmond District dinner house. To economize, take advantage of the weekday lunch special (call for current specifics). Geary Boulevard's tropical, romantic **Straits Cafe** features extraordinary food from Singapore—an exotic hybrid of European, Indian, Chinese, and Malaysian tastes that mixes spicy-hot peanut sauces with cool cucumbers and coconut-milk curries. Chef Chris Yeo uses all these flavors and textures to create extraordinary dishes like *laksa* (tamarind-scented broth with fish, chili peppers, onions, and rice noodles), and *satays* (chunks of meat). For great Vietnamese food, check out the **Golden Turtle**, a modestly elegant restaurant near Russian Hill that looks and tastes much more expensive than it is. A choice of several French wines complements the delicately spiced entrees, ranging from steamed sea bass with fresh ginger to grilled beef with lemongrass. There's also good star-spotting here, if you recognize Chinese movie stars. Otherwise you'll have to settle for the unpredictable occasional visit by Mick Jagger or Robin Williams. The **Saigon Sandwich Cafe** is a Civic Center take-out deli with incredible Vietnamese sandwiches—baguettes full of pork or chicken with spicy sauces, cilantro, and peppers, or the popular Vietnamese-style meatball sandwiches—both for around $2.

Japanese jewels... There are more than 75 sushi bars in San Francisco, but for a variety of Japanese country-style food—fluffy tempura, savory noodles, and dumplings—go to **Sanppo** in the heart of Japantown, a favorite of local Japanese, where you may be asked to share a table when the regular crowd elbows in. Sanppo's rustic, home-like decor is instantly cozy. The tempura is consistently excellent and the *gyoza nabe* (pot stickers in a savory broth with noodles and bean curd) is a wonderful meal in itself. For the freshest sushi in town, call in advance to **Hama-Ko**, a gracious little Cole Valley restaurant, and ask chef Ted Kashiyama to prepare his special deluxe meal of hot and cold dishes; the exact contents depend on what local fishermen have available that morning. There are four **We Be Sushi** locations in town, two of which are within a few blocks of each other on Valencia Street (16th and 22nd streets). Those two are usually crowded at night with hip locals who know the sushi is both good and cheap—$10 to $15 for an ample dinner. The other locations, on Geary Boulevard and Judah Street, also cater to locals, but in those neighborhoods the denizens are a bit less artsy than in the Mission District. Wallet alert: We Be Sushi is also We Be Cash Only.

The French connection... Masa's used to be the name bandied about most often when people were bragging about the best restaurants in town—chef Julian Serrano was virtually worshipped by food critics and fledgling chefs for his unflagging dedication to authentic, perfectly executed French cuisine. But Serrano moved to Las Vegas and left Masa's kitchen to his sous chef, Chad Callahan. The latest chef to try his hand there is award-winning Ron Siegel, who used to be the head honcho at Charles Nob Hill. **Fleur de Lys** is San Francisco's true gem among classic French restaurants. Chef/owner Hubert Keller—who was the first guest chef in White House history when he cooked for President Clinton—was named best chef in California by the James Beard Foundation (1997). It's tough to find anything critical to say about this romantic, elegant Union Square restaurant, where the regularly changing menu is full of sumptuous dishes like boneless quail stuffed with swiss chard and pine nuts, enhanced with foie gras and a rich Merlot sauce. This is the very best of French dining—without the snotty waiters. Three bits of advice: Reserve well in advance, try the "Symphony of Fleur de Lys Appetizers," and don't be surprised if a dinner for two costs as much as your plane ticket. And if you really want to go out of your way for great food, take a 90-minute trip from the city to **French Laundry**, up in Yountville, a small wine-country village. You'll have to reserve several months in advance, but it's worth the drive, the wait, and the money. Fleur de Lys' Hubert Keller was named best chef in California, but French Laundry's Thomas Keller snagged the title of best chef in the entire country that same year, and has been the center of rave reviews all over the nation ever since. A young, enthusiastic California chef, Keller grows at least half of what he cooks in three gardens on the premises of this tiny three-star restaurant that has the feel of a private country home. He oversees every bite that ends up on a diner's plate. You'll find far less expensive French food in more modest bistros such as **Fringale** (South of Market). Fringale's menu reflects the chef's Basque origins and his classic training; the place is reasonably priced, and so friendly and comfortable that you never feel self-conscious, despite the studied indifference of much of the too-hip-for-words clientele. The frisée salad with warm bacon dressing and croutons is exquisite—soft but not soggy—and the pork tenderloin with onion and apple marmalade is rich and velvety without being overly sweet. If you want to feel as though you *are* in Paris, stop in at a Financial District treasure, **Cafe Claude**, where every fixture, chair, dish, and spoon has been imported from France. It's jammed with a lively, youngish crowd who come to enjoy both the atmosphere and the inexpensive but oh-so-French sandwiches along with a glass or two of Rhine, Beaujolais, or Mâcon Blanc wine.

Super supper clubs... You don't have to line up and wait an hour just to get in the door of a supper club anymore, but the best ones are still extremely popular, and new ones that hope to last longer than a Kleenex have to be both good restaurants and good nightclubs at the same time. **Bruno's** is super-hip, incredibly gauche, or wonderfully eclectic, depending on how you feel about savoring (and paying large for) a scrumptious Mediterranean-style dinner in an atmosphere that has been described as a cross between Frank Sinatra fifties posh and Midwest basement rec room. Chef Ola Fendert has done a fabulous job of building on former famous big-time chef James Ormsby's French-Italian soul-food shtick with her own hearty meat and fresh fish creations and a yummy oxtail dish. The food is unquestionably worth the money, but it's not what keeps Bruno's on the A-list (no matter how many times it closes, reopens, or changes chefs). The real deal here is the after-dinner entertainment, which has folks jammed like sardines into the adjoining lounges to dance, sweat, and get totally up-close-and-personal with hip young locals decked out in slinky cocktail dresses, dinner jackets, and chic thrift-store finds. The live music calendar is packed with contemporary jazz and Latin dance music. The atmosphere at **Mecca** is more rough-edged opulence, a perfect fit for its Upper Market address and for some of its famous customers, like Joan Jett. The circular bar is the centerpiece of the restaurant, which features gender-illusionist cabaret shows and an eclectic mix of live music ranging from soul to classic jazz. But forget about the great atmosphere—the food alone is reason enough to make a pilgrimage to Mecca. Chef Michael Fennelly mixes Creole and Asian influences with California cuisine, and the result is unforgettable. Try the fresh stone crab legs with spicy *remoulade* for an appetizer and follow it up with rock shrimp *pad Thai* rice noodles (tons of shrimp, peanuts, carrots, asparagus, and cilantro) or a grilled pork chop with apple and date chutney. And save room for the unbelievably delicious desserts. Union Square's **Biscuits and Blues,** named 1999 Blues Club of the Year by the Memphis Blues Foundation, isn't quite as funky as it sounds, though it definitely takes pride in presenting down-home food at its dressed-up best. Original owner Regina Charboneau sold the place, but new chef Jose Carbanara has kept the menu on track with solid Southern-style cooking, while some of the best blues acts in the country keep the crowds coming.

Vegging out… The Mother of All Vegetarian Restaurants once was **Greens**, where there's a two-week waiting list to sample the fare that has spawned several cookbooks, international acclaim, and a devoted following. This is no hippie-veggie-health-food cafe; it is meatless *haute cuisine*, combining the best of French, Mediterranean, and California cookery. Unfortunately the service has become inconsistent and the menu has lost its edge. Still, it retains its status as a classic and is worth a visit for yummy breakfasts and romantic late-night desserts—the dining room's view of the marina and the bay is stunning. For a spectacular vegan meal, you're better off at **Millennium.** Even carnivores have given rave reviews to this hip, beautiful Civic Center restaurant that, says the *Chronicle,* has moved vegetarian cuisine to a new level. Chef Eric Tucker, a lifelong vegan, is a daredevil in the kitchen, concocting exotic entrées and outlandish, architectural-looking, scrumptious desserts. The staff is knowledgeable but never stuffy. Signature special: monthly "Full Moon Aphrodisiac Special," including a four-course prix fixe menu with a Chinese Herbal Love Potion and a room in the adjoining Abigail Hotel. Feeling frisky yet? **Ganges Vegetarian Restaurant** is a great spot for people who love traditional Indian food but would prefer not to lay their eyes on any cooked flesh.

North Beach classics... Columbus Avenue's main strip (between Broadway and Washington Square) is loaded with calzone joints and trattorias, but one of the more recent "classics" in San Francisco's "little Italy" is **Rose Pistola,** named the best new restaurant in the country by the James Beard Foundation when it opened in 1996. It continues to attract the rich and famous as well as the hungry. Superstar guests range from Kirk Hammett (Metallica) to Francis Ford Coppola. The sleek decor might have been out of place in the midst of North Beach's unpretentious little cafes, but owner Reed Hearon (who previously turned a South of Market warehouse into the loud and trendy Restaurant Lulu) has managed to keep the place warm and inviting with a friendly bar and sidewalk tables for people-watching. The menu runs from snacks to full meals, so you can stop for a minute or stay for as long as you want. Try the *cioppino,* a classic fish soup that was originally brought by Italian immigrants to San Francisco, where local Dungeness crab became the central ingredient. Meanwhile, Rose Pistola's popular chef, Scott Warner, went around the corner to help Hearon open **Black Cat and Blue Bar,** a jazz club on Broadway that started with an eclectic menu meant to reflect the diversity of cuisines that have thrived in North Beach. But eclectic turned out to be unidentifiable-mediocre, so Hearon and Warner ditched the idea and turned the club into a cozy bistro that *Examiner* food critic/chef/author Patricia Unterman says is now so French, it might as well be called *Chat Noir.* With leather banquettes, dark wood tables covered in butcher paper, and lace curtains, the place that was originally named for the neighborhood's "cool cat" beatniks now "looks as if it were airlifted from the Montparnasse," Unterman observes. And she, like most guests there, absolutely loves it. Celebs haunt the place; actors Michael Tucker and Jill Eikenberry (and tables full of major-league baseball players) come for the classic food, service, and wine. You won't find fussy hybrids here—the hamburgers are a slice of heaven. Farther up Columbus Avenue at Greenwich Street, you'll find rich, authentic Tuscan food that locals love at **Buca Giovanni**. Garlic lovers should be in heaven here—the smell of the stinking rose greets you well before you descend into the downstairs dining room (*buca* means "hole" in Italian) that gave the place its name. A couple of years ago, chef Giovanni Leone turned over the run of his beloved kitchen to a third-generation Brooklyn Italian, Michael Aofieri, who was given the task of continuing the tradition of home-style cooking while updating the menu. Aofieri's hearty dishes rival Leone's in richness and proportion—specialties include *coniglio umido con olive nereb* (baby rabbit stew with black olives, roasted tomatoes, fresh thyme and sage over grilled herb polenta), *ravioli di anitra-porcini* (ravioli stuffed with veal and ricotta cheese, served with a roasted red pepper and toasted walnut cream sauce), and *maiale alla griglia* (grilled double-cut pork chops topped with sautéed chanterelle mushrooms and baby arugula, with garlic mashed potatoes). Plan on two to three hours for dinner—Aofieri's hearty, mega-caloric cuisine requires plenty of time to savor and digest.

The rest of the world... You'd be missing out on three of San Francisco's most fun—and unusual—dining experiences if you bypassed Suppenküche, Yaya Cuisine, or Helmand. Fans of German food may find **Suppenküche** one of the only places in town to satisfy their appetite. A small, spirited Hayes Valley beer hall and cafe, it serves delicious German food and drink to a good-humored, youngish crowd. The staples, served at plain wood tables, are variations of sauerkraut and sausage—flanked by baskets full of fresh-baked breads or mounds of buttery Bavarian-style mashed potatoes—supplemented by the more refined choices on the daily special chalkboard. At **Yaya Cuisine**, Chef Yehya Salih, who learned at the stove of superchef Jeremiah Tower, has transformed the cuisine of his native Iraq into a mouth-watering Mediterranean/California hybrid. Salih's enthusiasm is evident in every aspect of this Sunset District restaurant: his giant mural of Babylon that covers an entire wall, his habit of leaving the kitchen to chat with customers, and an ambitious menu. Tables are set with Iraqi-style flatbread to be dipped in thyme-sesame olive oil and savored while you mull over your order: Try the steamed oysters or vege-

DINING AND CAFES | THE LOWDOWN

tarian dolmas (his are whole vegetables stuffed with bulgur and chili peppers), both dressed in yogurt-mint sauce, or such main dishes as a hearty lamb stew or the California-style roasted baby chicken. The Helmand River flows out of Iran through Afghanistan; the formal dinner house **Helmand** rests on the shores of Broadway, which flows from North Beach to Pacific Heights. The Afghani food here is exquisite, with flavors from Central Asia, India, and the Middle East, and owner Mahmood Karzai has done Westerners the favor of removing much of the fat from the traditional recipes. We recommend *aushak,* a delicate, triangular-shaped wheat dumpling filled with leek and served in a yogurt-mint or beef sauce reminiscent of the Far East, and *chowpan seekh,* a grilled rack of lamb on Iranian-style flatbread; don't be afraid to try lots of new things, like *kaddo borawni,* an appetizer of baked pumpkin with garlic-yogurt sauce.

Goofy decor, fabulous food... What used to be Miss Pearl's Jam House, the cartoon version of "Abbott and Costello Go to Gilligan's Island," has been reincarnated as **Backflip,** a poolside cocktail party at the Tenderloin's Phoenix Motel. Entering through the modernistic cocktail lounge, you may go temporarily blind from the iridescent blue pool-color theme. Either float into the circular bar or swim upstream to the dining room, where the young and beautiful staff is outfitted head to toe in, you guessed it, iridescent blue. Once you settle into your faux cabana—a table enclosed on the sides by curtains—a wandering 7-foot drag queen (very tall platform shoes) may stop by to talk a little harmless trash and make sure you're having a good time. And you will be. This place is fun and the food is fabulous. The menu is "cocktail food," a whimsical variation on tapas that ranges from gourmet nibbles like smoked pork bruschetta with fig jam and shaved asiago to "tater tots" (potato and spring onion croquettes). Have a chocolate "martini" for dessert (a rich mousse served in an oversized martini glass).

The **Cypress Club,** though reminiscent of a grand, baroque opium den, is the opposite of funky. The ultra-chic backdrop once made this North Beach dining room a temple of trendiness, with more patrons jockeying for a strategic spot at the "see-and-be-seen" bar than ordering food at the tables. You might rub shoulders with Johnny Depp, Don Johnson, or any of the 49ers.

The Trend Factor has waned a bit, but the menu remains impressive; it's as rich as the decor. Don't miss the venison.

Kid pleasers... Dining with the family can be tricky business, especially if your children vary in age, but you're always safe in any of the neighborhood eateries in the Mission District, where there is usually at least one six-year-old running between tables while apologetic parents try to pull in the reins. **El Nuevo Frutilandia** (24th Street) is an especially good choice, because the fruit shakes will appeal to all ages, even if the Puerto Rican food is a bit too spicy for some younger palates. **La Rondalla** (Valencia Street) is fun for lunch or early dinner because of the goofy decorations and the traditional Mexican food, familiar to most kids—and not too fiery. (Later in the evening, the bar livens up and the atmosphere is less suitable for younger children.) If the kids do like hot-and-spicy treats, take them to **Heavenly Hot** or **Coriya Hot Pot City** (Richmond District), where they can have a ball playing chef and cooking their own meat on the grills.

Where to seal a deal... This, of course, depends upon the client. The Old-Boy network tends to be wary of fancy food and effusive waiters, which you'll never find at **Harris'** (Van Ness Avenue). It's not cheap, but it's the best steak house in the city, and a few of Harris' martinis can soften up even the toughest old buzzard. If your client is of the artistic persuasion, go to the **Cypress Club** (North Beach), where the ingenious, surrealistic decor is matched by the superb menu. Attorneys love the **Fly Trap Restaurant**, the traditional San Francisco grill (with a few culinary updates) across the street from the courthouse. If your clients are food lovers who don't want to be bothered with trendy trappings, take them to our favorite small French bistro, **Fringale** (South of Market).

Cheap eats... The Mission District is jammed with great food at inexpensive prices, but the best buy of all is **El Trebol** (24th Street), where a full Salvadoran dinner including rice and beans comes in at around $4. You'll also find good food for next to nothing at **La Taqueria** (Mission Street near 24th Street), a family-oriented

DINING AND CAFES | THE LOWDOWN

Mexican cafe, and **El Nuevo Frutilandia** (24th St.), where the fruit shakes are as popular as the Puerto Rican food. The best Vietnamese deli in the city is the **Saigon Sandwich Cafe** (near Civic Center), where $2 buys a delectable pork or chicken sandwich with spicy sauce.

Eating with insomniacs... San Francisco is not known as an all-night town, but there are a couple of spots that stay open until the wee hours, if not all night, and are a cut above the 24-hour Market Street joints where the coffee is as greasy as the bacon and eggs. Hamburger Mary's was our favorite, with its wonderful kitschy decor, creamers made from baby bottles with the nipples snipped off, and gender-bender waitstaff (not to mention the wicked margaritas)—but to the entire city's great disappointment, it closed its doors in April 2001. The all-night good-bye bash was a fitting wake for what had been a countercultural institution of the gay/queer/radical community for almost 30 years. On the other side of the coin, one of the city's most-missed late-night burger joints, **Clown Alley,** reopened at its original location on the corner of Columbus Avenue and Jackson Street in North Beach. It closed several years ago, then reopened as an upscale and thoroughly point-less reincarnation of its former self, which was thankfully very short-lived. Clown Alley has now been resurrected as a cheapo burger joint where you can walk up to the window and order a gooey chili-cheese with fries until 3am. And if you're too drunk to drive, eat outside—the cold air will sober you up in a hurry. Another place to eat after the bars close is **Sparky's Diner**, a 24-hour Church Street diner that serves a decent burger and a hearty breakfast to Castro and Upper Market locals. The lights are a tad too bright and the wait staff a bit too dim, but at least the breakfasts here avoid the white-bread toast and frozen-hash-brown-type food substance that seem to be standard issue at all-night coffee shops. It was good enough for Queen Latifah when she was in town.

The morning after... Two breakfast stops are mandatory when you visit San Francisco—Sear's, in Union Square, and the Seal Rock Inn, near the ocean. **Sear's Fine Foods** is best visited after 9 on weekday mornings, when the Financial District crowd has had time to get to work. Its coin-size Swedish pancakes are marvelous—

thin and sweet like the best French crêpes—and you get almost a million of them (well, 18) stacked high on your plate. A family-owned coffee shop attached to a small inn, **Seal Rock Inn** is one of those breakfast places you can go to on a Saturday or Sunday morning and see who slept with whom the night before. The scenic location is unbeatable (two blocks from the Pacific Ocean, near the Cliff House), the eggs Benedict and omelettes are a local legend, and you can actually find a place to park on the street. There is also patio dining. If you don't have a night-before paramour, take your kids here and walk down afterward to the Musée Mechanique at the Cliff House.

The cafe superhighway... Just a couple of years ago, SF Net coin-operated computer terminals were sucking down quarters like parking meters on speed. For a quarter for five minutes, cafe rats could log on and chat with simpatico souls at other cafes around town, send and receive e-mail, and post messages on cyberspace bulletin boards. Coins are still clinking at more than two dozen locations in the Bay Area, including **Jammin' Java Coffee House**, **Horseshoe Coffee House**, **Muddy Waters Coffee House**, and **Brain Wash Cafe**, to name a few, but SF Net's limited services have taken a back seat to the city's new "cybercafes." The dot-com invasion has pretty much gone the way of the Gold Rush, and most of the cybernerds who were banking on stock options have packed up their laptops and dot-gone back to wherever they came from (nobody ever seemed to know for sure), but there is still life in San Francisco's cyberspace. South of Market's "Multimedia Gulch" includes such digital diners as **Internet Alfredo**, where you can sip a latte while you hook up to the World Wide Web; SF Net doesn't have direct Internet access. Internet Alfredo has eight full-access terminals and is open 24 hours a day; you can do everything from desktop publishing to surfing the net and creating your own web page ($6 per hour). Cowabunga!

Wake-up call: cafes that open before 8am... When you're up and at 'em at the crack of dawn and you need a serious caffeine jolt, only a select number of cafes are open and ready to pamper you with a perfectly frothy cappuccino or cafe au lait, airy croissants, and the morning paper to boot. If you're staying in a downtown hotel, try one of Courtney Cox's favorites, the Financial District's **Cafe de la Presse**, a subdued French-owned refuge that is also an international newsstand. In North Beach, **Caffe Greco**, **Caffe Trieste**, and **Stella Pastry & Caffe** are early-morning favorites. There are even a few bohemian types who open their eyes before noon—**Cafe La Bohème** and **Muddy Waters Coffee House** serve daybreak espresso in the Mission District, while Haight Street early-birds go to **Jammin' Java Coffee House**.

How about a little fresh air?... San Francisco's narrow sidewalks leave little room for outdoor seating, and some neighborhoods strictly enforce ordinances against al fresco impediments to pedestrian traffic. A typical sidewalk seat is a bench—sans tables—in front of the building. There are some notable exceptions, however. At the granddaddy of the city's sidewalk cafes, **Enrico's Sidewalk Cafe** (North Beach), huge awnings overhang a table-seating area that provides Broadway's best people-watching—you feel as though you have box seats at the opera. Then there's the elevated wooden deck outside the gay hangout **Cafe Flore** in the Castro. On a foggy day, it's like being in one of those pensive French B-movies. On a sunny day, it's like being on the French Riviera. But no matter what the weather, it's almost impossible to get a deck seat unless you're there at opening time (7am) or have the patience to wait for someone to leave—and can sprint to the open table faster than anyone else. Our favorite backyard "garden," at Mad Magda's Russian Tea Room in the sunny Hayes Valley, is now closed, but you can still bask at **Red Dora's Bearded Lady** in the city's other sunbelt, the Mission District.

Cafe con angst... Every once in a while, every self-respecting cafe-dweller must disregard the sheer bliss of everyday life and slump over a coffee-stained table to agonize over some irresolvable existential dilemma. The absurdist population is high at **Brain Wash Cafe**, surrounded as it is by not only the endless spinning of clothes in dryers, but by the barren industrial architecture of South of Market warehouses. Still haven't met your angst quota? Go back to the Haight and listen to the lyrics blasting from the sound system at the **Horse-shoe Coffee House**. If the Horseshoe's whining, dysfunctional, alternative soundtrack doesn't send you running for the Prozac, nothing will.

All-day hangouts... One of the unwritten rules of cafe life is that customers get to linger as long as they wish, even if all they buy is one cup of coffee. But certain places are more conducive than others to the all-day, write-in-your-journal type of pause. **Cafe La Bohème** (Mission District) is the ultimate spot to waste a day—dozens of unemployed poets, artists, and general layabouts have made a career of it. If you sit there long enough, you'll see—and maybe meet—people of all ages, ethnic backgrounds, professions, and talents. (You'll probably also be asked for spare change a dozen times.) The location of **South Park Cafe** makes it possible to hang out all day within arm's length of an espresso without having to stay inside the whole time. It's one of a Victorian necklace of stylish eateries that circles the oval lawn of South Park.

Live music... The North Beach institution **Enrico's Side-walk Cafe** (also see Nightlife) presents live jazz seven nights a week, ranging from Brazilian, bebop, and swing to Dixieland and jump & jive. For opera buffs, North Beach's **Caffe Trieste** has live opera music on Sunday afternoons. Other cafes that occasionally present live music include **Brain Wash Cafe** and **Red Dora's Bearded Lady.**

Jack Kerouac woke up here... Legendary writers have scribbled on napkins all over North Beach. Jack Kerouac and Allen Ginsberg were regulars at **Caffe Trieste**; Richard Brautigan hawked homemade copies of his poems and stories there. Francis Ford Coppola drafted a screenplay at one of the small tables at **Mario's Bohemian Cigar Store Cafe.** Lawrence Ferlinghetti is a regular at **Caffe Puccini**, where every seat is a window seat, and he still displays his artwork at both Puccini and **Enrico's Sidewalk Cafe.**

Hippie holdouts... One of the few true hippie cafes left over from the sixties—it was a crash pad then—is **Sacred Grounds Cafe**, a Haight-Ashbury classic that will make you want to tie-dye your entire wardrobe. The atmosphere is gentle, but not nostalgic. The Mission District's **Cafe La Bohème** welcomes virtually everybody, and always has its share of customers who look like extras from *Woodstock*.

The Index

$$$$	over $30
$$$	$18–$30
$$	$10–$17
$	under $10

Angkor Borei. This small, unpretentious neighborhood restaurant serves fine Cambodian cuisine at Mission District prices. Try the delicate vegetable-filled spring rolls to warm up, then go for a spicy noodle dish.... *Tel 415/550-8417. 3471 Mission St., 14 or 49 MUNI bus.* $ **(see p. 63)**

Angkor Wat. Possibly the best Cambodian restaurant in the western hemisphere. On Friday or Saturday night, you'll be treated not only to exquisite tropical-French dishes, but also to performances by the Cambodian Royal Ballet.... *Tel 415/221-7887. 4217 Geary Blvd., 38 MUNI bus. Reservations recommended.* $$–$$$ **(see p. 64)**

Aqua. Celebrity lovebirds and hungry powerbrokers frequent this elegant seafood restaurant. Chef Michael Mina was named rising star chef of the year by the James Beard Foundation (1997).... *Tel 415/956-9662. 252 California St., Financial District, Embarcadero BART/MUNI Metro station; 42 MUNI bus. Reservations highly recommended.* $$$–$$$$ **(see p. 56)**

Backflip. Join rock stars, trendsetters, and people-watchers at this poolside restaurant/cocktail lounge adjacent to the

Phoenix Motel.... *Tel 415/771-FLIP. 601 Eddy St. (at Larkin St.), Civic Center BART/MUNI Metro station; 5 or 38 MUNI bus. Reservations recommended for "cabana" tables. $$* **(see p. 70)**

Biscuits and Blues. The dressed-up, down-home menu at this supper club includes treats like yam fries, along with jambalaya, chicken, catfish, and, of course, biscuits.... *Tel 415/292-BLUE. 401 Mason St., Union Square, Powell-Mason or Powell-Hyde cable car; Powell St. BART/MUNI Metro station; 38 MUNI bus. $$–$$$*
(see p. 67)

Black Cat and Blue Bar. One of the big bonuses of this fabulous little French brasserie in North Beach is that it serves both food and jazz until about 2am—a late bite in this town.... *Tel 415/981-2233. 501 Broadway, North Beach, 15 or 30 MUNI bus. $$–$$$* **(see p. 68)**

Brain Wash Cafe. Hang with the post-punkers or go online while you wash 'n' dry.... *Tel 415/861-3663. 1122 Folsom St. (near 7th St.), Civic Center BART station; 12 or 19 MUNI bus. $* **(see pp. 73, 74, 75)**

Brothers Restaurant. This Korean barbecue spot has wood-fired hibachis at each table, plus a host of other dishes for those who choose not to barbecue.... *Tel 415/387-7991. 4128 Geary Blvd., 38 MUNI bus. Reservations recommended. AE, DC not accepted. $$* **(see p. 62)**

Bruno's. This swanky, retro supper club has a huge local following, not only because of its hip Mission District location, but because of chef Ola Fendert's yummy Mediterranean food.... *Tel 415/648-7701. 2389 Mission St., 24th St. BART station. $$$* **(see p. 66)**

Buca Giovanni. Chef Michael Aofieri's authentic Tuscan cuisine—created from home-grown produce—is sinfully rich and hearty.... *Tel 415/776-7766. 800 Greenwich St., Powell-Mason cable car; 30 MUNI bus. Reservations recommended. $$* **(see p. 69)**

Cafe Claude. This great lunch spot tucked away in the Financial District is the most authentic Parisian-style cafe in the city; wonderful sandwiches and wines by the glass.... *Tel*

415/392-3505. 7 Claude Lane (near Bush and Kearny Sts.), Montgomery St. BART/MUNI Metro station; 38 MUNI bus. $ **(see p. 66)**

Cafe de la Presse. Escape from the shopping frenzy of Union Square into this oh-so-French cafe.... *Tel 415/398-2680. 352 Grant Ave. (near Sutter St.), 2, 3, 4, or 76 MUNI bus. $* **(see p. 74)**

Cafe Flore. The food is good (a bit pricey) and the outside sundeck is one of the prime people-watching spots in the Castro District.... *Tel 415/621-8579. 2298 Market St. (at Noe St.), Castro St. MUNI Metro station; 8, 24, or 37 MUNI bus. $* **(see p. 74)**

Cafe La Bohème. Share big, wooden tables with artistic and often terminally unemployed cafe-dwellers at this all-day hangout.... *Tel 415/643-0481. 3318 24th St., 24th St. BART station. $* **(see pp. 74, 75, 76)**

Caffe Greco. One of North Beach's most popular coffeehouses, partly because of its peerless espresso.... *Tel 415/397-6261. 423 Columbus Ave., 15, 30, 41, or 45 MUNI bus. $* **(see p. 74)**

Caffe Puccini. This cafe is deep Italian, and manages to avoid becoming a trend trap despite its fair share of noted patrons and artistic types.... *Tel 415/989-7033. 411 Columbus Ave., 15, 30, 41, or 45 MUNI bus. $* **(see p. 75)**

Caffe Trieste. One of the last remaining beatnik haunts—Jack Kerouac and Allen Ginsberg were regulars—this legendary little cafe is a must for visiting coffeehounds.... *Tel 415/392-6739. 601 Vallejo St. (at Grant St.), 15 or 41 MUNI bus. $* **(see pp. 74, 75)**

Carta. The "small plates" here come from a different country each month, but the fresh ingredients are always local.... *Tel 415/863-3516. 1760 Market St. (between Octavia and Gough Sts.), Van Ness MUNI Metro station or any Market Street MUNI bus. Reservations recommended. $$–$$$* **(see p. 59)**

Cha Cha Cha. Every dish in this funky tapas joint is a tongue-burner, as it should be in a Cuban/Cajun restaurant that looks like it was decorated by a voodoo queen on a sangria binge.... *Tel 415/386-5758. 1801 Haight St., 6, 7, 33, 66, or 71 MUNI bus. Second location: Tel 415/648–0504. 2327 Mission St., 24th St. BART/MUNI Metro station. No reservations.* $ **(see pp. 59, 60)**

Chez Panisse. Among restaurant reviewers, Berkeley's Chez Panisse is held sacred, but locals will tell you that it isn't consistent.... *Tel 510/548-5525. 1517 Shattuck Ave., Berkeley, North Berkeley BART station and a cab. Reservations essential.* $$$ **(see p. 59)**

Clown Alley. A late-night tradition for quick, cheap food, this North Beach burger joint has been an institution since 1962.... *Tel 415/421-2540. 42 Columbus Ave. (at Jackson St.), North Beach, 15 or 30 MUNI bus.* $ **(see p. 72)**

Coriya Hot Pot City. Load up your trays with the makings of a hearty meal, then play chef at your own table, where hot pots and grills are built in. You'll have to wait in line on weekends.... *Tel 415/387-7888, fax 415/387-7888. 852 Clement St. at 10th Ave., 38 MUNI bus.* $ **(pp. 63, 71)**

Cypress Club. It looks like Salvador Dali's impression of the Mad Hatter's tea party, but after one glance at the menu, you can rest assured this is a serious place to eat.... *Tel 415/296-8555. 500 Jackson St., 15 or 30 MUNI bus. Reservations recommended.* $$$ **(see pp. 70, 71)**

El Nuevo Frutilandia. One of the few places in San Francisco that serves authentic Puerto Rican and Cuban home cooking.... *Tel 415/648-2958. 3077 24th St., 24th St. BART/MUNI Metro station.* $ **(see pp. 62, 71, 72)**

El Trebol. This delightful little Salvadoran/Nicaraguan eatery in the Castro District is one of the best deals in the city.... *Tel 415/285-6298. 3324 24th St., 24th St. BART station. No credit cards.* $ **(see pp. 62, 71)**

Enrico's Sidewalk Cafe. New owners resurrected what may be the city's favorite cafe and transformed it into a casual supper club.... *Tel 415/982-6223. 504 Broadway, 15, 30, 41, 45, or 83 MUNI bus. Reservations recommended*

DINING AND CAFES | THE INDEX

for dinner (essential on weekends). $$

(see pp. 57, 74, 75)

Esperpento. Authentic, inexpensive Spanish paella and tapas in a jam-packed Mission District storefront.... *Tel 415/282-8867. 3295 22nd St., 24th St. BART station, 26 MUNI bus. Reservations recommended. $* **(see p. 58)**

Fina Estampa. Some of the most delectable Peruvian food you'll ever taste.... *Tel 415/824-4437. 2374 Mission St., 16th St. BART/MUNI Metro station; 14 or 49 MUNI bus. AE, DC not accepted. $* **(see p. 62)**

Firecracker. In case the name didn't make it obvious, the exquisite Mandarin food here is hot and spicy.... *Tel 415/642-3470. 1007½ Valencia St., Mission District, 24th St. BART station. $$–$$$* **(see pp. 58, 60)**

Fleur de Lys. The ultimate for a major splurge. Critics and customers alike call it the best classic French restaurant in the city.... *Tel 415/673-7779. 777 Sutter St. (at Taylor St.), Union Square, Powell-Mason or Powell-Hyde cable car. Reservations essential. $$$$* **(see p. 65)**

Flint's. It's worth a trip to Oakland to this famed barbecue pit where the sauce comes in a few choices—hot, hotter, and hottest. It's strictly takeout, but you can sit outside during the day.... *Tel 510/652-9605. 6609 Shattuck Ave. (at 66th St.), Ashby BART station. $* **(see p. 60)**

Fly Trap Restaurant. A long history of good humor and a menu based on traditional San Francisco grill food make this institution a refreshing choice amid the glut of tony, food-fad eateries.... *Tel 415/243-0580. 606 Folsom St., Montgomery St. BART/MUNI Metro station; 15 MUNI bus. Reservations recommended. $$* **(see pp. 55, 71)**

French Laundry. Thomas Keller, named 1997's best chef in the country by the James Beard Foundation, presides over this small gem out in the wine country.... *Tel 707/944-2380. 6640 Washington St., Yountville, CA. Reservations essential. $$$$* **(see p. 65)**

Fringale. A curved blond-wood bar greets you the moment you open the door of this chic South of Market bistro.

The food—French/Basque—is delightful.... *Tel 415/543-0573. 570 Fourth St., 30, 45, or 76 MUNI bus. DC not accepted. $$* **(see pp. 66, 71)**

Ganges Vegetarian Restaurant. Kukoo Singh runs his small Indian restaurant as though each patron were a long-lost friend.... *Tel 415/661-7290. 775 Frederick St., 33 MUNI bus. AE, DC not accepted. $* **(see pp. 63, 68)**

Gaylord of India. The furnishings are elegant and the view of the bay exquisite, but the prices are somewhat high.... *Tel 415/771-8822. Ghirardelli Square, 900 North Point (third floor); Powell-Hyde cable car; 19, 30, or 42 MUNI bus. Reservations recommended. $$$* **(see p. 63)**

Golden Turtle. Even the toughest food critics hail this modest but formal Vietnamese restaurant near Russian Hill.... *Tel 415/441-4419. 2211 Van Ness Ave., 42, 47, 49, or 76 MUNI bus. $* **(see p. 64)**

Greens. More than a decade ago there was a six-month waiting list for reservations here. Three cookbooks and a couple of chefs later, Greens can usually accommodate guests with just two weeks' notice.... *Tel 415/771-6222. Fort Mason, Bldg. A, Buchanan St. at Marina Blvd., 28 MUNI bus. AE not accepted. $$* **(see p. 67)**

Hama-Ko. Chef Ted Kashiyama's little Cole Valley restaurant offers a limited sushi-bar menu; for a full meal, order in advance.... *Tel 415/753-6808. 108 Carl St., 37 or 43 MUNI bus. Reservations essential except for sushi bar. AE, DC not accepted. $$* **(see p. 64)**

Harbor Village. The dinners are exquisite, but the real reason to go to Harbor Village is for the dim sum, served only at lunch.... *Tel 415/781-8833. 4 Embarcadero Center, Embarcadero BART/MUNI Metro station; 15, 45, or 76 MUNI bus. Reservations recommended. $$–$$$*
(see p. 61)

Harris'. Anne Harris cooks and serves damn fine steaks. The best steak house in the city.... *Tel 415/673-1888. 2100 Van Ness Ave., 42, 47, 49, or 76 MUNI bus. Reservations recommended. $$$* **(see pp. 56, 71)**

Hayes Street Grill. Superb fish and seafood are the main-stays of the menu, sautéed or mesquite-grilled with a Mexican, American, French, Italian, or Asian accent.... *Tel 415/863-5545. 320 Hayes St., Civic Center BART/MUNI Metro station; 21 MUNI bus. Reservations essential for tables before 8:30pm $$* **(see p. 55)**

Heavenly Hot. It's worth the wait (on weekends) to get into this festive tabletop hot pot house where the offerings range from Sizzling Hot Shabu-Shabu Pot to Ying-Yang Pot....*Tel 415/750-1818. 4627 Geary Blvd. (at 11th Ave.), 38 MUNI bus. $* **(see pp. 63, 71)**

Helmand. A formal dinner house on a stretch of Broadway between North Beach and Pacific Heights. Owner Mah-mood Karzai's Afghani menu—easily the best in the city—incorporates tastes of Central Asia, India, and the Middle East.... *Tel 415/362-0641. 430 Broadway, 15, 30 or 45 MUNI bus. Reservations recommended. $* **(see p. 70)**

Horseshoe Coffee House. The nose-ring and tattoo capital of the city, hands down.... *Tel 415/6260-8852. 566 Haight St. (near Fillmore St.), 6, 7, 66, or 71 MUNI bus. $* **(see pp. 73, 75)**

Internet Alfredo. Internet insomniacs can surf the web 24 hours a day at this "Multimedia Gulch" coffeehouse.... *Tel 415/437-3140. 790–A Brannan St. (near Eighth St.), South of Market, 42 MUNI bus. $* **(see p. 73)**

Izzy's Steaks and Chops. The steaks are thick, the drinks stiff and plentiful, the wait staff very friendly.... *Tel 415/563-0487. 3345 Steiner St., 10, 20, 30, 43, 60, 70, or 80 MUNI bus. Reservations recommended. $$* **(see p. 56)**

Jammin' Java Coffee House. A sidewalk seat at Jammin' Java can rejuvenate your trend-weary soul—especially on a sunny afternoon. The clientele is a harmonious blend of young hipsters and older bohemians.... *Tel 415/668-5282. 701 Cole St. (at Waller St.), 6, 7, 33, 37, 43, 66, and 71 MUNI bus. $* **(see pp. 73, 74)**

John's Grill. Now nearly 90 years old, this is a fun place to get a juicy steak or have a late-afternoon cocktail.... *Tel 415/986-0069. 63 Ellis St., Powell St. BART/MUNI Metro station. Reservations recommended. $$* **(see p. 55)**

La Rondalla. The traditional Mexican fare is tasty and substantial, a perfect prelude to a few gigantic margaritas at the crowded, lively bar.... *Tel 415/647-7474. 901 Valencia St., 16th or 24th St. BART station; 26 MUNI bus. No credit cards. $–$$* **(see pp. 62, 71)**

La Taqueria. A Mission District favorite, with its clean, comfortable cantina-style atmosphere.... *Tel 415/285-7117. 2889 Mission St., 24th St. BART station, 14 or 49 MUNI bus. No credit cards. $* **(see pp. 62, 71)**

Los Jarritos. Anything you order at this friendly Mexican eatery will be authentic and tasty, but make sure you don't miss the homemade tortillas.... *Tel 415/648-8383. 901 South Van Ness Ave., 16th or 24th St. BART station; 33 MUNI bus. AE, DC not accepted. $* **(see p. 61)**

Mario's Bohemian Cigar Store Cafe. This is our favorite North Beach cafe, not just because it has the best focaccia sandwiches in the city, but because it's still a closet-size corner cafe (P.S.: There are hardly any tourists.).... *Tel 415/362-0536. 566 Columbus Ave. (at Union St.), 15, 30, 41, or 45 MUNI bus. $* **(see p. 75)**

Masa's. If you want a three-star meal so classically French it will rival the best of Paris—and you don't mind spending $300 or so for two people—by all means, sign up four weeks in advance for dinner at Masa's.... *Tel 415/989-7154. Adjacent to Hotel Vintage Court, 648 Bush St., any Powell St. cable car. Jacket and tie recommended; reservations essential. $$$$* **(see p. 65)**

Mecca. Cozy into a black-leather booth and be pampered by the attentive waitstaff while you enjoy jazz or cabaret at this sensual supper club.... *Tel 415/621-7000. 2029 Market St. (between Dolores and 14th Sts.), Upper Market, any Market St. MUNI bus. Reservations recommended. $$$* **(see p. 67)**

Millennium. This stylish vegan restaurant's inventive menu is the culinary equivalent of a world-beat concert.... *Tel*

415/487-9800. 246 McAllister St., Civic Center BART/ MUNI Metro station, 5, 10, 20, 60, 70, or 80 MUNI bus. Reservations accepted. $–$$ **(see p. 67)**

MoMo's. The best part about this trendy scene across the street from Pac Bell Park is that you can eat, drink, and be merry on the outdoor patio day and night—major heaters keep the chill off.... *Tel 415/227-8660. 760 Second St., 15, 30, or 42 MUNI bus. $$–$$$* **(see p. 57)**

Moose's. Proprietor Ed Moose's innovative menu—combining Southwestern, Italian, and Californian delicacies—is exceptional, and the scene is glam.... *Tel415/989-7800. 1652 Stockton St., 15, or 30 MUNI bus. Reservations essential. $$–$$$* **(see p. 57)**

Muddy Waters Coffee House. The atmosphere here is funky, bohemian, punked-out cyber-nerd—with an eclectic clientele to match.... *Tel 415/863-8006. 521 Valencia St. (near 16th St.), 16th St. BART station or 26 MUNI bus. $* **(see pp. 73, 74)**

R & G Lounge. The name sounds like a booze joint where a guy named Sam might be playing the piano, but it's actually a Chinatown restaurant offering some of the best seafood in the area.... *Tel 415/982-7877. 631 Kearny St., 15, 30, or 45 MUNI bus. $–$$* **(see p. 61)**

Ramblas Tapas Bar. The sumptuous Spanish tapas served in this extremely popular Mission District restaurant were voted best in the Bay Area by the *Guardian*. Reservations are strongly recommended.... *Tel 415/565-0207. 557 Valencia St., 16th St. BART/MUNI Metro station. $$–$$$* **(see pp. 57, 58)**

Red Dora's Bearded Lady. This is a popular lesbian hangout, but the crowd is definitely mixed at this delightful, eccentric, Mission District cafe.... *Tel 415/626-2805. 485 14th St. (at Guerrero St.), 16th St. BART station. $* **(see pp. 74, 75)**

Rose Pistola. This popular trattoria was voted best new restaurant in the country (1997) by the James Beard Foundation.... *Tel 415/399-0499. 532 Columbus Ave., North Beach, 15 or 30 MUNI bus. $$–$$$* **(see p. 68)**

Sacred Grounds Cafe. This sixties throwback—eclectic furnishings and works by local artists share the room with fine, Victorian-style wood paneling—is still a vital part of the Haight-Ashbury scene.... *Tel 415/387-3859. 2095 Hayes St. (at Cole St.), 21 MUNI bus. $* **(see p. 75)**

Saigon Sandwich Cafe. Not a full-fledged restaurant, but it makes the best Vietnamese sandwiches in town—for around $2. Lunch only.... *Tel 415/474-5698. 560 Larkin St., Civic Center BART/MUNI Metro station, 19, 31, or 38 MUNI bus. No credit cards. $* **(see pp. 64, 72)**

Sanppo. Comfortable, inexpensive, and very good, it's right in the heart of Japantown.... *Tel 415/346-3486. Japan Center, 1702 Post St., 38 MUNI bus. $* **(see p. 64)**

Seal Rock Inn. Join the crew of "Nash Bridges" or Carlos Santana for breakfast at this neighborhood coffee shop just footsteps away from Sutro Park, which overlooks the Pacific Ocean.... *Tel 415/386-6518. 545 Point Lobos Ave., Ocean Beach, 38 MUNI bus. $–$$* **(see p. 73)**

Sear's Fine Foods. If you're anywhere near Union Square at breakfast time, it is mandatory to eat at Sear's diner, beloved for its teeny-tiny, rich, sweet Swedish pancakes.... *Tel 415/986-1160. 439 Powell St., Powell St. BART/MUNI Metro station; any Powell St. cable car; 76 MUNI bus. No credit cards. $* **(see p. 72)**

Slanted Door. The biggest problem at this highly lauded Vietnamese eatery—one of Bill Clinton's favorite places to chow down in the city—is getting in the door. The luscious menu, including Chef Charles Pham's signature crepes, is exquisite for both lunch and dinner.... *Tel 415/861-8032. 584 Valencia St., 16th St. BART/MUNI Metro station. $$$-$$$$* **(see p. 57)**

South Park Cafe. This little South of Market spot starts as a casual cafe in the morning, then turns into a super-hip lunch bistro, then goes back to its casual cafe persona for the rest of the day.... *Tel 415/495-7275. 108 South Park (near 2nd and Bryant Sts.), Montgomery St. BART station; 15, 30, or 45 MUNI bus. $$* **(see p. 75)**

Sparky's Diner. The wee-hours crowd at Sparky's can be a

DINING AND CAFES | THE INDEX

bit eccentric—and sometimes a tad inebriated—but just mind your own business and pass the ketchup.... *Tel 415/621-6001. 242 Church St., Church St. MUNI Metro station. DC not accepted. $* **(see p. 72)**

Stella Pastry & Caffe. Owner Franco Santucci will be happy to expound on the virtues of his patented *Sacripantina*, one of many delectable pastries baked on Stella's premises.... *Tel 415/986--2914. 446 Columbus Ave., 15, 30, 41, or 45 MUNI bus. $* **(see p. 74)**

Straits Cafe. The coconut-milk chicken curry is as exotically delicious as the Singapore-style decor.... *Tel 415/ 668-1783. 3300 Geary Blvd., 38 MUNI bus. Reservations recommended. $$* **(see p. 64)**

Suppenküche. This small, inviting (often crowded and noisy) Hayes Valley beer hall/dining room steadily attracts a young crowd looking for good food, good beer, and good company all in the same place. The weekend brunch (Sun 10am–2:30pm) is a special treat.... *Tel 415/252-9289. 601 Hayes St., Civic Center BART/MUNI Metro station, 21 MUNI bus. DC not accepted. $$* **(see p. 69)**

Tadich Grill. This landmark steak-and-seafood house has been run by the same family since the turn of the century..... *Tel 415/391-1849. 240 California St., Embarcadero St. BART/MUNI Metro station. No reservations accepted. AE, DC not accepted. $$–$$$* **(see p. 55)**

Thep Phanom. It's a good thing Thep Phanom is located in California, land of a zillion chili farmers, because it use stons of the red-hot peppers in its fiery Thai food. Keep plenty of water at your table—you'll need it.... *Tel 415/ 431-2526. 900 Waller St., 3, 6, 7, 22, 66, or 71 MUNI bus. DC not accepted. $–$$* **(see p. 60)**

Timo's in the Zanzibar. There are two major draws to quirky Timo's: the tapas, which locals insist are the best in town, and the adjoining bar, the Zanzibar.... *Tel 415/647-0558. 842 Valencia St., 16th St. BART/MUNI Metro station; 26 MUNI bus. DC not accepted. $$*

(see p. 59)

Tommy Toy's. This chi-chi Chinese dinner house is a favorite of visiting dignitaries and Hollywood stars.... *Tel 397-4888. 655 Montgomery St., Financial District, Montgomery St. BART/MUNI Metro station. Reservations highly recommended. $$$–$$$$* **(see p. 61)**

Watergate. The French-Asian food is truly splendid, but the formal, wood-paneled atmosphere may have a tough time surviving the trendy interior design–driven restaurant scene on hip Valencia Street.... *Tel 415/648-6000. 1152 Valencia St., 24th St. BART station. $$–$$$* **(see p. 58)**

We Be Sushi. The two We Be Sushi locations on Valencia Street are jammed with hip locals at dinnertime. No credit cards... *Tel 415/826-0607. 538 Valencia St., 16th St. BART station; 1031 Valencia St., 24th St. BART station.... Tel 415/221-9960. 3226 Geary Blvd., Richmond District, 38 MUNI bus. Tel 415/681-4010. 94 Judah St., Sunset District, N Judah MUNI Metro streetcar. $–$$* **(see pp. 57, 65)**

Yank Sing. A guidebook staple that's worth the trip. The dim sum is always satisfying, especially the dumplings, which include many vegetarian options.... *Tel 415/957-9300. 101 Spear St. (corner of Mission St.), Embarcadero BART/MUNI Metro station. $–$$* **(see p. 61)**

Yaya Cuisine. Chef Yahya Salih's native Iraq flavors the exuberant Mediterranean/California hybrid cuisine.... *Tel 415/434-3567. 663 Clay St., Montgomery St. BART/MUNI Metro station; 1 MUNI bus. Reservations recommended. DC not accepted. $$* **(see p. 69)**

THE INDEX | DINING AND CAFES

San Francisco Dining

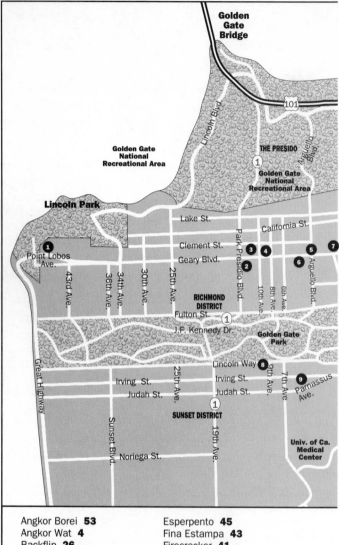

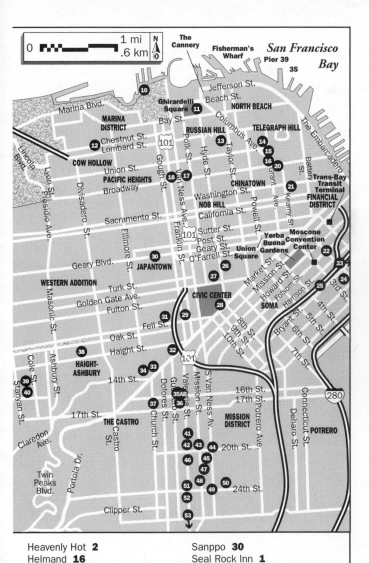

Map Legend:

- 0 — 1 mi / .6 km
- N

Labels on map:

The Cannery
Fisherman's Wharf
Pier 39 — 35
San Francisco Bay
Jefferson St.
Beach St.
Marina Blvd.
Ghirardelli Square — 11
Bay St.
NORTH BEACH
10
MARINA DISTRICT
Chestnut St. — 12
Lombard St.
RUSSIAN HILL — 13
Columbus Ave.
Taylor St.
Hyde St.
TELEGRAPH HILL
14
15
16 20
The Embarcadero
101
COW HOLLOW
Union St.
PACIFIC HEIGHTS
Broadway
18 17
Gough St.
Van Ness Ave.
Polk St.
CHINATOWN
Washington St.
Grant Ave.
Kearny St.
21
Battery St.
Trans-Bay Transit Terminal
FINANCIAL DISTRICT
Lincoln Blvd.
Lyon St.
Presidio Ave.
Divisadero St.
NOB HILL
California St.
Powell St.
Sacramento St.
Fillmore St.
Franklin St.
Sutter St.
101
Post St.
Geary St.
O'Farrell St.
Union Square
Yerba Buena Gardens
Moscone Convention Center
22
23
Geary Blvd.
JAPANTOWN
30
WESTERN ADDITION
Turk St.
Golden Gate Ave.
Fulton St.
26
27
Market St.
Mission St.
Howard St.
Folsom St.
Harrison St.
SOMA
24
25
3rd St.
4th St.
5th St.
6th St.
7th St.
Masonic St.
CIVIC CENTER
28
29
31
Fell St.
Oak St.
Haight St.
8th St.
9th St.
10th St.
101
Ashbury St.
HAIGHT-ASHBURY
38
14th St.
32
34 33
Cole St.
Stanyan St.
39
40
Guerrero St.
Dolores St.
Valencia St.
Mission St.
S. Van Ness Ave.
35AB
36
16th St.
17th St.
MISSION DISTRICT
Potrero Ave.
Deharo St.
POTRERO
280
37
Church St.
Castro St.
THE CASTRO
17th St.
Claredon Ave.
Portola Dr.
Twin Peaks Blvd.
41
42 43
44
46
45
47
48
49
50
24th St.
51
52
53
Clipper St.
Connecticut St.

Restaurant listings:

Heavenly Hot **2**
Helmand **16**
Izzy's Steaks and Chops **12**
La Rondalla **46**
La Taqueria **48**
Los Jarritos **44**
Mecca **33**
Millennium **28**
MoMo's **23**
Moose's **14**
Ramblas **35B**
Rose Pistola **15**
Saigon Sandwich Cafe **27**

Sanppo **30**
Seal Rock Inn **1**
Slanted Door **35A**
South Park Café **24**
Sparky's Diner **37**
Straits Cafe **5**
Suppenküche **31**
Thep Phanom **34**
Timo's in the Zanzibar **42**
Watergate **51**
We Be Sushi **36, 52, 7, 9**
Yaya Cuisine **8**

Union Square & Financial District Dining

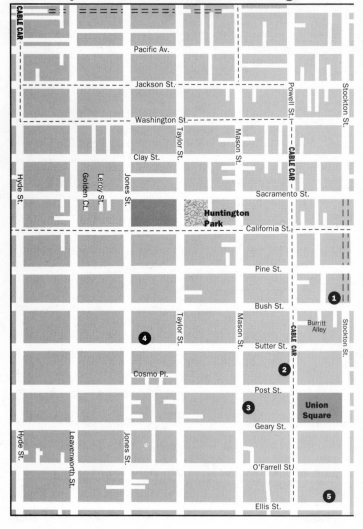

CABLE CAR

Pacific Av.

Jackson St.

Washington St.

Powell St.

Stockton St.

Taylor St.

Mason St.

CABLE CAR

Clay St.

Hyde St.

Golden Ct.

Leroy St.

Jones St.

Sacramento St.

Huntington Park

California St.

Pine St.

Bush St.

1

Taylor St.

Mason St.

CABLE CAR

Burritt Alley

Stockton St.

4

Sutter St.

2

Cosmo Pl.

Post St.

3

Union Square

Geary St.

Hyde St.

Leavenworth St.

Jones St.

O'Farrell St.

5

Ellis St.

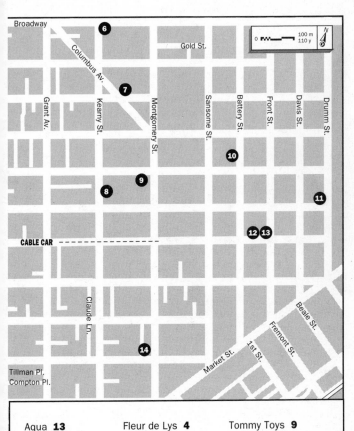

Aqua **13**

Biscuits and
  Blues **3**

Cafe Claude **14**

Cypress Club **7**

Enrico's Sidewalk
  Cafe **6**

Fleur de Lys **4**

Harbor Village **11**

John's Grill **5**

Masa's **1**

R & G Lounge **8**

Sear's Fine Foods **2**

Tadich Grill **12**

Tommy Toys **9**

Yank Sing **10**

3

sions

First word of
advice: Stay away
from Fisherman's
Wharf. Ditto for
Pier 39 and the
cable-car turn-
arounds. That

is, unless your purpose in traveling all the way to San Francisco is to rub elbows with throngs of tourists, shivering in their shorts and souvenir tank tops despite repeated warnings about how cold it is in July. If you brought the kids, you may have to surrender, but get your wharf duty out of the way as quickly as possible (we give you a few survival tips later on in the chapter) so you can move on to the city's true delights.

There are a few things that are so utterly San Francisco that they absolutely must be experienced at some point during your visit—a cable-car ride to the Buena Vista Cafe for a cup of Irish coffee, a trip to Coit Tower, a walk across the Golden Gate Bridge, the view from the elevator at the top of the Fairmont Hotel—but the best way to get to know the city is to explore the neighborhoods where people actually live. Skip the taxicabs (unless it's after dark or you're in a questionable neighborhood): Take a bus or a streetcar instead, then poke around on foot. Wander around the Haight and count the shrines to Jerry Garcia. Take in the Spoken Word or an avant cha-cha band at a hip, side-street bar in the Mission District. Practice your tai chi with the Chinese senior citizens in Washington Square (North Beach). Gawk at the mansions in Pacific Heights. Visit the Castro for an undiluted dose of the predominant—and wonderfully irreverent—influence gay culture has on every aspect of life in San Francisco.

Lombard Street
The zigzags of "the crookedest street in the world" are negotiated by so many tourists that the bricks finally cracked and popped out of the pavement a few years ago. But the city never would have let one of the jewels of its tourist trade fall into disrepair for long. The famous block between Hyde and Leavenworth streets was closed to automobile traffic for around two years while work crews painstakingly repaired or replaced every errant brick. The street is again open to cars, but the best way to enjoy the view is still to walk down the staircases on either side.

No matter what neighborhood you visit, the best seat in the house is any table at a cozy cafe (see Dining and Cafes). Pull up a chair. Have a nice, frothy cappuccino. There is plenty of time for that trip to the museum—mañana.

Getting Your Bearings
Get a map. There's no other way to visualize San Francisco's irregular layout. The city is not one big grid like Manhattan;

it is totally akimbo with sub-grids that skirt its many hills and valleys in a roundabout way. You can rarely see what's over the next hill, so you may not realize that North Beach is the uphill next-door neighbor of Fisherman's Wharf (north) and Chinatown (south). That may not seem important to you yet, but when you think you're trapped at Pier 39, you'll be relieved to realize that the inviting cafes of North Beach are just a few blocks away.

When it comes to maps, you need two kinds—an overall view of the neighborhoods in relation to each other, and a comprehensive street map. A neighborhood map will show clearly, for example, that Haight-Ashbury is right next to Golden Gate Park, which stretches from the middle of the city all the way to the Pacific Ocean (at Ocean Beach, near the Cliff House). You'll see that the Castro and the Mission District—right next to each other, and not too far east of Haight-Ashbury—are both south of Market Street, but the neighborhood officially known as South of Market is quite a distance farther east, in the downtown area.

You'll also see that San Francisco—a city and county unto itself—is at the northern tip of a peninsula flanked by the San Francisco Bay on the east and the Pacific Ocean on

Pick a Card, Any Card
If you've already seen the in-flight movie nine times—before the airline censored it—and you're looking for a good way to amuse yourself on the plane ride to San Francisco, why not play cards? Forget Solitaire and Old Maid—you'll have much more fun with Lynn Gordon's special deck, "52 Adventures in San Francisco." There are no hearts, diamonds, clubs, or spades, but each card does bear a lively illustration on the front and directions for an enticing adventure on the back. Pick cards at random and find the best places to get ice cream—or to go bird-watching—or go through the whole deck and relish the thought of how much fun you're going to have when you finally land in the city. The decks are inexpensive ($6.95) and also double as souvenirs or substitutes for all those postcards you didn't send because you were having way too much fun to stop at the post office. Find them at your local bookstore or contact Chronicle Books, tel 800/722-6657.

the west. The Financial District sits on the eastern shore of the city, which curves northward as the Embarcadero passes North Beach and Fisherman's Wharf, eventually turning almost due west to the Golden Gate, where the Pacific Ocean meets the bay. If you stand just about anywhere in the city, you can see a tower that looks like a miniature space needle sitting atop Twin Peaks, the geographical center of the city.

The front section of the San Francisco Yellow Pages has several excellent maps, including transit maps, but if you want to get your bearings in advance, send $2 for a complete packet including useful booklets and a comprehensive visitor map to: San Francisco Convention and Visitors Bureau, P.O. Box 429097, San Francisco, CA 94102-9097 (allow three weeks for U.S. delivery; international mail sent via surface). You can also pick up a copy of the visitor map for free at the Visitor Center at Hallidie Plaza when you arrive. To get the official transit map by mail, send $2 to: MUNI MAP, 1145 Market St., 3rd floor, San Francisco, CA 94103; or call 415/673-MUNI or 415/817-1717 (allow two weeks for delivery). It includes all MUNI routes (cable cars, buses, and Metro streetcars), regional transit connections, frequency guide, travel hints, and points of interest. Transit maps, fares, schedules, and tours are downloadable (free) at www.sfmuni.com.

The Lowdown

Must-sees for first-time visitors from Peoria...

There is one sure-fire perfect way to spend your first afternoon in San Francisco—take $2 out of your pocket, walk five or ten blocks up Powell from Market Street (away from the turnaround), and hop on the **Powell-Hyde cable car**. Don't even think about not doing it because it seems too "touristy"—locals have been known to invite out-of-town guests purely for an excuse to take this ride. The Powell-Hyde line is our favorite because it ends up just footsteps away from the **Buena Vista Cafe** (2765 Hyde St., tel 415/474–5044), a National Historic Landmark where a post-cable-car Irish coffee is an esteemed tradition, especially on a foggy afternoon. (The first Irish coffees ever served in America were mixed at the Buena Vista in 1952.) The ride itself twists through the city, climbing "halfway to the stars" atop Nob Hill, then plummeting back down on a breathtaking roller-coaster ride that levels out around the famous crooked section of Lombard Street ("The Crookedest Street in the World") before coasting down to the bay. No post-card can possibly capture what it feels like the first moment you glimpse that million-dollar view. (By the way, watch your teeth—many first-timers smile so broadly they collect stray bugs like radiator grills.)

Another mandatory awe-inspiring adventure is a bracing 15-minute walk across the **Golden Gate Bridge**. There is simply no other way to truly appreciate its immense scale and beauty. The best part is that the weather is absolutely predictable—it always feels cold and windy on the bridge (wear layers). To get an unbelievable view before you actually set foot on the bridge, take the 28 MUNI bus to Fort Point—a brick-and-granite strong-hold built in 1861—where you can climb up to the roof and behold the bridge above you before you set out on the pedestrian walkway. Once you are on the bridge, you'll feel it sway and vibrate as gusty ocean winds whip through its cables. Don't be alarmed. The bridge is not about to collapse. It held up under the ballast of more than a hundred thousand revelers who congregated there to celebrate its 50th anniversary (1987), and it didn't flinch during the 1989 earthquake.

Unless you take the lazy—and boring—way out (the 30, 39, or 45 MUNI bus), you'll probably need to fuel up for the steep hike to **Coit Tower**. We suggest starting out with a cup of super-strength coffee at **Caffe Trieste** (601 Vallejo St., tel 415/392–6739; see Dining and Cafes) because it's right on the corner of Grant Street, the most interesting route to the famous fire-hose-nozzle spire atop Telegraph Hill (where you turn right and head up the hill to the tower). Then head up Grant to Greenwich Street. Once you've actually begun the ascent, you may want to distract yourself from the daunting incline by imagining the tower's namesake—Lillie Hitchcock Coit (1843–1929)—dressed as a fireman and racing around town with the volunteer brigade. Rumor has it that Ms. Coit found men's clothes appealing in other circumstances as well, particularly when she wanted to get into places where "ladies" weren't allowed. Though Ms. Coit's greatest achievement was to be made mascot of Engine Company 5—a reward for her help in fighting a fire—we love to think of Ms. Coit as San Francisco's most famous cross-dresser. No one really knows if Coit Tower was deliberately designed in the shape of a fire-hose nozzle. Up close, it doesn't matter. The Depression-era murals inside the lobby at the base of the tower are haunting images of Americans at labor, and the 360-degree view from the top of the tower (elevator ride $3.75) is unbeatable.

DIVERSIONS | THE LOWDOWN

Only in San Francisco... San Francisco is full of sights
and sounds that simply don't exist in other cities. Where
else would a major-league baseball team blast a foghorn
to celebrate home runs, or a county fair include a "fog
calling" contest? The fog and the hills are San Francisco's
natural treasures.

One of the best ways to enjoy the trademark topog-
raphy is to hike down some of the stairways that have been
built into the city's steep sidewalks and pathways. Allow at
least an hour or two to walk the **Filbert Street Steps**
(between Sansome Street and Telegraph Hill), a romantic
favorite with locals because the path feels
hidden from urban clamor as it winds past enchanting
hundred-year-old cottages and lush gardens. The breathtaking view of the bay from the top of the hill has attracted
artists, writers, and singers for years (Joan Baez and
Armistead Maupin are among past residents). Start there,
at Telegraph Hill Boulevard near Coit Tower, and work
your way down. When you cross Montgomery Street to
the lower steps, take a look at the art-deco apartment complex at 1930 Montgomery—you might recognize it from
the movie *Dark Passage* (Humphrey Bogart and Lauren
Bacall). You may want to take a sidetrack along Napier
Lane, a lovely wooden walkway that leads to the public
Grace Marchant Gardens, a particularly enchanting sight
on Halloween, when more than 200 jack-o'-lanterns light
up the night for local trick-or-treaters.

Chinatown is one of the most celebrated neighborhoods in San Francisco, but it has never become merely a
tourist trap—above all else it is a place where people *live*,
the largest Chinese community outside of Asia. As soon
as you cross under the ornate, dragon-crested gateway on
Grant Avenue (at Bush Street), you're no longer in the
Western world. Street signs are marked in Chinese characters, lamp posts are encircled by dragons, and store windows display strange medicinal herbs and animal parts
you'd never find at a suburban drugstore. The best time to
see this teeming neighborhood is early in the morning,
when merchants deliver their wares in pushcarts and
mothers rush down the street toting live chickens for that
night's dinner. Wander up Grant Avenue or Stockton
Street to Sacramento and find Waverly Place, where
you'll find **Tien Hon Temple** (125 Waverly Place, top
floor) among the many brightly painted balconies. Back
on Grant Avenue, a tiny bar with the single word

"**Buddha**" on a sign over the door sits on the corner of Washington Street. Look inside. Old men with long braids and "thinking caps" sit at the bar. You're not only on a different continent, you're in a different century.

Every city has churches, but only San Francisco has the **Church of John Coltrane,** an African Orthodox church that has been using Coltrane's music for the divine liturgy—and serving free food three days a week—since 1971. It has moved from its original location near the Panhandle, but jazz lovers from all over the world still flock to hear the house band, Ohnedaruth (the Sanskrit word for compassion and the spiritual name Alice Coltrane gave her husband when he died), play their patron saint's music every Sunday. You never know who will be in attendance—or sitting in with the band. Bobby Hutcherson stopped by more than once, along with Rashid Ali, Coltrane's last drummer. Once you get inside, you'll be in Coltrane heaven—the walls are adorned with more than a dozen contemporary versions of traditional Russian-style icons, including, of course, ones of Coltrane. The music seems to come from everywhere—the band sits near the altar, the choir takes up the entire first row of seats, and there are saxophones and other instruments spread throughout the congregation. It really is a divine spectacle. Come early to get a good seat; services usually start around noon and last for at least an hour-and-a-half. Visit the church's web site (www.saintjohncoltrane.org).

Special moments... If a ride on the Powell-Hyde cable car or the view from Coit Tower hasn't already made you fall hopelessly in love with San Francisco, perhaps what you need is a view of the sun virtually melting into an orange-red-fuchsia pool as it sets on the blue Pacific. The ultimate spot is a window table at the pub in the **Cliff House** restaurant (1090 Point Lobos Ave., tel 415/386–3330), facing directly out to sea. The funky-nautical motif pub is a bit tacky, but it fades into the distant background the moment the sun begins its dazzling nightly show. Even the most jaded urbanites ooh and ahh at the display, so be sure to go at least an hour before sundown if you expect to get a good seat—or go outside and find a spot along the cliff.

If you have access to a car, don't leave the Bay Area without watching a sunset from the top of **Grizzly Peak** in the Berkeley Hills. Cars start lining up about a half-hour before sundown to watch the transformation from daylight to shimmering night lights—a magnificent sight in any weather, clear or foggy. The vista covers the entire bay, from San Mateo to the south, the city and the Golden Gate Bridge straight ahead, and Marin County to the north.

On Sundays, soak up the true "spirit" of the city with hundreds of other foot-tapping, hand-clapping, shoulder-swaying sinners at **Glide Memorial Church**'s morning celebrations. An hour or so with Reverend Cecil Williams and his exuberant gospel choir will surely shake your soul and let the glory out, no matter what your religious beliefs may be—everybody leaves this Tenderloin church wearing a major smile. Glide brings out the best in everyone—Bobby McFerrin drops by often, Maya Angelou visits when she's in town; even President Clinton has joined the crowd (fortunately he left his saxophone at home).

Morbid landmarks... For those who enjoy excursions to the dark side, here are a few points of interest that will never make it into San Francisco's public relations hall of fame.

The People's Temple, where crusader Jim Jones gathered disciples before leading them to their eventual death at a tragic mass suicide in Guyana, still stands at 1859 Geary Street. (It is now a Korean Presbyterian Church.)

It's hard to believe that Charles Manson recruited some of his deadliest "family" members—including Susan Atkins and Squeaky Fromme—during the peak of Haight-Ashbury's peace-and-love scene, but he lived at 636 Cole Street for a few months in 1967 before heading to Southern California to organize his horrifying killing spree. (Manson now lives about 80 miles north of San Francisco at Folsom Prison, isolated from other inmates for his own protection.)

San Quentin State Prison, fondly known to its residents simply as "Q," has hosted some of California's most notorious criminals, including the aforementioned Mr. Manson, Sirhan Sirhan, and William Harris (one of Patty Hearst's kidnappers). They don't give tours of death row or anything like that, but you can take a ferry to Larkspur and hoof it to the prison, where there is a small museum (gas-chamber mementos and such) and a gift shop that sells items made by prisoners (no license plates).

Every hotel has gruesome moments it would rather not recall, but the **Westin Saint Francis** (see Accomodations) has a couple of whoppers—**President Ford's assassination attempt** (September 23, 1975) and **Fatty Arbuckle's lost weekend** (Labor Day weekend, 1921). President Ford was leaving the hotel through the Post Street entrance when Sara Jane Moore whipped out a gun and fired at him from across the street, but an ex-Marine standing next to her grabbed her arm, redirecting the bullet. (It was the second assassination attempt in one two-week trip to California.) Fatty Arbuckle was celebrating a multimillion-dollar movie contract inside the hotel at what has often been described as a drunken orgy when a young female guest was found unconscious in Room 1219. She died a few days later and Arbuckle was tried three times for her murder before finally being acquitted.

The roar of the fish stalls, the smell of the crowd... It has been decades since **Fisherman's Wharf** was actually a bustling fresh-fish market, and equally as long since **Pier 39** and the Port of San Francisco were a thriving part of the city's mercantile economy. Yet these two tourist traps are the first stop for most sightseers. (Pier 39, converted in the early '80s to an outdoor mall of shops and restaurants, is third on the list of the world's top 10 attractions, with more than 10.5 million guests each year.) There are precious few reasons to go near either place, but if you must (your kids will probably insist), here are some ways to make the best of it: Buy a fresh, whole crab at **Nick's** seafood stall (make sure it's still alive and wiggling), get them to cook and crack it for you on the spot, then pick up a sourdough baguette from **Boudin Sourdough Bakery**, and savor one of the best crab sandwiches around. Visit the sea lions—hundreds of them hang around Pier 39's K-Dock, where docents from the Marine Mammal Center (remember it from *Star Trek IV*?) give out free books and teach visitors all about the barking pinnipeds (11am–5pm). Then escape to **Pier 23 Cafe**, an almost-unnoticeable shack that attracts a local crowd with jazz, reggae, and calypso, as well as a beautiful view.

Looking for a few good whales: Marine World... One of the best ways to take the family to Pier 39 without actually lingering there is via a ferry excursion on the Blue & Gold Fleet to **Six Flags Marine World**, a unique, hands-on wildlife park across the bay in Vallejo. The hour-long passenger-ferry ride provides incredible views of the city, Alcatraz, Angel Island, four bridges, and many tiny islets, some with lighthouses. One of the most popular park features is its spectacular whale and dolphin show—where kids love getting splashed by giant killer whales—but there are plenty of other fine entertainers among its sea lions, walruses, lions and tigers, primates, and exotic and predatory birds. You can ride elephants, feed giraffes, walk though a glass atrium filled with butterflies from all over the world, or roam through a "walkabout" with kangaroos, wallaroos, wallabies, and an occasional emu.

Urban ferry tales... There are plenty of bay cruises that pick up tourists at Fisherman's Wharf and Pier 39, but it's more fun to go to the Ferry Building at the foot of Market Street and ride with the locals on an afternoon **Golden Gate Ferry** to the seaside village of Sausalito. You can do a one-hour round-tripper or stop to explore Sausalito. There is really just one main street—Bridgeway—so it's easy to walk around the yuppie/nautical/ex-Bohemian enclave and find a perfect spot to watch the sun set behind the San Francisco skyline. If sunsets aren't your thing, and you'd sooner toss back a pint at a rowdy tavern full of live music and boisterous baby boomers, try the **No Name Bar**, but don't drink too many happy-hour specials unless you intend to spend the night—the last ferry departs for San Francisco just after 7.

Cruising Golden Gate Park... The city's reigning playground, Golden Gate Park has been home to the 49ers football team and all the city's major hippie happenings (including Jerry Garcia's memorial service in 1995); it still is home to Sunday strollers, skaters, and joggers, to museums, to free operas, even to a herd of buffalo. Most of the park's recreational facilities are covered in the Getting Outside chapter, but Golden Gate also probably has more museums than any other urban oasis in the world. The **Asian Art Museum**, which was the largest museum outside of Asia devoted exclusively to Asian art (more than 12,000 pieces in the permanent collection) closed its doors in the park, but it's relocating to a new, expanded facility in the Civic Center and will open in early 2003. Stay tuned at www.asianart.org. Its collection comprises more than 500 Korean and Chinese masterpieces—including the world's oldest-dated Chinese Buddha—plus hundreds of exquisite works from India, Tibet, Nepal, Pakistan, and Southeast Asia. The massive **California Academy of Sciences** complex (off Martin Luther King Jr. Drive, opposite Ninth Avenue) is a great place to take your kids, but be sure to allow plenty of time—it includes the Natural History Museum, the Steinhart Aquarium, and the Morrison Planetarium. The most fun shows at the Natural History Museum have always been in the Earth and Space Hall, with a simulated earthquake and lots of good "Star Trek" souvenirs in the gift shop. Sadly, the Earth and Space Hall was wrecked by a fire in August 2001, and there is no set date to reopen (get the latest details at www.calacademy.org). The aquarium and planetarium are still open, though the nighttime laser shows, which used to delight teenagers with blasting heavy metal music, have been discontinued. The planetarium's 50-minute sky shows—projected on a huge domed ceiling—are a hit with adults, but young children tend to get bored and restless. The **M. H. de Young Memorial Museum** (formerly housed next to the Asian Art Museum) was San Francisco's scaled-down, unobtrusive answer to New York's Metropolitan Museum of Art. The major international exhibits drew art lovers from miles around, but it was the museum's exhaustive collection of American art—from Paul Revere to Georgia O'Keeffe—that put it on the map. Like its neighbor, the deYoung closed its doors in 2001. But the new, improved version is scheduled to reopen on the same site in Golden Gate Park in the spring of 2005. Meanwhile, check out the blueprints and take a virtual tour of both the museum and the park at www.thinker.org.

Then there are the gardens. The 5-acre Japanese Tea Garden (adjacent to the **Asian Art Museum**) is the oldest in America. When you enter through the hand-carved gate, you really feel as though you are in Japan. The bamboo-lined footpaths and bridges pass ponds full of koi fish, tiny Bonsai trees, stone lanterns, Shinto shrines, and a serene 18th-century Buddha. In early spring, the garden is ablaze with cherry blossoms. (Go early in the morning to avoid crowds.) Cap your visit with a rest stop at the tea pavilion for a fortune cookie (they were first introduced there) and a relaxing cup of green tea served by women in traditional Japanese costume. The **Conservatory of Flowers** (on Conservatory Way, near Arguello Boulevard) is a massive glass Victorian greenhouse that was built in Ireland and shipped to San Francisco piece by piece. It is stunning from the outside, and utterly magnificent on the inside, where beautiful exotic flowers and tropical trees are always in season. We suspect the orchids possess magic restorative powers—especially on drab, foggy days.

Museum meccas outside Golden Gate Park...

From a half-block away, the huge circular skylight atop Swiss architect Mario Botta's **Museum of Modern Art** (South of Market) looks like some sort of signaling device for extraterrestrial art collectors. Inside, earthlings have been known to be utterly dazzled by the West Coast's most extensive collection of 20th-century art, which fills 50,000 square feet of gallery space. Botta's magnificent structure is a work of art in itself, and one of the primary reasons to visit.

The city's ethnic diversity and social compassion fuel most of the art displayed in the celebrated **Yerba Buena Center for the Arts,** a multigallery center adjacent to the new Museum of Modern Art. Exhibits have included panels from the NAMES Project Memorial Quilt and works by prison inmates and residents of local halfway houses. There is also a theater, which hosts a variety of local performances from multicultural groups.

The **Palace of Fine Arts** is a must-see, not just because it houses the Exploratorium, but because it looks just like an ancient Roman temple—where's Nero when we really need him?—and it's the only building that remains from the 1915 Panama Pacific Exposition (held to celebrate the opening of the Panama Canal). A trip to the **Exploratorium** is also mandatory. (If you brought your kids, it is a ticket to heaven.) Seasoned locals will assure you it's the most fun you can have without hallucinogenic drugs, especially if you crawl through the dark, sensual Tactile Dome or try any of the other hands-on games designed to totally twist your mind. You never know what the mad scientists will have in store for you at this wonderfully fun, interactive science museum—and the gift shop is the best of any museum in the galaxy.

San Francisco's cable-car system is still run out of a 3-story red-brick barn, and you can watch it in action from several special spectator galleries. The **Cable Car Barn and Museum** includes the original prototype cable car (1873) along with other cars and models. Yes, there is a gift shop full of cable-car souvenirs.

The literally shipshape **Maritime Museum** looks like a set for an old Hollywood romantic-cruise movie. Nautical types will go nuts when they see all the ship models, relics, figureheads, photographs, scrimshaw—you know, your basic sailor stuff.

Freebies at the major museums... Most major museums set aside special free-admission days; some are free year-round. The free days tend to occur during the first week of the month, so keep that in mind when planning your trip, and always call for the most current schedule. The **Cable Car Barn and Museum** is free every day from 10 to 6; the **California Academy of Sciences** in Golden Gate Park is free the first Wednesday of every month; the **Yerba Buena Center for the Arts** offers free gallery admission the first Thursday of every month from 5 to 8pm, and to seniors every Thursday from 11 to 8; the **Exploratorium** at the Palace of Fine Arts is free the first Wednesday of every month from 10 to 9; the **Museum of Modern Art** is free the first Tuesday of every month from 11 to 6; and the **Maritime Museum** at Aquatic Park is free every day from 10 to 5. (See the Index for descriptions of each museum.)

Museums for special interests... When Pogo would make a more entertaining afternoon companion than Picasso, it's time to quit the cathedrals of culture and head for smaller houses of object worship, like the **Cartoon Art Museum** (tel 415/227-8666). Once tucked away in a largely ignored warehouse space, then an esteemed neighbor of the Museum of Modern Art, the comic book heroes are on the road again, looking for a new home (go to www.cartoonart.org for their new address—when they find one). The museum has thousands of pieces in its permanent collection, from original Krazy Kat watercolors and Pogo comic strips to storyboards from the Disney classic, *Fantasia*. Some of the donors include "Peanuts" artist Charles Schulz and rock star Graham Nash.

DIVERSIONS | THE LOWDOWN

If you can't resist penny arcades, you'll love the quirky little **Musée Mecanique** at the Cliff House. It's packed with antique mechanical gadgets, from old carnival fortune-tellers to marionette shows and player pianos. Admission is free, which is a good thing because you'll easily drop a small fortune in coins playing with all the doohickeys and thingamabobs. One really strange exhibit is a miniature amusement park made out of toothpicks. The fact that the piece was glued together by prisoners at San Quentin kind of makes you wonder.

Galeria de la Raza and the **Mexican Museum** feature Mexican and Chicano art. The Mexican Museum's permanent collection—more than 9,000 pieces—makes it a "serious" museum (with plans to relocate to Yerba Buena Gardens, by the Museum of Modern Art), but the atmosphere is as informal and friendly as Mexico itself. It showcases the best in Mexican and Chicano culture, from folk art to Frida Kahlo, and has one of the best gift shops in the city. Be sure to check out the many whimsical Dia de los Muertos (Day of the Dead) objects, including the perfect wedding gift—a skeleton bride-and-groom to top the cake. The Galeria de la Raza was the first Mexican museum in the United States. It is more locally oriented than the Mexican Museum, and often more innovative, presenting fine examples of work by community artists, as well as major national exhibits.

The **Jewish Museum** (121 Steuart Street) has two primary focal points—history and art. Exhibits have featured a variety of works by Jewish artists, from emerging current artists to masters like Marc Chagall. The gallery is known for presenting shows that challenge visitors to critically examine what they see.

The West Coast's largest photography collection is housed at the **Ansel Adams Center for Photography**. Holdings range from Annie Liebovitz's irreverent portraits to Ansel Adams' awesome images of the American West. This remarkable museum houses five exhibition halls and extensive bookstore. Exhibits change, but one of the galleries is devoted solely to Adams' own work.

To get a virtually private glimpse of the history of one of San Francisco's most intriguing neighborhoods, go to the **North Beach Museum**, tucked away on the mezzanine of the Bay View Street Bank. This delightful little museum traces North Beach's past with photographs and artifacts dating back to the turn of the century. Hardly anybody knows the museum is there, so you may have it all to yourself, but you must go during regular banking hours.

Museums for really special interests... Ghia Gallery/Discount Caskets and Urns is a favorite among necro-kitsch fans, but you don't have to be morbid to like designer coffins. Just ask Cher—she bought two of Ghia's "King Tut" sarcophaguses and turned them into wine bars. Other creative coffins include the all-glass "Here's Lookin' At You" models and a variety of custom designs that have been used as phone booths, vanity tables, and nightstands. Some people have been so inspired by Ghia's furniture for the hereafter, they've staged their own funerals while they were still alive.

For flesh freaks, we have two recommendations: **Lyle Tuttle's Tattoo Museum** and **Good Vibrations** (also see Shopping). Lyle Tuttle, undisputed king of the San Francisco tattoo empire, moved his mini-museum from a seedy location at Seventh and Market streets long after he had already engraved Janis Joplin's flesh, but you can still see his collection of tattoo art—including candid shots of himself, covered head-to-toe with indelible designs—at his tiny little shop in North Beach. More pleasurable pleasures of the flesh are explored at Good Vibrations, where the contraptions in the window display look like old-time hair dryers or permanent-wave doodads, but are actually part of an eclectic collection of sex toys and vibratorana, including the "Queen Victoria," a wooden hand-crank model from turn-of-the-century London. The museum/store—which tends to favor women's interests—is almost cheery; if it weren't for the dozens of plastic penises on the shelves, you'd expect a young Henry Fonda to appear from behind the counter and offer you an ice cream soda.

At the **Keane Eyes Gallery**, those tacky bug-eyed waif paintings from the '60s—portrait after portrait of small children with oversized heads and eyes so huge and round they make Liza Minelli look like a squinter—are celebrated as high kitsch.

Outlandish out-of-town archives... Heading south from the city, US 101 is dotted with weird little wayside collections. The first stop is the **Burlingame Museum of**

DIVERSIONS | THE LOWDOWN

Pez Memorabilia, not far from the airport. Remember those tiny little candies spit from the mouths of plastic cartoon characters? Since the first Pez-spitter hit the shelves in 1952, hundreds of models have been issued, and the museum's collection of them is exhaustive. Moving right along to the Silicon Valley, you'll find the perfect antidote to Apple, Intel, and the rest of the area's high-tech cathedrals: the **Rosicrucian Egyptian Museum**. One of the mummies on display at this San Jose park was actually a post-mortem hitchhiker discovered by the shippers at Neiman Marcus, who packaged up what was supposed to be a "vacant" case. The store graciously offered to dispose of the uninvited mummy, but the Rosicrucians were delighted to keep it as one of their many permanent guests. Last stop, Surf City. The **Santa Cruz Surfing Museum** is as close as you can get to a surfin' safari without climbing on a board and catching a wave. The museum itself overlooks Steamer Lane, time-honored haunt of inveterate Santa Cruz surfers and home to many championship surfing contests. The view is spectacular, and the exhibits inside are totally awesome, dude.

The bongo-rama beatnik tour... Bohemian-history buffs won't want to leave San Francisco without paying homage to some of the hallowed grounds that have made the city a capital of late 20th-century counterculture. One might say the beat movement, for instance, was born in 1953, when Allen Ginsberg moved to San Francisco and Lawrence Ferlinghetti opened **City Lights Bookstore** (see also Shopping) at 261 Columbus Avenue, even though Neal Cassady and Jack Kerouac already lived in the city at **29 Russell Street** (a small alley off Hyde Street between Union and Grand streets). One weekend in 1955, stoned to the gills, Ginsberg wrote his magnum opus, "Howl," in his apartment at **1214 Polk Street** (between Bush and Sutter streets), and read it for the first time two weeks later to a spellbound audience at the tiny **Six Gallery** at 3119 Fillmore Street (between Filbert and Greenwich streets). City Lights published the poem in 1956, and the police immediately declared it obscene, focusing national attention on North Beach. *Chronicle* columnist Herb Caen coined the term "beatnik" to describe the disheveled literati, who dug poetry and jazz at places like **Vesuvio** (255 Columbus Avenue), on the corner of what is now Jack Kerouac Alley; **The Place** (1546 Grant Ave.), which Jack Kerouac described in *The Dharma Bums* as "the favorite bar of the hepcats around the Beach"; the **Cellar** (576 Green St.); and **Specs** (12 Adler Place). In 1958, after Kerouac's *On the Road* became a best-seller and Hollywood producers came up with the watered-down TV series "Route 66" to exploit the theme, tour-bus gawkers descended on North Beach to stare at the beatniks, making popular hangouts like **Caffe Trieste** (601 Vallejo Street; see Dining and Cafes), the now defunct **Co-Existence Bagel Shop** (1398 Grant Avenue), and **Enrico's** (504 Broadway; see Dining and Cafes) feel like zoos for the caged poets. In 1960, The Place and the Co-Existence Bagel Shop closed, and the fuss over beatniks died down for a while.

Tune in, turn on, drop out... Just a few years later, the city was the center of a cultural convulsion of a more Day-Glo shade. By the time the infamous Summer of Love rolled around in 1967, San Francisco's psychedelic scene had actually been in full swing for more than two years, since *One Flew Over the Cuckoo's Nest* author Ken Kesey introduced Owsley acid (known as the "cadillac of LSD") to the Grateful Dead, and acid rock was born. Another acid-powered band, the Jefferson Airplane, first played at a little club called the **Matrix** (3138 Fillmore Street, near Union Street) in August 1965, but the club got too loud for the neighbors, so the acidheads moved on and it evolved into a rowdy singles bar still doing business as **Pierce Street Annex**.

Examiner writer Michael Fallon coined the term "hippie" to distinguish the new hipsters from their beatnik predecessors shortly before the first big psychedelic concert was staged in October 1965 at **Longshoreman's Hall** in Fisherman's Wharf (400 North Point) by Chet Helms and his production company, the Family Dog. The Family Dog later moved its gigs to the **Avalon Ballroom** at 1268 Sutter Street (near Van Ness Avenue), now a multiplex movie theater. Meanwhile, Bill Graham entered the scene with a benefit for the San Francisco Mime Troupe (December 1965) at the **Fillmore Auditorium** (1805 Geary Blvd., at the corner of Fillmore Street; see Nightlife), which would become his virtual kingdom and the undisputed center of the psychedelic rock universe.

In January 1967, 20,000 people showed up for the first "Human Be-In" at the **Polo Field** (just off Middle Drive between 30th and 36th avenues in Golden Gate Park) covered in luminous detail by the *Oracle*, a popular underground newspaper headquartered at **1371 Haight Street**. The Haight had become the center of hippie culture— Janis Joplin lived at **112 Lyon Street** (corner of Oak Street), the Grateful Dead around the corner at **710 Ashbury Street** (near Haight Street), and the Jefferson Airplane at **2400 Fulton Street** (closer to the park). By the summer of 1967, the whole world was watching the Haight, especially when Rudolf Nureyev and Margot Fonteyn were arrested at a pot party at **42 Belvedere Street** (near Haight Street). Drug busts became a priority—if not a sport—for San Francisco's Finest, and the October 1967 raid of the Dead house was the top feature of the premiere issue of *Rolling Stone*, which was produced in a small loft at 746 Brannan Street, South of Market. Drug busts and a massive influx of unenlightened strangers were ruining the scene; that same month, the **Psychedelic Shop** (1535 Haight St.) closed its doors and a march through the neighborhood declared the death of the true hippie movement. The party was over.

The last-call saloon crawl... The party is never over at some good old watering holes—these historic saloons are still full of characters and stories. There are at least a half-dozen classic booze joints in North Beach, from beatnik haunts that orbit City Lights—**Specs**, **Tosca Cafe**, and **Vesuvio's**—to beloved neighborhood dives like **Gino and Carlo** and literary hangouts like **Washington Square Bar & Grill**. Many of the best old downtown retreats, like the Templebar (1 Tillman Place, now a popular restaurant called Rumpus), have given way to more stylish ventures, but a few remnants of Old San Francisco remain, the best of which is **Harrington's**, a landmark Irish bar that has never been tamed by the genteel Financial District that surrounds it.

Painted ladies... Some 14,000 Victorian buildings— mostly private homes—are scattered throughout San Francisco, but the ones you usually see on the postcards (the 700 block of Steiner Street) are lined up around Alamo Square, the center of a small, wealthy neighborhood bordered by Golden Gate Avenue on the north, Fell

Street on the south, Webster Street on the east, and Divisadero Street on the west. These ornate wooden homes range from gracious to almost garish, depending upon how much gingerbread is involved and who has been choosing the color scheme, but most of them have been meticulously restored. For a famous view, with the painted ladies in the foreground and the city and bay in the background, find a high spot anywhere in **Alamo Square** and face due east (toward Steiner Street), or stand on the corner of Hayes and Steiner streets. The **Archbishop's Mansion** (1000 Fell St., see Accommodations), now an exclusive bed-and-breakfast inn, is a huge blue Victorian mansion right at the northern edge of the Painted Ladies postcard block. (A word of caution: This affluent area is the southwestern neighbor of the Western Addition, which can be dangerous near the public-housing projects, especially at night. If you're not familiar with the area, you may prefer to take a bus or a cab instead of walking.)

If picture-pretty private residences are less intriguing to you than time-worn structures in a working-class neighborhood, head over to the inner Mission District, where several types of the city's oldest Victorians—stick, Italianate, and Queen Anne—can be found on or near **Liberty Street**, a small side street between 20th and 21st streets. These structures survived the 1906 earthquake because the fires stopped at 20th Street. An 1878 stick-style building, characterized by square bay windows with flat wooden "sticks" that have carved scrolls, leaves, and flowers, stands at 956 Valencia Street, on the corner of Liberty. Head north on Liberty, and you'll see rows of Victorians built between 1870 and 1894. At least five of them (19, 23, 35, 43, and 77) are Italianate style, distinguished by ornate porticos, facades above the rooflines, and slanted bay windows designed to bring in more light on foggy San Francisco days. The house at 27 Liberty is a local adaptation of a Queen Anne, identifiable primarily because of the shingled walls (most Queen Annes have rounded corner towers, but there are many variations on this theme). Some of the most interesting houses in the Mission District combined several architectural styles to get just the right amount of gewgaw and curlicues—the house at 827 Guerrero Street (corner of Liberty Street) has a Queen Anne tower, a Gothic front window, and a Moorish doorway. The Mission is full of wonderful houses; walk around and explore for yourself.

Mural, mural on the wall... The 200 or so brilliant murals painted on the walls, fences, and sides of buildings in the Mission District are famous around the world, but often overlooked by visitors and locals alike. There are at least 250 more murals in other neighborhoods around the city—including the stunning Depression-era murals that cover the interior walls of the base of **Coit Tower**. Keep your eyes open wherever you venture, but here's a tip for quick total immersion in the art of the streets: Take BART to the 24th Street station and head up 24th toward Potrero Hill—you'll see it looming in front of you—until you come to **Balmy Alley**, nestled between Treat Avenue and Harrison Street. This one-block lane has one of the most dense collections of murals anywhere in the world—practically every inch of every fence, wall, and garage door is covered with color. Many of the alley's most cherished murals were defaced or destroyed by vandals in the past, but local muralists have painted new images and restored old ones. After you've marveled at Balmy Alley, go back out to 24th Street and head farther toward the hill until you reach **York Street**, about four blocks away. Again you will be treated to a marvelous assortment of brilliantly colored murals. **Precita Eyes Mural Center**, a community resource center, hosts a tour of this area that will show you at least 60 Mission District murals in one eight-block stretch.

Are we there yet? (Fun with the kids)... The top family attractions besides Fisherman's Wharf and Pier 39 (sorry) are the **Exploratorium**, Alcatraz, the Zoo (**San Francisco Zoological Gardens and Children's Zoo**), and the **Steinhart Aquarium**. You simply cannot escape these places if your kids are even slightly persuasive. The latest hot spot for kids is a place called **Zeum**. Its official tag is "art and technology center for ages 8-18," but that title doesn't do it justice. The events calendar features everything from live hip-hop concerts (free with admission) to interactive art studios where teen-artists-in-residence get visitors to help create projects like Megaopolis 3000, "a futuristic cityscape" that teaches kids how to make their own miniature film sets at home. There is also an animator's studio and a film production lab. This is hot, hot stuff for kids. One look at the web site (www.zeum.org)—which has a "Teen Zone" created by and for teenagers—will have your kids begging to go. It's a much better way to spend your time—and money—

than the big-hype **Metreon,** Sony's huge, slick South of Market entertainment center that is a glorified shopping mall/video arcade/movie-plex. The only good thing about the Metreon is that you can drop your teenagers off there for a few hours while you walk around the corner to SF MoMa, a museum they're almost certain to hate. But there are other places they're likely to enjoy as well, depending on their ages. Youngsters love the **Children's Playground** in Golden Gate Park, just off Waller Street, opposite Arguello Boulevard, with all the requisite paraphernalia, plus wheelchair-accessible equipment. If they get bored with the slides/swings/sandbox routine, there is a restored 1912 carousel right next door. The last thing most teenagers want to do is go *anywhere* with their parents, but if you promise to hide across the room and pretend not to know them, they might just love you for taking them to the **Hard Rock Cafe**, where you'll need earplugs and they'll need enough money to buy expensive souvenir T-shirts.

Fabulous footsteps... Hills, schmills. Don't let a few slopes here and there deter you from one of San Francisco's greatest pleasures—walking around the neighborhoods and exploring the city for yourself. Before you set out on your own, however, pick up some free walking-tour guides from the Visitor Information Center (Hallidie Plaza, 900 Market St., Powell Street BART/MUNI Metro stop, tel 415/391–2000). The public library also offers about 20 free walking tours led by **City Guides**, volunteers who have completed an exhaustive training program in San Franciscan history, art, and architecture. Tours range from hidden rooftop gardens to brothels and boardinghouses. Some of the city's most unusual tours are organized by local individuals who love to show off their favorite parts of San Francisco. Rachel Heller leads the **Flower Power** Haight-Ashbury tour, with stops at erstwhile crash pads of famous hippies (Janis Joplin and the Grateful Dead) and other lost psychedelic ports of call, such as the Straight Theater, where Bill Graham first staged his dance con-certs. Host Trevor Hailey, a beloved—and very friendly—local historian, will take you **Cruisin' the Castro**, where you'll visit only-in-San Francisco businesses, chat with the shopkeepers, enjoy brunch in a local hot spot, and discover why gay men have been migrating to San Francisco since the Gold Rush. Television chef and cookbook author Shirley Fong-Torres is the mastermind of the **I Can't**

Believe I Ate My Way Through Chinatown tour, which treats walkers to a private tea ceremony, snacks, a visit to a rice-noodle factory, more snacks, visits with local food merchants, just one last snack, and a full Chinese luncheon. Fong-Torres' Wok Wiz Tour and Cooking Center also features a "Ciao Chow Multicultural Stroll" that includes stops in North Beach as well, and a short "Yin Yang" tour for visitors in a bit of a hurry. There are no hills to climb in Elaine Sosa's **Javawalk**, a 2-hour jaunt through Union Square, Chinatown, Jackson Square, and North Beach, with pit stops along the way for—what else?—cups of joe. A multicourse lunch at Cobalt Tavern is the highlight of *Chronicle* food writer GraceAnn Walden's **Mangia North Beach** tour that goes behind the scenes at brick-oven bakeries, delis, and sausage makers to show what life is like for serious Italian foodies in San Francisco's favorite neighborhood. For lust and crime, get up early and join author John McCarroll on his **A.M. Walks** through the Barbary Coast, Chinatown, and Union Square, where gold rushers found "the best bad things obtainable in America." Then hook up with another local author, Mark Gordon, on his **Frisco Productions Crime Tour**, where you'll visit infamous crime scenes like the Hibernia Bank, robbed by Patty Hearst and the Symbionese Liberation Army in the mid-1970s.

The Index

A.M. Walks. You've got to get up at about 8am to find a little peace and quiet while you roam Chinatown, Union Square, and the Barbary Coast as author John McCarroll recounts tales of unbridled lust, scandal, and crime.... *Tel 415/928-5965. Admission charged.* **(see p. 114)**

Ansel Adams Center for Photography. The largest collection of photography on the West Coast, with one gallery devoted solely to Adams' work.... *Tel 415/495-7000. 655 Mission St., Montgomery St. BART/MUNI Metro station. Open Tue–Sun 11–5, first Thur of every month until 8. Admission charged.* **(see p. 106)**

Asian Art Museum. If you're in town in 2003, do not miss this under any circumstances. It is the largest museum outside of Asia devoted exclusively to Asian art but its new 165,000-square-foot home in the 1917 Beaux Arts building that used to be the city's main library won't open until January 2003.... *Tel 415/668-8921; TDD 415/752-2635. 200 Larkin St., Civic Center Plaza, Civic Center BART/MUNI Metro Station. Hours TBA* **(see p. 102)**

Boudin Sourdough Bakery. When you're at Fisherman's Wharf or Pier 39, nothing tastes better than a San Francisco–style round sourdough bread from Boudin's.... *Tel 415/928-1849. 156 Jefferson St., 32 MUNI bus. Open daily until 5:30.* **(see p. 101)**

Burlingame Museum of Pez Memorabilia. One of the world's most exhaustive collections of Pez dispensers.... *Tel 650/347-2301. 214 California Dr., Burlingame. Closed Sun, Mon. Admission free.* **(see p. 107)**

Cable Car Barn and Museum. San Francisco's cable-car system is still run out of this museum, which also houses the original prototype cable car.... *Tel 415/474-1887. 1201 Mason St., Powell-Hyde or Powell-Mason cable car. Open daily 10–6, Oct–March 10–5. Admission free.* **(see p. 105)**

California Academy of Sciences. This huge science museum complex is a major kid-pleaser, but the biggest draw—the Earth and Space Hall—was closed after a major fire, so be sure to call in advance to make sure it is open again. Meanwhile, the fish roundabout at Steinhart Aquarium puts you inside an enormous tank, and the Morrison Planetarium offers night-sky shows that delight adults and bore kids to death.... *Tel 415/221-5100 or 415/750-7145 (recorded message). Golden Gate Park, near Eighth Ave. and Lincoln Way, 44 MUNI bus. Open 10–5; 9–6, June–Sept. Admission charged.* **(see pp. 103, 105)**

Cartoon Art Museum. In fancy digs near the Museum of Modern Art, cartoon artists are taken seriously but not enough to pay for the rent. In the next episode, the comic book heroes will reopen their doors in a new location—call Visitor Information (Tel 415/283-0177) to find out where. This is one of the few art museums where your kids will have as much fun as you will.... **(see p. 105)**

Church of John Coltrane. An absolute must for jazz fans, the Saint John Coltrane African Orthodox Church has been a dynamic force in the community—and a magnet for musicians as well as music-lovers—since 1971. The live jazz on Sunday is divine. Don't miss it. *Tel 415/673-3572. 930 Gough St. (near Turk St.), 5 MUNI bus. Divine liturgy Sun noon, midweek service Wed 6pm.* **(see p. 99)**

City Guides. Free walking tours offered by the public library range from Mission murals, hidden rooftop gardens, and Pacific Heights mansions to brothels, boardinghouses, and bawds.... *Tel 415/557-4266.* **(see p. 113)**

Coit Tower. Depression-era murals cover the interior walls at the base of the tower, while the top offers a 360-degree view.... *Tel 415/362-0808. 39 MUNI bus. Open daily 10–7. Base admission free, elevator $3.75.* **(see pp. 97, 112)**

Cruisin' the Castro. Walk through the city's gay mecca with a local historian who knows every nook and cranny. Brunch at a popular cafe included. Host: Trevor Hailey.... *Tel 415/550-8110. Admission charged.* **(see p. 113)**

Exploratorium. Kids love this wacky, blow-your-mind science circus—especially the dark and often creepy crawl-through Tactile Dome. The gift shop is probably the best you'll ever encounter at a museum. (Don't miss the Einstein relativity theory wristwatches.).... *Tel 415/561-0360. Palace of Fine Arts, 3601 Lyon St., 30 MUNI bus. Open Tue–Sun 10–5, Wed until 9. Admission charged.* **(see pp. 104, 105, 112)**

Fisherman's Wharf. It's a tacky tourist trap, but if you have to go there, try to save your sanity by feasting on some fresh crab from a sidewalk stall and remembering that it used to be a real fishing port. Your kids may want to hit the Wax Museum and the Ripley's Believe It or Not Museum. To get to the wharf, take any Powell Street cable car or the 15, 30, or 42 MUNI bus. **(see p. 101)**

DIVERSIONS | THE INDEX

Flower Power. Take a walking tour through Haight-Ashbury, and check out the crash pads, concert halls, and psychedelic shops that gave birth to the Hippie era. Host: Rachel Heller.... *Tel 415/863-1621. Admission charged.* **(see p. 113)**

Frisco Productions Crime Tour. Get a vicarious thrill as you visit infamous crime scenes—real and fictional—with local author Mark Gordon, who also offers a Bar Crawl tour, a Sentimental Journey Nostalgia tour, and a Hollywood in San Francisco tour.... *Tel 415/681-5555.* **(see p. 114)**

Galeria de la Raza. The first Mexican museum in the United States, it is still a major art and cultural center in the Latino community.... *Tel 415/826-8009. 2857 24th St., 24th St. at Bryant St. BART station; 48 or 67 MUNI bus. Tue–Sat, noon–6. Admission free.* **(see p. 106)**

Ghia Gallery/Discount Caskets and Urns. If the Addams Family had an art gallery, there's no question this would be it. Not only is the gallows humor good-natured, the coffins are actually fun to look at. (Cher is a customer—is that a surprise?).... *Tel 415/282-2832. 2648 Third St., 15, 30, or 45 MUNI bus. Admission free.* **(see p. 107)**

Gino and Carlo. No bar in North Beach has more loyal regulars than this classic neighborhood dive almost invariably free of tourists. Venture through the double doors, and be prepared for spirited arguments (mostly about sports) and patrons who will undoubtedly retell at least one episode from the bar's long history.... *Tel 415/421-0896. 548 Green St.* **(see p. 110)**

Glide Memorial Church. Charismatic civic leader Reverend Cecil Williams and his gospel choir host services every Sunday morning that seem to lift the spirits of the whole city.... *Tel 415/771-6300. 330 Ellis St. Services Sun at 9 and 11.* **(see p. 100)**

Golden Gate Ferry. Join the locals who ride from San Francisco's Ferry Building at the foot of Market Street to downtown Sausalito, a scenic seaside village with lots of expensive stores, expensive restaurants, expensive real estate, expensive boats—and gorgeous sunsets. The ride takes about a half-hour. Fare is $5.30 each way for adults, $4 for children, and $2.65 for seniors. Call for schedule....

DIVERSIONS | THE INDEX

Tel 415/923-2000, TDD 415/257-4554. Embarcadero BART/MUNI Metro stop. **(see pp. 99, 102)**

Good Vibrations. An eclectic collection of sex toys and vibrators. Workshops offered after hours range from safer-sex education (led by the Safer Sex Sluts) to erotic reading circles.... *Tel 415/974-8980. 1210 Valencia St. 25th St. BART station; 26 MUNI bus. Open Mon–Tue 11–7, Wed–Sun until 8. Admission free.* **(see p. 107)**

Grizzly Peak. A popular Berkeley Hills perch for a great sunset vista of the entire bay. From San Francisco: Drive across the Oakland–San Francisco Bay Bridge, follow the signs to Highway 24 toward Walnut Creek (via Interstate 580), go through the Caldecott Tunnel (stay to the far right), and exit immediately after the tunnel at Fish Ranch Road. (The exit turns sharply right, then right again over the freeway.) Drive up to the top of the hill on Fish Ranch Road, turn right at the stop sign onto Grizzly Peak Boulevard, and drive about a half-mile or so until you find a turnout that appeals to you (the view parking spots will be on your left). **(see p. 99)**

Hard Rock Cafe. Teenagers love the super-loud rock music, juicy hamburgers, and T-shirts that prove they've been there.... *Tel 415/885-1699. 1699 Van Ness Ave. (at Sacramento St.), California St. cable car; 1 MUNI bus. Reservations not accepted.* **(see p. 113)**

Harrington's. When original owner Leo Harrington died in 1959, a procession of motorcycle police led a mile-long cortege in his honor—that's how beloved this Irish bar is. The old building is wonderfully creaky and the floors have been known to get ankle-deep in green beer on St. Patrick's Day.... *Tel 415/392-7595. 245 Front St., California St. cable car.* **(see p. 110)**

I Can't Believe I Ate My Way Through Chinatown. Shirley Fong-Torres lets you in on a private tea ceremony, among other gustatory delights, before you reach your final destination: a huge Chinese luncheon.... *Tel 415/981-8989. Admission charged.* **(see p. 113)**

Javawalk. Walk the coffee trail in Chinatown, Jackson Square, and North Beach with Elaine Sosa.... *Tel 415/673-9255. Apr–Oct. Admission charged.* **(see p. 114)**

Jewish Museum. This fine museum highlights important events in Jewish history as well as contemporary Jewish themes and artists.... *Tel 415/591-8800 (recording). 121 Steuart St., Embarcadero BART/MUNI Metro station. Open Sun–Thur noon–5 (closed on all Jewish holidays). Admission charged.* **(see p. 106)**

Keane Eyes Gallery. Portraits of small children with oversized heads and huge waifish eyes. The gallery used to be open to the walk-in public, but now you need to call for an appointment.... *3036 Larkin St., across from the Ghirardelli Chocolate Factory, Powell cable car; 30 MUNI bus. Admission free.* **(see p. 107)**

Lyle Tuttle's Tattoo Museum. Lyle Tuttle is the undisputed king of the San Francisco tattoo empire. His list of satisfied clients includes Gregg Allman, Cher, Joan Baez, and Peter Fonda.... *Tel 415/775-4991. 841 Columbus Ave., 15 or 30 MUNI bus. Open daily noon–9. Admission free.* **(see p. 107)**

M. H. de Young Memorial Museum. This beautiful Golden Gate Park art museum is closed for renovations until 2005, but in the meantime you can take a virtual tour of the new facility at www.thinker.org. The deYoung hosts most of the major international shows that come to town, but is best known for an impressive collection of American art that dates back to the 1600s.... *Tel 415/750-3600 or 415/863-3330 (recording). Golden Gate Park, near Tenth Ave. and Fulton St., 44 MUNI bus.* **(see p. 103)**

Mangia of North Beach. This 5-hour tour is worth taking for one simple reason: It ends up with a full, multicourse lunch at Cobalt Tavern. Host: GraceAnn Walden.... *Tel 415/397-8530. Saturdays only; during the week by prior arrangement. Admission charged.* **(see p. 114)**

Maritime Museum. Kids like it because it looks like a life-size plaster model of a ship. Inside, the nautical exhibits—models, relics, and other inanimate sailor stuff—might bore the youngsters, but the macramé knots are kind of fun for parents with a twinge of '70s arts-and-crafts nostalgia.... *Tel 415/556-3002. Fisherman's Wharf, 900 Beach St., Powell-Hyde cable car; 15, 30, 42, or 69 MUNI bus. Open daily 10–5. Admission free.* **(see p. 105)**

The Metreon. Sony's four-story, 350,000-square-foot entertainment arcade is a real money-sucker, from the themed attractions at $5–$6 a pop and 15 movie theaters at $8.75 (adult), to the overdose of gift and theme stores. Both Sony and Microsoft have major stores here, with all items at full retail. It's crowded, it's commercial, and the only real reason to go there is to park your kids while you visit nearby SF MoMa.... *Tel 415/369-6000. 101 Fourth St. at Market St.; Powell-Hyde or Powell-Mason cable car; Powell St. or Montgomery St. BART/MUNI Metro station; any Market St. MUNI bus. Open 10–9 Mon–Thur, Fri-Sat until 10. $20 and $10 attraction samplers or pay as you go.* **(see p. 113)**

Mexican Museum. Some people go for the huge permanent collection, others go for the changing exhibits that range from Diego Rivera to graffiti art. We go for the gift shop.... *Tel 415/202-9700. Fort Mason Center, Bldg. D, 28 MUNI bus. Open Mon–Fri 9–5:30. Admission charged.* **(see p. 106)**

Musée Mecanique. This ingenious little museum inside the Cliff House restaurant is full of mechanical gadgets you can actually play with, from player pianos and old carnival fortune-tellers to an entire miniature amusement park. Bring your own quarters.... *Tel 415/386-1170. 1090 Point Lobos Ave., 18 or 38 MUNI bus. Open Mon–Fri 11–7, weekends 10–8. Admission free.* **(see p. 106)**

Museum of Modern Art. Opened in 1995, this ultramodern skylit structure set in the middle of the city's art center, South of Market, features major modern and postmodern artists, but the best part is its huge collection of art photography.... *Tel 415/357-4000. 151 Third St., Montgomery St. BART/MUNI Metro station; 15, 30, or 45 MUNI bus. Open daily 11–5:45, Thur until 8:45, closed Wed. Admission charged.* **(see pp. 104, 105)**

Nick's. Located right on Fisherman's Wharf, Nick's funky sidewalk seafood stall recalls the way things used to be when the area was still a bustling wharf.... *Tel 415/929-1300. Fisherman's Wharf (Jefferson St.), 32 MUNI bus.* **(see p. 101)**

No Name Bar. The music is live (blues and jazz) and the rowdy baby boomers are always in the mood to dance, 7 nights a week.... *Tel 415/332-1392. 757 Bridgeway, Sausalito.* **(see p. 102)**

North Beach Museum. Tucked away on the mezzanine of a small bank, this delightful little museum traces North Beach's history with photographs and artifacts dating back to the turn of the century. Call for schedule.... *Tel 415/391-6210. Bay View Bank, 1435 Stockton St. (at Columbus Ave.), 15, 30, or 45 MUNI bus. Closed weekends. Admission free.* **(see p. 106)**

Palace of Fine Arts. This wonderful old building resembling a Roman ruin is home to the **Exploratorium** (see above) and the sole surviving structure from the 1915 Panama Pacific Exposition.... *Tel 415/567-6642. 3601 Lyon St., 30 MUNI bus. Open Tue–Sun 10–5, Wed until 9.* **(see p. 104)**

Pier 23 Cafe. Great views of the bay and live jazz , R&B, salsa, and reggae for a $5 cover charge.... *Tel 415/362-5125. Pier 23 (the Embarcadero), 32 MUNI bus.* **(see p. 101)**

Pier 39. Basically a glorified shopping mall/carnival, but not so bad if you steer toward the sea lions (K-dock).... *Tel 415/705-5500. 15, 30, or 42 MUNI bus. Open Sun–Thur 11-7, Fri–Sat 10–9, restaurants until 11:30.* **(see p. 101)**

Precita Eyes Mural Center. This community resource center for murals and muralists offers information, tours, and workshops.... *Tel 415/285-2287. 2981 24th St. (near Harrison St.), 24th St. BART/MUNI Metro Station. Tours Sat 1:30pm. Admission charged.* **(see p. 112)**

Rosicrucian Egyptian Museum. The West Coast's largest collection of Egyptian, Babylonian, and Assyrian antiquities: jewelry, pottery, tools, textiles, mummies, and funerary exotica.... *Tel 408/947-3636. Park and Naglee Aves., San Jose. Admission charged.* **(see p. 108)**

San Francisco Zoological Gardens and Children's Zoo. At this 65-acre zoo, nothing can top Gorilla World, one of the world's largest assortments of the big guys. Other delights include the Children's Zoo, adjacent to the main park, where kids can pet baby animals in the zoo nursery or visit the Insect Zoo (more than 6,000 specimens).... *Tel 415/753--7080. Sloat Blvd. and 45th Ave., L Taraval MUNI Metro streetcar to the end of the line. Open daily 10–5, children's zoo 11–4. Admission charged, under 2 free. Free first Wed of every month.* **(see p. 112)**

Santa Cruz Surfing Museum. Cowabunga! This beachside museum features surfboards (from the old redwood "planks" to today's high-tech designs), ancient wetsuits, photos, and other artifacts from 100 years of surfing.... *Tel 831/420-6289. Mark Abbott Memorial Lighthouse, West Cliff Dr., Santa Cruz. Admission charged.* **(see p. 108)**

Six Flags Marine World. Kiss a whale, let an exotic butterfly land on your nose, ride an elephant, feed a giraffe, or get soaked by a mighty splash from the tail of a gigantic killer whale in a million-gallon pool. The wildlife park is an hour from the city via high-speed Blue & Gold ferry from Pier 39; the fleet's package deal—round-trip ferry transportation, shuttle to the park, and all-day park admission is available May–Sept. Call for prices. Reservations recommended.... *Tel 415/705-5555 (ferry information), 707/643-6722 (park information, including driving directions).* **(see p. 102)**

Specs. This tiny brick-walled bar, a beatnik landmark, is cluttered with mementos including a whale's penis bone that hangs over the bar.... *Tel 415/421-4112. 12 Adler Place.* **(see pp. 109, 110)**

Steinhart Aquarium. Part of the California Academy of Sciences, the aquarium is one of the largest in the United States—more than 14,000 species. It's tough to say which is most popular with kids—the 10,000-gallon fish round-about (a miniature ocean that surrounds you) or the feeding of the dolphins, seals, and penguins. There are also tide-pools and a living coral reef.... *Tel 415/221-5100, 415/750-7145 for recorded information. California Academy of Sciences, Golden Gate Park, near Eighth Ave. and Lincoln Way, 44 MUNI bus. Open 10–5, 9–6 during the summer. Admission charged.* **(see p. 112)**

Tosca Cafe. Everyone who stays in San Francisco long enough eventually ends up at Tosca, where the jukebox plays Pavarotti and the cappuccino automatically comes with a shot of booze.... *Tel 415/391-1244. 242 Columbus Ave.; 15, 30 MUNI bus.* **(see p. 110)**

Vesuvio. The list of poets who have spent hours at Vesuvio's getting anywhere from pleasantly buzzed to totally soused stretches from Dylan Thomas (soused) and his namesake

Bob Dylan (buzzed) to Jack Kerouac (soused) and Allen Ginsberg (soused and buzzed).... *Tel 415/362-3370. 255 Columbus Ave.; 15, 30 MUNI bus.* **(see p. 108)**

Washington Square Bar & Grill. Whatever it is, it's already been done at the "Washbag"—weddings, wakes, funerals, deals, scandals—during the past quarter-century.... *Tel 415/982-8123. 1707 Powell St., 15, 30 MUNI bus.* **(see p. 110)**

Yerba Buena Center for the Arts. This dynamic multigallery center focuses on emerging local and regional artists. *Tel 415/978-2700. 701 Mission St., Montgomery St. BART/MUNI Metro station; 14, 15, 30, or 45 MUNI bus. Open Tue–Sun 11–6; Thurs–Fri until 8. Gallery admission charged.* **(see pp. 104, 105)**

Zeum. This is a cutting-edge funhouse where kids not only can see art, film, and computer exhibits, they can help make them. The events calendar includes everything from live hip-hop concerts to workshops with Australian Aboriginal didjeridoo masters. You can't miss the vintage Playland at the Beach carousel at the entrance atop Yerba Buena Gardens.... *Tel 415/777-3500. 221 Fourth St., Yerba Buena Gardens, Moscone Center, Powell St. BART/Metro MUNI station. Open Sat–Sun 11–5 during the school year. Admission $5 for ages 5–18, $6 for students over 18, $7 adults.* **(see p. 112)**

getting

4
outside

At first glance, it
might seem that
San Franciscans'
favorite outdoor
activity is
lounging at side-
walk cafes—a

respectable pastime, to be sure, though hardly a hallmark of physical fitness. But very little is as it seems in this unorthodox city. A magnificent natural environment distinguishes it from most others, and even the most impassive urbanites eagerly embrace any diversion that takes place outdoors, from picnics to surfing. San Francisco may not be Montana or Wyoming, but there's still so much open space around it that cattle ranching remains a major industry in the East Bay. The Bay Area's public greenbelt—more than 860,000 acres of open land and watershed—is probably the largest of any major metropolitan center in the country, according to Greenbelt Alliance, a regional land conservation organization. Add undeveloped private land and there is easily more than a million acres of open space in and around the city, with almost a third of that set aside as public park and recreation areas, including such huge, inviting parks as Golden Gate Park and the Presidio. There's a lot of fun stuff offshore, too, on the islands that dot San Francisco Bay, some of which are just a short ferry ride from the heart of the city, and a great escape—so to speak—from the hubbub. And, of course, there is the spectacular **Golden Gate Bridge**, which you must walk across before you can truly claim to have seen San Francisco.

The Lowdown

Parks... Two dozen neighborhood parks within the city limits include facilities for baseball, basketball, barbecues, boating, bird-watching, bocce, bicycling, cricket, jogging, football, fishing, picnics, swimming, tennis, golf, soccer, volleyball, windsurfing, handball, and lawn bowling. Some even have gyms. **Golden Gate Park** covers 1,000 acres stretching from the Panhandle to the beach. Besides various major attractions covered in the Diversions chapter, it has 11 lakes, 2 waterfalls, 21 tennis courts, horseshoe pits (off Conservatory Way near Grove Street; bring your own horseshoes), a nine-hole golf course, flycasting pools, a miniature yacht club, a 5-acre Japanese tea garden, a primitive garden featuring plants from the dinosaur era, and the very same polo grounds where Allen Ginsberg and Timothy Leary ushered in the Summer of Love at the first "Human Be-In" in 1967. The horseback-riding stables were closed in September 2001, but there's still a resident herd of bison

at the Buffalo Paddock on John F. Kennedy Drive (parallel to 38th Avenue), adjacent to the Chain of Lakes. The
breeding herd of bison are particularly fond of stale bread
tossed to them by passersby. The animals are the progeny
of two cows, Sarah Bernhardt and Princess, and a bull
named Ben Harrison, who were purchased by the city in
1890 and brought down from the Montana plains. Not far
from the buffalo paddock is the Model Yacht Club Boat
House, where miniature yachts are prepared for racing on
Spreckels Lake by the second-oldest miniature yacht club
in America, founded in 1901. Another goofy little wonder
in the park is near the M. H. de Young Memorial
Museum, off Tenth Avenue and Fulton Street. Called the
Forgotten Works, it's a field of carved rocks (some hidden
beneath the grass) which are actually part of the ruins of
El Monasterio de Santa Maria de Avila, a monastery near
Madrid, Spain, part of which was reassembled in the
museum nearby. Another fun spot is **Marina Green**, a
bayshore strip of park where you can listen to the **Wave
Organ**, a bizarre contrivance made of different lengths of
pipes that extend into the bay and resonate to the motion
of the waves. (To reach the green from the Golden Gate
Promenade, turn off at the St. Francis Yacht Club and
take a short walk east past the lighthouse and the Golden
Gate Yacht Club.) Sometimes it's so quiet you can barely
hear it; other times it's like a soothing liquid mantra. Just
west of Marina Green, the **Presidio**—where the city was
originally founded as Yerba Buena in 1776—is now a
national park, with spectacular views of the Golden Gate
Bridge, beautiful hiking and biking trails, a fishing
stream, and other diversions, not the least of which is the
city's pet cemetery. At Crissy Field, at the west end of the
Golden Gate Promenade in the Presidio, you can watch
kite-flyers strut their stuff or windsurfers whizzing around
on the bay. **Mountain Lake Park**, at the edge of the Presidio, has great running trails, four tennis courts, and
fishing; **Lake Merced Park**, near the zoo and Fort Funston, has all the water sports you can imagine, plus two golf
courses and lots of jogging trails. It's also the city's best
park for bird-watching.

Stretching your legs... Some of the most beautiful—and
least hilly—places to jog or walk in San Francisco are its
promenades, which trace the shoreline of the bay from the
Embarcadero's South Beach area to the foot of the

Golden Gate Bridge at Fort Point. The 42 MUNI bus will drop you off near China Basin, a block from King Street and the Embarcadero, which is a good place to start your trek along the **South Promenade**. Heading north, you'll experience a stunning perspective change as you approach and then pass directly under the Oakland–San Francisco Bay Bridge. On your left, across the street, you'll see tempting sidewalk cafes and lush palm trees. On your right, nothing but a railing separates you from the bay itself. It's the most spectacular sea-level view in the city. At Pier 24, the **Waterfront Promenade** features a nearly mile-long staircase that leads down into the water and continues to the Ferry Building. On Saturdays, you may want to stop there and wander through the outdoor farmer's market at the Ferry Plaza (across from the Embarcadero, at the end of Market Street). If you continue along the Embarcadero, you'll pass Pier 39 on your right and end up at Fisherman's Wharf within $1^1/2$ miles. **Golden Gate Promenade** starts at Aquatic Park/Fort Mason at the western edge of Fisherman's Wharf—the 28 MUNI bus route runs near the trail, so you can go one-way or round-trip, or stop anywhere along the way. The Golden Gate Promenade, which is marked by blue-and-white signs, ends at Fort Point, where steps lead up to the Golden Gate Bridge's pedestrian walkway; the entire route is less than 4 miles long (not counting the walk across the bridge), and is popular with cyclists, because of the beautiful views, varied terrain, and decided lack of automobile traffic. Heading west, there's a $2^1/2$-mile parcourse loop for fitness buffs who aren't satisfied with a simple walk or jog, as the trail follows the seawall along the Marina Green. Look over your left shoulder and you'll see the Marin Headlands, Mount Tamalpais, Angel Island, and Alcatraz. When you get to the Palace of Fine Arts, you will have gone a bit more than $1^1/2$ miles. Continue along the promenade to the St. Francis Yacht Club, where, if you want to distract yourself for a quiet moment, you can go east past the lighthouse and the Golden Gate Yacht Club to find the Wave Organ (see "Parks," above). Head back out to the promenade, pass Crissy Field, and you'll have another mile to your credit. From there, it's about 1 more mile to Fort Point; on a windy day, the ocean may spray its mist onto your face as you pass. On Sundays and holidays, **Golden Gate Park** is great for jogging; John F.

Kennedy Drive is closed to vehicular traffic from 19th Avenue to Kezar Stadium—about $2^1/2$–3 miles. To get there, take the N. Judah MUNI Metro streetcar or the 7 MUNI bus to Kezar, or the 5 MUNI bus to Park Presidio and Fulton Street, then walk into the park to John F. Kennedy Drive. You'll pass many potential diversions along the way, so just pretend it's a form of interval training and stop often to indulge yourself. Neighborhood parks with running trails include the 700-acre **Lake Merced** (tel 415/681-3310) at Harding Road off Skyline Boulevard, and the 15-acre **Mountain Lake Park** (tel 415/666-7005) at Lake Street and 12th Avenue. Slightly wacky joggers and walkers—two-, four-, or many-legged—are always welcome to join the **Bay to Breakers** in May, one of America's favorite footraces, when more than 100,000 revelers in goofy costumes make their way from the Embarcadero to the ocean. If you aren't in shape to run the distance ($7^1/2$ miles), you'll have plenty of company—most people walk, trot, dance, or just sort of drift along with the crowd. It's a popular race; register well in advance (call 415/359-2604 for info) to ensure getting your T-shirt at the finish line. There is no more intimate view of the city than the fantastic scenery along the route of the **Chronicle Marathon**, run in early July (register by June—call 800/698-8699), a time of year when the oddball weather here is generally pleasantly cool. The 26.2-mile race takes runners through some of the city's most scenic areas—the Presidio, the Marina, Ghirardelli Square, PacBell Park, downtown's "Wall Street West"—and the vibrant neighborhoods of North Beach, Chinatown, the Mission District, and Haight-Ashbury. For more information, visit the website (www.chroniclemarathon.com).

Pedal pushing... It's no accident that mountain bikes were were invented in the Bay Area. There are two basic ways to ride a bicycle in San Francisco—laboring up the hills and zooming back down. Fortunately, however, there are exceptions—most notably Golden Gate Park, the Great Highway, the Golden Gate Promenade, and the Golden Gate Bridge—which are relatively easy to ride and absolutely gorgeous to behold. The best time to ride in **Golden Gate Park** is ostensibly on Sunday, when John F. Kennedy Drive ($7^1/2$ miles) is closed to automobile traffic, but since that fact is well known to every cyclist, scooter geek, in-line skater, jogger, and baby stroller in the city, congestion can be a bit of a nuisance for cyclists, even without cars. A good alternative is to use the park during the week and steer clear of the area between Arguello Street and 19th Avenue, where most of the museums and other popular attractions are located. The **Great Highway,** from Ocean Beach (at the end of Golden Gate Park) to Lake Merced (turn right on Sloat Boulevard), is an easy 3-mile ride along the ocean on a flat sidewalk with three bike lanes. Add-ons: a 5-mile ride around Lake Merced or a 200-foot ascent on Point Lobos Avenue (near the Cliff House) on your return trip to the park. You can rent a bike for these rides at **Golden Gate Park Skate & Bike** (tel 415/668-1117, 3038 Fulton St.), but if you're more interested in riding across the **Golden Gate Bridge** or into the village of **Sausalito,** you'd be better off picking up your wheels at **Blazing Saddles** (tel 415/202-8888, www.blazingsaddles.com, 1095 Columbus Ave.) or the **Adventure Bicycle Company** (tel 415/771-8735, 888/544-2453, www.adventurebike.com, 968 Columbus Ave.). They're both at the end of the Powell-Mason cable-car line near the foot of the bridge, and as their names imply, they rent the latest, grittiest mountain bikes (as well as cool kids' bikes and tandems). They throw in everything from maps, handlebar bags, water bottles, and cycling computers to windbreakers for the chilly mile-and-a-half ride across the bridge. When you do get to the other side of the bridge—if you're still going for thighs of steel—take the bike lane (parallel to Highway 101) from the Vista Point parking lot and turn off onto Alexander Avenue for a downhill jaunt to Sausalito, another 2 miles. Just remember: What goes down, must come up. Way up, if you make the 2,500-foot climb to the top of **Mount Tamalpais,** birthplace of the mountain bike. This ride is not for wimps. Nor is it for wannabes. In fact, it's pretty much for maniacs and ironmen, so make sure somebody takes your picture at the summit to prove you actually did it. The rest of us can enjoy the view from a convertible with the top down. (Get ride maps and details at www.blazing saddles.com or www.adventurebike.com.) **Angel Island** is also a great place to explore on two wheels. Take a ferry (see "Islands with a past," below) to the state park, then rent a mountain bike at Ayala Cove for $10 per hour or $30 per day (helmet included). There are about 8 miles of beginning and intermediate trails and many steeper advanced trails. Finally, keep in mind that BART allows cyclists to board on off-peak hours. Bike route maps and information are available from the **San Francisco Recreation and Park Department** (tel 415/831-2700) and the **East Bay Regional Park District** (tel 510/635-0135).

Working up a sweat... If you're staying at any of the city's major hotels, you're probably eligible for the special $10 daily guest package (regularly $15) at the state-of-the-art **Pinnacle Fitness Club**, voted best in the Bay Area by the *San Francisco Bay Guardian*. This immaculate club with new and perfectly maintained equipment is frequented by locals as well as hotel guests; the majority tend be young (20–35), fitness-conscious professional types rather than bulky bodybuilders. The price is fantastic, but the only pool is a small lap pool at the Post Street location. The list of participating hotels is far too long to give here; ask your concierge or call one of the three facilities (tel 415/ 495-1939, 345 Spear Street, near Embarcadero BART or MUNI Metro stops; tel 415/781-6400, 1 Post Street, or tel 415/543-1110, 61 New Montgomery Street, both near Montgomery Street BART or MUNI Metro stops). If you get the urge to pump iron in the middle of the night, there's always **24 Hour Fitness**, with five huge facilities in the city. You won't find many "gym rats" there, nor will you find many women in the middle of the night, but at other hours there's a fairly even mix of men and women, varied according to the neighborhood. Daily fee is $15 (tel 415/776-2200, 1200 Van Ness Avenue; tel 415/395-9595, 350 Bay Street; tel 415/543-7808, 303 Second Street; tel 415/334-1400, 1850 Ocean Avenue; and tel 415/434-5080, 100 California Street). Of the city's four YMCA health clubs, the cream of the crop is the **Embarcadero YMCA** (tel 415/957-9622, 169 Steuart Street, $12 a day), with a sparkling pool, state-of-the-art exercise equipment, and a spectacular view of the bay from the Life-cycle machines. During the week, the club is filled with financial district types—especially at lunchtime—but on weekends, you're likely to see locals just in from their morning espresso at a North Beach cafe.

Hitting the beach... Can we talk? Northern California ain't Hawaii, kids. The water is usually as cold as ice, the wind can be fierce enough to blow your tuna sandwich into

SAN FRANCISCO | GETTING OUTSIDE

the next person's picnic basket, and the summer sky is generally overcast—though it will give you a dreadful sunburn if you don't wear sunblock. So don't look for swaying palms and white-sand beaches. That's a different California. The rugged, cliffside beaches here are some of the most spectacular in the world. Huge waves crash against sheer walls of rock, but a treacherous undertow and unpredictable surf conditions make them dangerous for swimming.

Ocean Beach (at the end of Golden Gate Park, near the Cliff House) is surely the most dramatic seaside vista in the city—at least the sea lions that gather on Seal Rocks seem to think so—but it is absolutely forbidden to swim there. You can enjoy sunbathing, beachcombing, hiking, sipping a drink at the **Cliff House** (tel 415/386-3330, 1090 Point Lobos Avenue), but don't even think about dipping your little toe in the water. Swimming is also prohibited at **Land's End Beach** (north of the Cliff House), **Kirby Beach** (below the northern end of the Golden Gate Bridge), **Rodeo Beach** (at Fort Cronkite, Marin Headlands), and **Tennessee Beach** (north of Rodeo Beach), though beachcombing can be fun if you stay a safe distance from the water. There are safe swimming beaches in the city, if you can stand the cold water: **China Beach** (28th Avenue and Sea Cliff Drive) and **Aquatic Park** (end of Hyde Street). Both are sandy coves where lifeguards are on duty during the summer; they're open April 15–October 15, 7am–dusk. More popular with adventurous locals is **Baker Beach**, where nude sunbathing is fashionable for both gay and straight sunbathers. Officially designated clothing-optional by the city, it's easily reached by public transportation (you might want to keep your clothes on while you're riding the bus). The truly gay men's section, according to that indispensable, outrageous local guide *Betty and Pansy's Severe Queer Review*, is beyond the large rock formations, which are most easily navigated at low tide. That part of the beach is definitely a cruise scene. The rest of the beach, however, has a predominant atmosphere of comfortable indifference to the fact that many people are not wearing clothes. Swimming is not prohibited but is definitely very dangerous and should be avoided. No lifeguards are on duty; there are changing rooms, which seem rather pointless when no one's wearing clothes anyway. The beach is open April 15–October 15, 7am–9pm. If you want to meet some real-

live local maniacs, get out the wetsuit and join in the **Alcatraz Shark Fest**, a 1^1/$_2$-mile swim from the Rock to the
city shore. Believe it or not, it's a pretty popular event, so
preregister (tel 415/868-1829, www.environ sports.com).
For beachcombing, tide-pool exploring, hiking, camping,
or bed-and-breakfast getaways, a trip to **Point Reyes
National Seashore** is without equal. At 65,000 acres, it's
the largest and wildest section of the Bay Area's greenbelt—32,000 acres of designated wilderness. You may
even be lucky enough to spot a great white shark out in the
water. Point Reyes' beaches and tiny villages are accessible
by Golden Gate Transit public transportation (tel
415/923-2000, TDD 415/257-4554), but are much easier
to reach by car, less than an hour from the city.

Bathing in the buff: beyond Baker Beach... While
Baker Beach (see "Hitting the beach," above) is the most
popular, three other city beaches are also clothing-
optional—**Land's End**, **Fort Funston Beach**, and
Golden Gate Bridge Beach—and bare-butt bathing is
allowed at all Golden Gate National Recreation Area
beaches as long as nobody complains (which they rarely
do). Marin County's nude beaches are generally sunnier
and less crowded than those in the city. The best is **Muir
Beach** (Pacific Way, off US 1), where there is plenty of
sand and privacy, but no cops or poison oak. The crowd
is mixed—gay, straight, singles, families. Get there before
11:30 on weekends to find a parking lot space. On the
other side of San Francisco, head south on US 1 past the
town of Pacifica to **Devil's Slide**. Turn left onto the
unmarked road 3 miles south of the Denny's restaurant
in Linda Mar and you'll find an immaculate, privately
operated beach. Gays, straights, singles, and families
flock to this little cove, even though swimming in the
freezing-cold water is dangerous and sharks occasionally
have been spotted offshore. Privately operated **San Gre-
gorio Beach** (about an hour south of San Francisco, near
the junction of US 84 and US 101) claims to have been
the first nude beach in America, established as clothing-
optional in the '30s. It's warm enough here to run around
naked on the 2 miles of rolling sand as early as February,
but it's often very windy with water usually too cold and
dangerous for swimming. To get the skinny on any—or
all—of California's nude beaches, check out the *Bay
Guardian's* online guide at www.sfbg.com.

SAN FRANCISCO | GETTING OUTSIDE

Poolside plunges... OK, the beaches weren't made for swimming, and not many of the hotels have pools, but if you really want to take off your summer cold-weather gear and dive in, the best poolside scene in the city is at **The Phoenix** (tel. 415/776-1380, 601 Eddy Street), where rock stars and their attendant groupies lounge, socialize, sip cocktails, and sometimes even swim—but you must be a hotel guest (or invited by one) to join in. The abstract mural on the bottom of the pool—painted by New York City artist Francis Forienza—was almost outlawed by state inspectors, who insisted it was a hazard and claimed: "People have been hurt by art before." Ultimately the governor of California enacted a bill exempting the mural from an antiquated law that requires all pool bottoms to be painted white.

Water sports... You won't have to worry about dangerous murals lurking at the bottom of the bay when you go sea kayaking, windsurfing, sailing, or fishing. Watching the windsurfers on the bay just off Crissy Field, it's easy to forget there are skyscrapers a few minutes away. On an ideal day, the waves are high and the wind is strong enough to give advanced windsurfers a ride that would make anyone forget the stress of urban life; beginners should definitely stick with calmer waters. The **San Francisco School of Windsurfing** (tel 415/753-3235, www.sfwindsurf.com, Candlestick State Park) offers lessons and rentals. All-day kayaking trips (weekends only) are definitely the up-close-and-personal way to enjoy the dramatic cliffs, secluded beaches, and unbelievable views on **Angel Island**—and you don't even have to know how to paddle. All trips are led by expert naturalists and require specific advance reservations; the $95 to $135 fee includes lunch. Paddlers may rent single kayaks for $15 the first hour and $10 per each additional hour; doubles rent for $30 the first hour and $10 per each additional hour (tel 415/488-1000; fax 415/332-8790, www.seatrekkayak.com). Sailing is kind of a misnomer for what one does in a rented boat on **Stow Lake** in Golden Gate Park (tel 415/752-0347), but few things in life are more fun than getting in a pedal boat with someone else and simply pretending to pedal while your friend does all the work. At Stow Lake, you can also rent rowboats, which are especially suitable for afternoon trysts or for dressing up fancy and pretending you're in an

Impressionist painting. If you're feeling sort of Hemingway-esque and you just have to get out on the bay in a real boat, both **Spinnaker Sailing** (tel 415/543-7333, Pier 40, South Beach Harbor) and **A Day on the Bay** (tel 415/922-0227, San Francisco Marina) offer sailing instruction and rentals. If you'd rather sip cocktails and let the captain sail the ship, there are dozens of charters, from dinner cruises to overnighters aboard yachts (see Diversions).

Reeling them in... If that Hemingway thing just won't go away, you could always pay your money and take your chances on a fishing boat. There are dozens of charters, but only one is owned and operated by a woman: **Wacky Jacky** (tel 415/586-9800). Skipper Jacky has been having a great time on the bay for almost 30 years, and her sense of humor makes even the most inexperienced angler have fun—and catch fish. A day on Jacky's sleek, fast 50-footer (board at Fisherman's Wharf at 5:30am, depart 6am, return 3pm) will cost around $85.50, including license, rod, tackle, and anything else you'll need to land a big fish. Here's an inside tip: When you choose a rod, ask for the Green Weenie. It has brought in so many big ones, Jacky is considering retiring it for good behavior.

For tasty little trout, **Lake Merced** is a good stop. The **Lake Merced Boating and Fishing Company** (tel 415/681-3310) can set you up with boats, rods and reels, bait, and licenses (California requires a state fishing license that costs $10 for a two-day permit or $29.40 annually; Lake Merced charges an additional $4 for a daily use permit). And if the swoosh-swoosh-plop of a perfect flycast is your cup of tea, bring your own rod to the **Golden Gate Park Fly Casting Pools** (tel 415/386-2630, opposite the Buffalo Paddock off John F. Kennedy Drive), where tournament-level fly casters can be found practicing (ask them for pointers). Tuesdays, Saturdays, and Sundays are the best days; there's no fee, but then there are no fish here either—it's strictly for practice.

Par for the course... If you suddenly get the urge to sink one but you didn't bring your clubs, don't worry. The **Lincoln Park Golf Course** (tel 415/221-9911, 34th Avenue and Clement Street, near the California Palace of the Legion of Honor) will rent you a set of clubs for $25 and send you out to try your luck on this 18-hole, par-68 course, where you may get distracted by the vista of the Pacific Ocean and the Golden Gate Bridge. Greens fees are $23 weekdays, $27 weekends; golf carts are $22. The magnificent **Presidio Golf Course** (Tel 415/561-GOLF, 300 Finley Road)—where Teddy Roosevelt, Dwight Eisenhower, and even Babe Ruth used to play—was opened to the public in 1995 when the Presidio became a national park. The 18-hole, par-72 course—San Francisco's oldest—overlooks the Pacific Ocean, San Francisco Bay, and the city itself. It is spectacular, immensely popular, and expensive: Greens fees are $57 to $87 in peak season, plus $15 cart rental fee. You can book a tee time, preferably well in advance, online at www.presidiogolf.com (click on reservations). The **Golden Gate Golf Course** (tel 415/751-8987, 47th Avenue and Fulton Street) is less challenging—9 holes, par 27, and 1,357 yards—but it's three blocks from the Pacific Ocean and is a great place to practice your swing and stay in shape without spending a fortune. Greens fees are just $10 weekdays, $13 weekends.

Lawn bowling... At the opposite end of the park, you'll find another delightfully peculiar sport—lawn bowling. Free lessons are offered at the **Golden Gate Park Bowling Green** (tel 415/753-9298, just south of the tennis courts on Bowling Green Drive).

Islands with a past... **Alcatraz** is certainly the most commemorated of the San Francisco Bay's 14 islands—virtually every souvenir stand in the city sells a variety of tacky T-shirts proclaiming the wearer to be an inmate, escapee, or survivor of the notorious island prison, once home to folks like Al Capone and Machine Gun Kelly. But far from being a tourist trap, it's more like a set for a nightmarish Fellini movie co-authored by Stephen King—part bucolic Mediterranean island, part claustrophobic cell-block nightmare. Truly masochistic visitors can ask to be enclosed in deep six, a solitary confinement cell. After the prison was closed down, fitness guru Jack LaLanne once swam from Alcatraz to the city's shore handcuffed or blindfolded or both (who can remember?), perhaps inspiring today's Escape from Alcatraz triathlon, which originally included a bicycle ride to Marin County and a brutal Double Dipsea run over a twisted, mountainous course—better designed for billy goats—from

Stinson Beach to Mill Valley and back. The race now finishes with a 12-mile run through the Golden Gate National Recreation Area, and has 500 competitors. Aside from morbid and/or historical fascination, however, the jagged island, 135 feet above the bay, is a surprisingly lovely spot for walking, with views of the city's skyline and the Golden Gate Bridge that are worth every penny of the $12.25 round-trip ferry ride (children $7, seniors $10.50; ferries operated by Blue & Gold Fleet, tel 415/773-1188). Admission to the island park is free. Ferry reservations are suggested at least two weeks in advance during the summer.

Angel Island—a 640-acre state park with a 360-degree view of the bay from atop Mount Livermore (781 feet)—is a favorite with locals for cycling, hiking, sea-kayaking, and overnight camping, but, besides being a quarantine station and a Nike missile base, it was once a detention center for more than 175,000 Chinese and other Pacific Rim immigrants (1910–1940). It used to be nearly impossible to explore that immigration station, but now the park offers an open-air TramTour through the area, with a narrated history and aerial views that evoke audible sighs from passengers. The tram departs the Cove Cafe weekdays at 10:30, 12:15, and 1:30; weekends and holidays at 10:30, 12:15, 1:30, and 3:15. Fare is $11.50, $7 for children 6-12, $10.50 for seniors. Ferries to Angel Island, operated by Blue & Gold Fleet (415/773-1188), cost $10.50 round-trip, $5.50 for children 5-11. For cycling information, see "Pedal pushing"; for kayaking, see "Water sports."

Fantasy islands... It takes a little more work to get to the bay's undiscovered islets, but if you want to see a part of outdoor San Francisco rarely experienced even by locals, it's worth the effort. The bed-and-breakfast innkeepers on **East Brother Island** ferry visitors to the island in a tiny boat, but you have to go to the San Pablo Yacht Harbor (Point Molate exit off Highway 580, east of the Richmond–San Rafael Bridge) to catch it. A defunct lighthouse station (1874–1969) has now been replaced with an automated signal, and the elegant Victorian structures that once served as the light tower and signal building have been converted into a four-bedroom bed-and-breakfast. It's a wonderfully quiet (and often sunny) retreat from the city during the summer, but be warned:

From October 1 to April 1, the foghorn sounds every 30 seconds. Day visits, 11:15–3:30, cost just $15 (bring your own picnic lunch). Reservations should be made a month in advance for day visits and six months in advance for overnight stays (tel 510/233-2385, www.ebls.org).

The wine country... Most people, including locals, don't realize that California's famous Napa Valley wine country is less than an hour and a half from downtown San Francisco by car. If you leave the city around 10:30 or 11, you'll miss the morning traffic and be in the heart of vineyard-and-spa land in time for a yummy lunch on the sunlit terrace at **Pinot Blanc** (tel 707/963-6191, 641 Main Street, St. Helena). Take the Golden Gate Bridge out of town and stay on Highway 101 North about 15 miles to Highway 37 East (toward Napa). After about 20 miles, you'll wind through the town of Napa on Sonoma Boulevard, which becomes Highway 12 West, then 121 North, then 29 North. Highway 29 is the main road through the Napa Valley. As you drive along it, you'll see dozens of "No Winery Here" signs on side roads and driveways, a testament to the hundreds of wineries—and millions of visitors—in the area.

It's possible to check out a few choice wineries in an afternoon, without straying far from Highway 29. Be sure to stop in at the first winery you see when you leave the town of Napa: **Trefethen** (tel 707/255-7700, 1160 Oak Knoll Avenue, Napa; www.trefethen.com). Built in 1886 and meticulously restored, it is the only existing wooden "gravity-flow" winery in Napa County and is on the National Register of Historic Places. A bit farther up the highway, one of the largest modern art collections in California is housed at what was once the Christian Brothers' first Napa Valley winery. **The Hess Collection** (tel 707/255-1144, 4411 Redwood Road, Napa; www.hesscollection.com) is a working winery, but its biggest draw is beautiful ivy-covered stone buildings (circa 1903) and a permanent exhibit of paintings and sculptures by contemporary artists such as Francis Bacon, Robert Motherwell, Frank Stella, Magdalena Abakano-wicz, and Gerhard Richter. The collection is open to the public daily 10–4. The next must-stop is **Niebaum-Coppola** (tel 707/968-1177, 1991 St. Helena Highway, Rutherford; www.niebaum-coppola.com), a magnificent

19th-century chateau that had been chopped up and sold to a huge vintner's conglomerate before Francis Ford Coppola and his family bought—and rescued—it in 1995. After three years of intensive restoration, the spectacular castle is again a thriving winery. But even if there wasn't a drop of vino, you wouldn't want to miss the terrific two-floor display of Coppola's personal movie memorabilia collection, including his Oscars, handwritten scripts and story boards, and Don Corleone's desk from *The Godfather*. Continuing to Calistoga, treat yourself to a bottle of bubbly at **Schramsberg** (tel 707/942-6668, 1400 Schramsberg Road, Calistoga; www.schramsberg.com). Immortalized by Robert Louis Stevenson, who called wine "bottled poetry," Schramsberg's sparkling wine was served as the "Toast to Peace" between President Nixon and Premier Chou En-lai in Beijing in 1972, and has been poured in the White House ever since. Ironically, it was Chinese "coolie" laborers who built most of the two miles of caves in which the wine is aged. Built in 1862, Schramsberg is a Historical Landmark.

Dozens of books, websites, and tours are devoted to California's wine country. The most comprehensive Napa Valley website, www.napavalleyonline.com, offers as many options on its home page as Yahoo plus detailed maps and a web cam stationed in Street Helena that updates photos hourly. Another good source is the Napa Valley Conference and Visitors Bureau (www.napavalley.com).

Insider's tip: Most small, family-owned wineries allow visitors only by appointment. It's worth a call to arrange a private tour, where you will likely get to meet and talk with the winemaker instead of a tour guide. For example, **Frog's Leap** (tel 800/959-4704, 8815 Conn Creek Road, Rutherford; www.frogsleap.com)—originally located on a farm that raised frogs for fine restaurants—provides welcome comic relief from the tiresome wine snobbery that affects so many tours. The wine is fine, but it's the fun that counts. Owner John Williams, who was also poking a little fun at the popular Stag's Leap vineyard when he named his winery, welcomes visitors Monday through Saturday 10-4, but you have to call ahead for an appointment.

St. Helena is a lovely little Old-West-Victorian town, perfect for strolling, shopping, and counting passing BMW convertibles. It's a bit precious, but just a few minutes away is its poor—and preferable—cousin, Calistoga. This unpretentious little community, famous for its mineral water, was supposedly named by an 1860s entrepreneur who tapped into the 212-degree water and proudly declared he was going to create "the Calistoga of Sarafornia." He meant to say "the Saratoga of California." How can you not love that? Today's spas range from places that look like veterinarians' offices with gooey mud baths to pristine salons with manicured attendants in white lab coats. **Lavender Hill Spa** (tel 707/942-4495 or 800/528-4772, 1015 Foothill Boulevard, Calistoga) definitely falls into the latter category, with spacious, private bathhouses surrounded by gardens. You won't be left to soak in a traditional thick mud bath that makes you wonder what might be crawling around in the muck. Lavender Hill's baths are prepared individually for you, with a combination of local volcanic ash; white sea kelp from France; Dead Sea salts; and essential oils infused into the clear, clean water ($68 for a one-hour treatment). To find a spa that suits you, check out the Chamber of Commerce's website (www.calistogafun.com).

There are tons of great places to stay. The charming, friendly **Calistoga Inn** (tel 707/942-4101, 1250 Lincoln Avenue, Calistoga) is a downtown hub with a restaurant and microbrewery; European-style rooms with a shared bath cost $65 to $90 a night. A few blocks away, at the splendid **Cottage Grove Inn** (tel 707/942-8400 or 800/799-2284, 1711 Lincoln Avenue), each private cottage has a wood-burning fireplace, a two-person whirlpool tub, a stereo system, all the amenities of a big-city luxury hotel, and a wide front porch with wicker rocking chairs ($235–295). If you want to stay overnight anywhere in the Napa Valley in peak season—June through October—or on weekends, you'll need reservations well in advance.

Soothing spas and marvelous massages... Meanwhile, back in the city, many hotels, such as the **Miyako** in Japantown, offer therapeutic massage as part of their service packages. If your hotel isn't one of these, get thee to a spa and find out why Californians rave about hot tubs and aromatherapy. The spa that's probably most recommended by locals to their out-of-town guests—but not yet discovered by throngs of weary tourists—is **Kabuki Springs & Spa** (tel 415/922-6000, www.kabukisprings.com, 1750 Geary Boulevard) in Japantown. There are few, if any, misfortunes that a soak in the Kabuki's communal hot pool can't cure. The ultimate city indulgence has separate days for men and women except coed Tuesdays (women's days are Sunday, Wednesday, and Friday; men are welcome Monday, Thursday, and Saturday) and costs a mere $15 to $18. The service menu also includes massage ($50–115), facials, seaweed wraps, and an hour-and-a-half Javanese body treatment that involves flower oil massage, a jasmine scrub, a yogurt massage, and an exotic flower bath ($115). If you want all of these spa services *and* one of the most beautiful urban resort settings in America, take BART just four stops across the bay to Rockridge and have a cab drop you off at the **Claremont Resort Hotel, Spa & Tennis Club** (tel 510/549–8566 for reservations, 510/843–3000 for information; Ashby and Domingo avenues, Oakland). This spectacular Victorian landmark hotel, nestled in 22 lush acres at the foot of the Oakland/Berkeley hills, is especially lovely during the summer—when San Francisco is foggy and cold, the Claremont is sunny and warm. The full-service European spa here offers nine different types of massage, seven body-care treatment packages (wraps, masks, scrubs, massages, Swiss showers, whirlpool baths), and many varieties of facials and salon treatments. Reservations are a must—one to two weeks in advance for weekend visits—but midweek visits can often be arranged on the same day. The best package deal is the $99 Refresher, which includes an aroma bath, neck and shoulder massage, manicure or shampoo/blow dry, gift, lunch, and use of all facilities. On the north side of the bay, just 12 miles from the city, is **Tea Garden Springs** (tel 415/389-7123, 38 Miller Avenue, Mill Valley), a holistic spa with a Chinese tea garden, where visitors are invited to sip tea or enjoy a vitalizing elixir before receiving massages or other treatments. The spa, designed in accordance with feng shui, is at the foot of Mount Tamalpais in Mill Valley. What set this spa apart from the others are its many ancient Chinese practices and meticulous attention to aesthetic detail. Massages cost $45 to $120, depending on the technique and duration; half-day retreats including several services and a meal are also available.

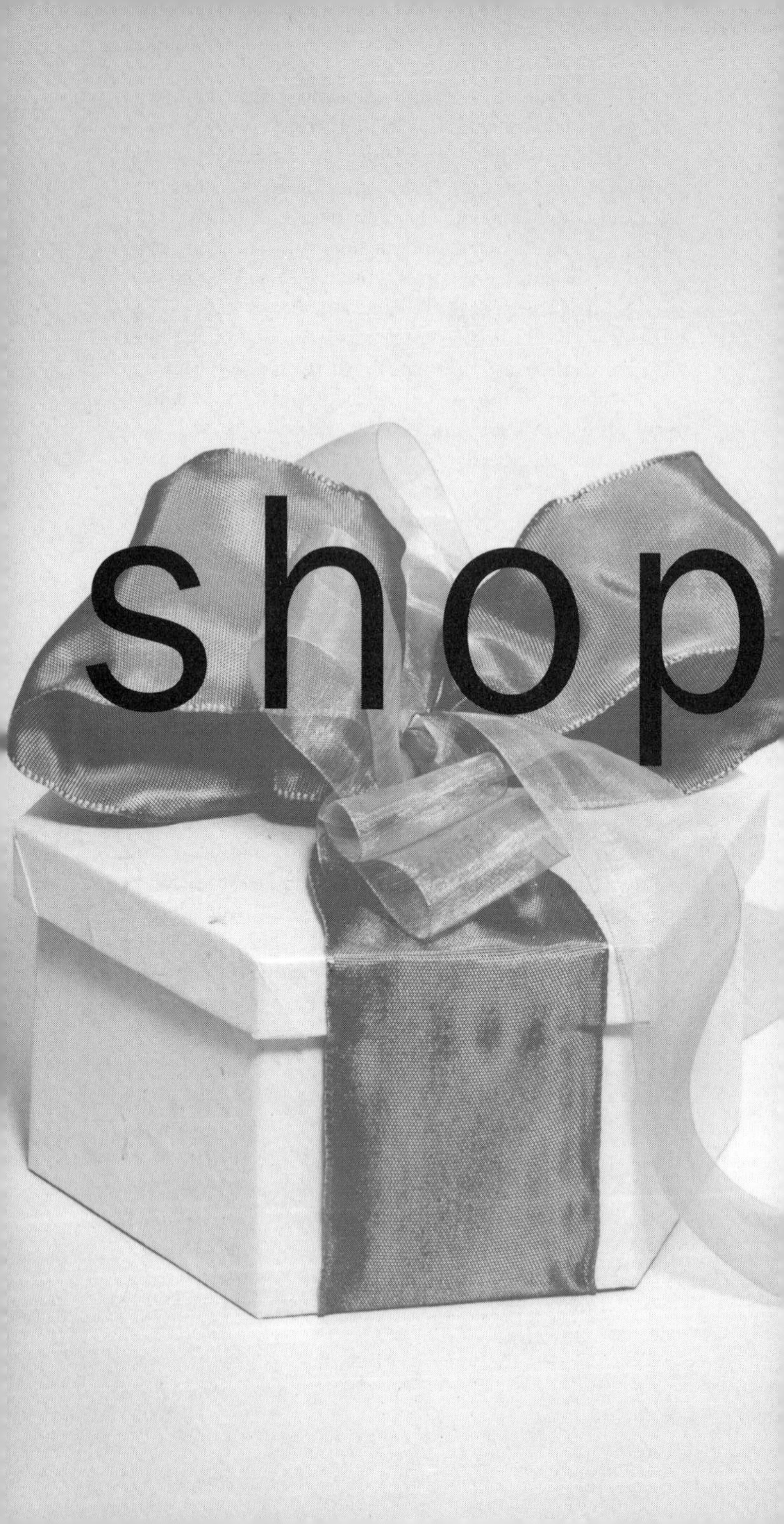
shop

5

ping

In San Francisco's neighborhood boutiques, the glorious hodgepodge of goods ranges from merely wacky to utterly bizarre.

Here lies the Bay Area's most memorable shopping. Vintage clothing, countercultural accoutrements, New Age paraphernalia, and all kinds of obscure books are the city's stock in trade, living up to San Francisco's reputation for the offbeat.

Then, of course, there's Union Square, where the city's conservative and classic side asserts itself with tiny department stores and designer boutiques. Refined little old ladies in prim white gloves still bemoan the loss of the landmark City of Paris building, on the corner of Stockton and Geary streets, which has been replaced by the modern Neiman Marcus store. But tradition is hardly threatened in this neighborhood.

Not much good can be said for San Francisco's shopping centers and malls. With few exceptions, an afternoon at the Anchorage, the Cannery, the Crocker Galleria, or Pier 39 isn't all that different from an afternoon in any other well-groomed mall. Some of the stores are housed in historic buildings—just as they are in Denver, Seattle, Sacramento, and dozens of other cities' old-town areas—but the intrigue tends to end with the architecture.

Target Zones

Union Square (bordered by Kearny and Mason streets, from Market Street to Bush Street) is the stop for department stores and exclusive designer shops that rival the world's best. Even the larger stores offer courteous personal service and at least a couple of small cafes; Saks and Neiman Marcus still provide elegant lounges where female shoppers can freshen their lipstick and rest on comfy chairs when a quick trip to the toilet just isn't enough. Nearby **Maiden Lane**, a hidden 2-block alley that runs from Kearny Street to Stockton Street (between Geary and Post streets), continues to count Brooks Brothers and Chanel among its many upscale tenants.

Oh-so-prettified **Union Street** (between Van Ness Avenue and Steiner Street) has become rather old-hat and overpriced, a favorite haunt of well-heeled tourists and visiting suburbanites. Union Street's shops seem to sell stuff from everywhere but San Francisco—New York bagels, Seattle coffee, European clothes. It's also a great place to find top-quality children's clothing and toys.

Fillmore Street (between Post and Jackson streets), the nouveau-chic area that proclaims itself a five-star neighborhood on obnoxious yellow banners at every street corner, is on the verge of becoming the next Union Street. A few short years ago, when there were just a handful of interesting little shops and cafes—and **D & M Wine and Liquor Co.**, the best wine store in the city—some of the merchants tried desperately to establish this small patch of real estate as part of wealthy Pacific Heights rather than the notoriously slummy Fillmore District. They succeeded. Now you have to wait in line to get a cup of coffee on a Sunday morning, the bars are jammed with *GQ*-model lookalikes, and the sidewalks are congested with yuppie baby strollers. Locals looking for something truly interesting to do look elsewhere.

Chinatown is one of the most popular neighborhoods among tourists, though the bounty to be found here is often of dubious value—tacky souvenirs made in Taiwan, jade jewelry at a discount, or XXX-rated fortune cookies. Hand-painted signs swear that everybody is going out of business and must sell everything at incredibly low prices right now. Sidewalk stalls are stuffed with every plastic and rubber item ever sold for less than $5. Herbalists sell dragon's blood and other exotic ingredients next to vegetable stands, jewelry stores, banks, and dim sum parlors. There are some fun bazaars, though, and the smells alone are worth the visit.

The **Hayes Valley** (Hayes Street between Franklin and Buchanan streets) is a happy byproduct of the 1989 earthquake, which brought down a nearby freeway and let the sunshine in. It's fun, hip, eclectic, friendly, and not yet full of itself. You can find local clothing designers, bead stores, vintage clothing, African artifacts, Mexican art and knickknacks, collectible furniture, junk stores, and tarot card readers, among other things.

Haight Street ain't what it used to be, but it's still quasi-psychedelic and filled with people and things you certainly won't see in Kansas. Vintage clothing stores are a big thing, but the value ranges from great deals on retro-fashions to ridiculously overpriced castoffs. Don't get caught paying $75 for a used Levi's jacket just because some guy with a mohawk cut the sleeves off it. If you're looking for avant-garde new clothing and shoes, this is the place. And if you're a man looking for a pair of shimmering red cha-cha heels in a perfect size 12, this may be the only place. Most of the shops are between Central and Stanyan streets.

North Beach will never leave you bored, with everything from beatnik bookstores and hippie poster shops to tattoo parlors and record stores. You can buy postcards, wigs, shoestrings, old clothes, new clothes, incense, bells, beads, crystals, jewelry, pasta machines, furniture, focaccia, and anything else you can imagine—even a new set of bocce balls.

The **Mission District** (between 16th and 24th streets) is a weird and wonderful place to shop, if you can handle being on two planets at once. Mission Street has the tightest cocktail dresses and shiniest spiked-heel shoes in town, alongside pure white confirmation and wedding dresses. Valencia Street sells used books and new vibrators, candles for Catholic and other rituals, expensive clothes that look like they've already been through the wringer, antiques, and thrift-shop treasures.

Bargain Hunting

San Francisco is loaded with thrift stores and secondhand clothing stores, a prime source of cool couture for local hipsters (though prices on quasi-vintage clothing, which can be very hip, can also be steep). Haight, Valencia, and Mission streets are the best spots for super scores. (Also see "Recycled regalia" and "Cheap thrills," below.) For discounts on all kinds of new merchandise, there are more than 40 factory outlets South of Market—you really need a guide to hit them all, especially since the city's only version of an outlet mall, Yerba Buena Square, is now defunct. All you'll find there now is a multilevel Burlington Coat Factory, and who would go all the way to San Francisco for that? (Also see "In the outlets," below.)

Trading with the Natives

San Francisco's merchants are by and large well-disposed toward out-of-towners. All major department stores will hold merchandise for a reasonable amount of time and will ship your packages home for you. (If you live out of state you won't have to pay sales tax.) Most will accept your personal check if you have proper identification, such as a driver's license with photo; it is illegal to ask for a credit card as a form of identification. Some small stores may not accept out-of-state checks, but as a rule, paying by check is not a problem in the Bay Area. It's not common practice to negotiate prices unless you're at a flea market, garage sale, or used-car lot, but it's always acceptable to point out a flaw or defect and ask for a reduction in price. (Whether you get it is up to the sales staff.) Most department stores will automatically give you 10% to 20% off for a broken zipper, missing button, or similar problem; smaller stores vary in their policies. Stores are not required to give refunds if you're not satisfied with your purchase—many stores will, though some will offer it only in the form of exchange credit. Stores cannot charge an extra fee for credit-card purchases, but they may offer a discount for cash payment.

Hours of Business
Most stores tend to open around 10 or 11am (noon on Sundays) and close up at times that suit the neighborhood and clientele. Department stores, for instance, usually stay open through early evening, while many neighborhood boutiques and bookstores don't close until 10 or 11 at night. Most are open seven days a week—the Index below notes if they're not.

Sales Tax
A sales tax of 8.5% is added to every purchase unless the store ships it out of state for you. This is a state tax, with a .25% surcharge for rapid-transit subsidy; some outlying areas don't include this surcharge, leaving the tax at 8.25%. To make matters more confusing, some items—including just about anything edible—are not taxable.

The Lowdown

Shopping bags to show off... When shopping in Union Square's exclusive stores, it's always wise to carry a shopping bag that proves you're buying—not just looking—and therefore deserve deferential treatment. Post Street is heaven for bourgeois bags; you can start small, with a cigar from **Alfred Dunhill of London** (250) or a few pieces of candy from **Saks Fifth Avenue** (384), so long as you get a nice big bag to carry it in. Then carry the bag with the logo in full view as you work your way down Post Street, visiting **Tiffany and Co.** (350), **Cartier** (231), **Louis Vuitton** (230), **Burberry's** (225), **Brooks Brothers** (150), **Gump's** (135), or **The Polo Store/Ralph Lauren** (90).

Are you being served?... The best service in town is definitely proffered by **Nordstrom**, in the San Francisco Centre. While you relax in the fitting room, sales assistants will run up and down the store's five floors to locate a blouse in the exact shade of ivory that flatters your face and matches the navy skirt you're thinking about buying. They'll even keep a customer card on file if you have particular needs and intend to return to shop some other time. If that's not enough to make you feel pampered, Nordstrom also offers a full-service European spa and four restaurants.

One-stop shopping... Head for the department stores. There's no shame in shopping at **Macy's**, especially now that it's got an entire building devoted strictly to men's clothing and accessories. Plus, there are almost always sales and clearance racks in every department. The other big department stores are **Neiman Marcus**, the super-upscale Texas implant that's sometimes bigger on price than on taste (it does offer a fur salon for those who aren't afraid of being pelted by animal-rights activists); **Saks Fifth Avenue**, where the sales staff can be a bit too uppity for the rather pedestrian merchandise on display; and, as mentioned above, **Nordstrom**, which is the most fun of any of them.

For foot fetishists... **Nordstrom** probably has the largest selection of women's and men's shoes in the city, in prices ranging from very reasonable to check-your-credit-limit. If expensive isn't a scary concept to you, head to **Kenneth Cole** (in the San Francisco Centre, the same mall that houses Nordstrom) for trendy, high-fashion numbers, or to **Stephane Kelian** (Crocker Galleria) for the most popular shoes made in Paris. **Gimme Shoes** on Hayes Street sells funky new designs from Belgium and France. **McB's Shoes** (which recently moved a few BART stops away, to Oakland) specializes in unusual sizes, from 9 AAAAA to 14 EE (drag queen alert). **East West Leather** in North Beach has cowboy boots galore. And don't forget those sensible shoes: Get 'em at **Ria's**, **Birkenstock Natural Footwear**, and **First Step**.

If it's July, you're going to need a sweater... **Dreamweaver** has fluffy American handknits to die for; **Tse Cashmere** features rich colors and luxurious 10-ply handknits; **House of Cashmere** is just what its name implies; and **Irish Castle Shop** has fisherman-knit sweaters and the claim to fame of having served Sinead O'Connor in the past.

For men who want to look like Cary Grant... It's tough to go wrong at **Wilkes-Bashford**, whose small line of impeccably tailored clothing has served as a mark of distinction in San Francisco for more than 30 years. **Courtoué** features both classic and avant-garde Italian designers and made-to-measure tailoring. If the tailoring idea appeals to you but you're in a rush, try **David Stephen**, a mostly sportswear store that offers same-day alterations.

For men who'd rather look like Lou Reed than Cary Grant... **Rolo SF**, **Dinostore**, and **Daljeets** will outfit you in off-the-rack alternative styles suitable for clubs, cafes, or taking a little walk on the wild side. **Citizen** is a bit more elegant, but still a good bet for hip men's clothes that you won't find in department stores, including a small selection of shoes. For specially designed clothes from Michael Cronan, stop by **Cronan Artefact** (South of Market), which features what it calls threshold attire. A less pretentious description might be "clothing for both work and play," but you're talking capital-D designer here.

If you can't make it to Hong Kong, but you're into custom-made shirts... The California Gentleman by Astanboos makes dress and casual shirts right there on the premises; a staff person will come to your hotel if you prefer. They also make suits and ties, and blouses for women. **Patrick James** also does custom shirts and clothing, and offers tailoring and alterations for the lifetime of the garment.

If you simply can't live without a feather boa and a new tiara... Go right to **Piedmont Boutique** in the Haight, where drag queens, strippers, and ultra-hip high-school girls buy their velvet-and-feather bell-bottoms, sequined micro-mini-skirts, and long chartreuse gloves. When you see Piedmont's wall of earrings (more than 18,000 pairs in stock) starting at a mere $2, and racks of fishnets and other outlandish tights, you'll know why Sister Dana van Iniquity, one of the drag nuns in the Sisters of Perpetual Indulgence, prays, "Please, God, let only my seams be straight."

Recycled regalia... We're not talking flannel shirts and dirty hair—that's Seattle's fashion problem—we're talking the hottest street couture around. Haight Street is the used-clothing mecca of San Francisco. The best prices are at **Buffalo Exchange** (1555), where you can also sell your clothes for cash or trade. **Aardvark's Odd Ark** (1501) has a huge and fairly boring collection, but it's good for simple items like jeans and vests. **Wasteland** (1660) is staffed by inattentive young hipsters who seem truly impressed with the loud music, high prices, and each other. You can occasionally find something great, but most of the ordinary stuff here is overpriced. Meanwhile, in other parts of the city: **American Rag Cie** has already sorted through the maybe rack and trimmed its stock down to the most desirable items; **Clothes Contact** sells clothing by the pound, which sounds terrific until you put an old leather jacket on the scale and see how much it weighs; **560 Hayes** sells high-end vintage clothing, much of which was bought from old stores' unsold stock and has never been worn. **Guys and Dolls** is the place to buy a used tuxedo and all the accessories to go with it.

Cheap thrills: nonprofit thrift shops... The trouble with thrift shops is that you could spend your entire vacation combing them and never turn up a thing, or you could spend an hour in one place and come out with the outfit of the century for a couple of dollars. There's no way to predict, but if a scavenger hunt appeals to you, try these favorites: **Goodwill Stores** (eight locations); **Community Thrift Store**; and **Thrift Town**.

In the outlets... Among San Francisco's many outlet stores, here are two of the best: the **Esprit Outlet Store,** where the bargain bins are not to be missed; and **North Face Factory Outlet** store, one of California's top outdoor-gear manufacturers.

Politically correct splurges... If you're ambling along Hayes Street and you come across a store that looks like Martha Stewart's ecologically correct attic, you've probably arrived at **Worldware**, where you can purchase sheets and towels made from organically grown cotton and linen, as well as housewares made of exotic hardwoods from sustainable forests. The goods are actually very nice, but they're rather expensive, and the atmosphere is a bit contrived. **Global Exchange** is part of a national network that buys crafts from third-world countries and pays the artisans roughly 40 percent of the retail price—far more than most importers share. Pick up that voodoo wall hanging you've always wanted, and you can sleep well knowing you've helped a Haitian artist pay the rent. **PlaNetweavers Treasure Store**, a UNICEF store located in the Haight, also sells crafts made by indigenous people around the world and doesn't rip them off in the process. The prices for these goods can be higher than some of the large import chains, but proceeds directly benefit UNICEF's programs to fight hunger and disease among the world's children.

Crystals and other assorted New Age voodoo...

What else would you expect from a city with a gigantic pyramid in the middle of its financial district? **Crystal Way** specializes in crystals, and will arrange psychic or tarot card readings for you by appointment. **Lady Luck Candle Shop** will supply you with candles and other ritual objects you might need. If you're really, truly sick and tired of watching the Yankees and the Braves in October, **Botanica Yoruba** is the place to do something about it. You can curse your enemies—and bring winning Lotto tickets to your friends and family—with the super-charged Santeria candles and charms in this Mission District shop. If you speak Spanish and are duly respectful, the owners may tell you how.

Baubles, bangles, and beads...

Be an artist for a day, or at least a wild-and-crazy jewelry maker. In true San Francisco style, local bead stores reflect the grab bag of artists and hangers-on who live and work in the city—hippie holdouts (and their kids and grandkids), European exiles, African Americans keeping their heritage alive, and, of course, assorted opportunists out to make a buck off unsuspecting tourists. So if you're truly a bead freak, you'll love this town, but choose your shops carefully. And if you're just looking, wander into any shop you see. No matter where you go, you'll find loads of beads, as well as a staff of artisans willing to help you make your own necklaces and earrings. **The Bead Store** is worth a visit to check out the sacred statues and ethnic jewelry; **African Safari** has beads to use in hair braiding; **Gargoyle Beads** specializes in Czech beads; **General Bead** is huge—3,000 square feet—and offers many closeouts at bargain prices; and **Yone of San Francisco** in North Beach is hailed by locals for its unusual beads.

Goofatoriums... (or is that goofatoria?) San Franciscans pride themselves on being a bit off center, and many of the city's small stores go out of their way to milk that image. The dusty, doodad-crammed Schlock Shop, a North Beach institution, closed its doors in 1996, but **Quantity Postcards** is alive and well across the street, still selling just one thing: postcards. This is the largest, goofiest collection you'll find anywhere—more than 10,000 different cards. Don't miss the Swingin' Fifties party cards (great for last-minute invitations) or the ridiculous dirty-joke section. Buy a card here, if only to get a close-up look at the funky cash register. At first, **Paxton Gate,** at the hub of the hip Mission District, seems to be a high-end gardening store—until you spot the mounted insects and glass eyes used for taxidermy. Then comes the kicker, the collection that recently made the store a huge favorite among avant-garde gift-givers: stuffed mice (real, dead mice) dressed up in costumes. You'll find Hamlet, the Pope, and many other "seasonal favorites." No doubt about it, you're nowhere near Kansas anymore. Actually, you're in a neighborhood where everybody goes to **Therapy,** not for analysis but for odd little knickknacks that were clutter in someone else's dream but are now incredibly cool home accessories in your reality. There's also some mighty tempting new and used retro-contemporary furniture, but it won't fit in your suitcase, so you might want to stick with the doodads.

Gumby for grown-ups... You don't have to be Jack Nicholson to know that all work and no play makes Jack a dull, dull boy. Toys for adults are a booming business, and San Francisco sells more than its share. **Uncle Mame** is Upper Market's one-stop shop for everything your parents wouldn't buy you when you were a kid—that bad-ass G.I. Joe with the Kung Fu grip, or "collectible" boxes of sticky sugar-coated cereal. Uncle Mame claims to have the West Coast's largest collection of currently available Pez dispensers; one of the first things you see when you walk into the store is a miniature football stadium fashioned from hundreds of unwrapped Pez candies. While not technically a toy store, Union Square's **Globetrotter** offers a complete library of beautifully illustrated books about the popular European comic-book adventurers Tin Tin and Asterix; it's the only official Tin Tin store in the United States. Globetrotter stocks the books in a variety of languages, along with watches, luggage, clocks, and other collectibles. The store's staff is helpful and friendly, and there are even bean-bag chairs up front to curl up in as you read.

If you've got an itch for leather... North Beach Leather is probably the city's most famous manufacturer of stylish leather clothing for men and women. The quality and prices are high, but the workmanship is unbeatable, and jackets can be custom-made for hard-to-fit customers. If, however, your interests tend toward leather in its more exotic sense, head for **Stormy Leather**, which bills itself as San Francisco's premier erotic-fetish boutique. It never disappoints the whip-and-chain crowd. **A Taste of Leather** deals in adult items including leather toys and body jewelry.

Everything you ever wanted to know about sex... Don't be afraid to ask at **Good Vibrations**, an airy, comfortable bookstore/sex-toy shop owned and run by women. Their mail-order business has become one of the most successful in the country, but this flagship store in the Mission District is still small, personal, and as far from sleazy as you could possibly get. The clientele is primarily women, but the books and toys are for both sexes.

Or sexy underwear... Now that the Wonder Bra has almost single-handedly taken the term "flat-chested" out of the popular American lexicon, you can walk into any KMart and buy the kind of seductive lingerie that once would've been found only at Frederick's of Hollywood. Still, there's something delicious about a small underwear boutique. Carol Doda, for years queen of the city's premier strip joint, the Condor, now sells all the expected sexy stuff for women at **Carol Doda's Champagne and Lace Lingerie Boutique**, along with some racier inducements for both sexes, including see-through underwear and G-strings for men, stripper's accoutrements, and other fun little objets d'amour. A visit to **Backseat Betty** makes lacy push-up bras seem ho-hum—this store is for people who think sex is fun, and looking sexy even more fun. Yeah, yeah, yeah, there's all the rubber and latex stuff, but the basic mode is Cher, all the way.

Uncommon scents... **Jacqueline Perfumery** has the best selection of scents in San Francisco, including some French perfumes that aren't available anywhere else in the United States. If you don't know what you want, simply ask her for a suggestion or two; her olfactory intuition is uncanny. Check your shopping bag when you get back to your hotel—Jacqueline has been known to tuck in samples of expensive and exotic perfumes with customers' purchases.

Sweets to go... At **Joseph Schmidt Confections**, feast your senses on the most delectable chocolate sculptures in the Western world. Buy at least a truffle or two (your taste buds will worship you for it), and do not miss the ever-changing, elaborate window displays. While you're there, step across 16th Street and peek at the outdoor mural entitled *La Madre Tonantsin*, to get in the mood for a trip to the **Pacitas Bakery** for *pan dulce*, sugary pastries in the Central American tradition, and *bolillos*, yummy little torpedo-shaped rolls that are especially wonderful dunked in Mexican hot chocolate. **Just Desserts** is full of fabulous, fattening goodies at all of its six locations, including an award-winning chocolate fudge cake that will put you on a sugar-high for hours (especially if you down it with a double cappuccino, as many locals do).

Italian treats to go... Just about any cafe in North Beach has great pastries, but **Stella Pastry & Caffe** has all that and *La Sacripantina*, too. Owner Frank Santucci will be happy to tell you about the patent he has on this puffy, sweet dessert that's one of Luciano Pavarotti's favorite confections. **Dianda's Italian American Pastry** has the best Italian cakes; **Danilo Bakery** bakes breads, *panettone*, tortes, and cookies for many of the top local restaurants; and **Italian French Baking Co.** still uses a brick oven and makes the best hand-rolled bread sticks you'll ever taste. While you're visiting North Beach, stop by the landmark deli **Molinari's** for a classic selection of Italian grocery and deli items; the old Italian locals shop there daily.

Oddly enough, another great Italian deli is in the Mission District: **Lucca Ravioli Co.**, a traditional full-service deli with good-humored employees in white aprons. Their takeout sandwiches are superb and inexpensive.

The best deal on the best bubbly... Don't even bother shopping around; this is the place to buy champagne. The staff at **D & M Wine and Liquor Co.** is friendly, funny, and more knowledgeable about champagne than all the wine editors in the country combined. They offer the largest selection of champagne in the United States and will steer you away from overpriced status wines to lesser-known and cheaper labels that will make you think you've died and floated away to heaven. Every wine in the store has been personally tasted by the staff—all of whom are inveterate oenophiles—and you can be absolutely certain that any bottle they suggest will meet your expectations, and then some. Their latest addition to the gourmet intoxicants repertoire is single-malt Scotch, of which they have the best selection in San Francisco.

Kid stuff... You probably won't see Tom Hanks running up and down a gigantic keyboard at **FAO Schwarz** like he did in the movie *Big*, but this branch of the famous New York store is still a fantasyland for kids and adult toy-lovers alike. Other terrific toy spots in San Francisco include **Jeffrey's Toys**, **Sanrio at Union Square**, and **Basic Brown Bear**, where you can watch teddy bears being made and even stuff your own, if you like. If you go in for designer clothing for kids, try **Dottie Doolittle** or **Minis By Profili**.

Words, words, words.... As befits a place with a heralded literary heritage, the city of San Francisco has a wealth of independent booksellers. **A Clean Well-Lighted Place For Books** is a favorite of author Armistead Maupin (who immortalized '60s San Francisco in *Tales of the City*); **The Booksmith** boasts more than 1,000 foreign and domestic magazines and newspapers; **City Lights Bookstore** is Lawrence Ferlinghetti's legendary '50s beatnik haunt and offers one of the best poetry sections in the United States; **A Different Light** is the foremost gay and lesbian bookstore in San Francisco, as well as a resource center for gay information. **The Anonymous Place** carries 12-step recovery books (it's become quite a budding genre); **The Buddhist Bookstore** represents many Buddhist traditions and also offers altar supplies; **Forever After Books** sells used books on spirituality, psychology, health, history, true crime, and other assorted topics. **McDonald's Bookshop** has more than a million used books and can get you a copy of *Life* magazine published when you were born. **Dog Eared Books** is a wonderful place to pick up some choice reading material—check out the Lust and Desire section before you settle in for an espresso at one of the neighboring cafes; **Argonaut Book Shop** is a rare-book shop that specializes in California history.

In search of 12-inch vinyl... If you're one of those people who understands the magic of a phonograph needle dropping softly into a groove, you're in luck. San Francisco has several record stores that still sell records: **Streetlight Records; The Record Finder;** and **Medium Rare Records.**

Music meccas... Every city in America has plenty of generic music stores that sell compact discs and cassette tapes, but San Francisco's music stores boldly go into musical niches that the MTV nation barely dreams of. **Open Mind Music**, for instance, is a clothing/music emporium that features "cool collectibles and the esoteric." **Let It Be** carries (naturally) Beatles memorabilia, rare and out-of-print records, assorted music collectibles, and concert items. For Latin and salsa selections, **Discolandia** is a good bet—you'll hear the music pounding long before you get close enough to see the Latin/psychedelic/airbrush/jukebox storefront. **Amoeba Music** in Berkeley offers more than 30,000 used CDs, plus original Fillmore and Avalon concert posters from the sixties; **Mod Lang**, also located in Berkeley, features imports, indies, acid jazz, ambient, trance, and reissues; Oakland's **Saturn Records** offers an eclectic collection of music in one of the most fun walking neighborhoods (Rockridge) in the East Bay; and the **Groove Yard**, also in Oakland, specializes in jazz, blues, and soul selections. Oakland is the blues capital of the West Coast, so get over there and groove.

The Index

A Clean Well-Lighted Place For Books. This independent bookstore has a very helpful and informed staff, who will be happy to ship internationally.... *Tel 415/441-6670. 601 Van Ness Ave., Opera Plaza, Civic Center BART station.* **(see p. 155)**

A Different Light. Gay and lesbian literature, magazines, and community resource information are sold here by a friendly staff.... *Tel 415/431-0891. 489 Castro St., Castro St. MUNI Metro station (K,L,M). Open 10am–10pm.* **(see p. 155)**

A Taste of Leather. Adult and custom-leather items.... *Tel 415/252-9166. 1285 Folsom, south of Market St. (near 8th St.), 42 MUNI bus.* **(see p. 153)**

Aardvark's Odd Ark. This huge store sells used clothing in current styles. It's not as eccentric as some other Haight Street shops.... *Tel 415/621-3141. 1501 Haight St., 7 MUNI bus.* **(see p. 150)**

African Safari. Beads for use in hair braiding are sold in this shop, both to wholesale and retail customers.... *Tel 415/922-2899. 1221 Divisidero St. between Eddy and Ellis Sts., Western Addition, 5, 38 MUNI buses. Closed Sun–Mon.* **(see p. 151)**

Alfred Dunhill of London. It's almost a shame San Francisco is so antismoking—there's nothing like a Dunhill lighter to make you feel decadently luxurious.... *Tel 415/781-3368. 250 Post St., Union Square, Powell St. BART station.* **(see p. 147)**

American Rag Cie. Stylish, contemporary secondhand and

vintage clothing—and not cheap. The staff ranges from friendly to way-too-hip.... *Tel 415/441-0537. 1305 Van Ness St. between Sutter and Bush Sts., 42 MUNI bus, California St. cable car.* **(see p. 150)**

Amoeba Music. This Berkeley store—voted best in the Bay Area by the *Guardian*—has a huge selection of used CDs.... *Tel 510/549-1125. 2455 Telegraph Ave., Berkeley, Berkeley BART station.* **(see p. 156)**

The Anonymous Place. The specialties here are 12-step recovery books and gifts—sold to customers by a supportive staff, as one might well imagine.... *Tel 415/923-0248. 1885A Lombard St., 28, 30 MUNI buses. Closed Sun.* **(see p. 155)**

Argonaut Book Shop. Fine and rare books and manuscripts are bought and sold here, especially volumes on California history. Established in 1941.... *Tel 415/474-9067. 786 Sutter St. at Jones St., Union Square, Powell St. BART station. Closed Sun.* **(see p. 156)**

Backseat Betty. Naughty underthings and outerwear for contemporary sex kittens.... *Tel 415/431-8393. 1584 Haight St., 7 MUNI bus.* **(see p. 155)**

Basic Brown Bear. Kids absolutely love this teddy-bear factory. Discount prices.... *Tel 415/626-0781, 444 DeHaro, Potrero Hill; 2801 Leavenworth, the Cannery, 30, 42 MUNI buses or Powell-Hyde, Powell-Mason cable cars.* **(see p. 154)**

The Bead Store. Come here for beads, sacred statues, ethnic jewelry.... *Tel 415/861-7332. 417 Castro St. at Market St., Castro St. MUNI Metro Station.* **(see p. 151)**

Birkenstock Natural Footwear. Comfort shoes, California-style.... *Tel 415/989-2475. 42 Stockton St., Union Square, 38 or 30 MUNI bus.* **(see p. 148)**

The Booksmith. A source for lots of books and a huge selection of domestic and foreign magazines and newspapers. Knowledgeable staff.... *Tel 415/863-8688. 1644 Haight St., 7 MUNI bus.* **(see p. 155)**

Botanica Yoruba. This is not a New Age emporium, folks. This is a down-home, dead-serious, we-mean-business Santeria supply shop with some of the most potent candles and charms in the city.... *Tel 415/826-4967. 998 Valencia St., 16th St. BART station.* **(see p. 151)**

Brooks Brothers. In any word association game, definitely traditional, but not as stodgy as you might think. Men's, women's, and boys' clothing.... *Tel 415/397-4500. 150 Post St., Union Square, Powell St. BART station.* **(see p. 147)**

The Buddhist Bookstore. As the name suggests—a source for Pure Land, Zen, Tibetan literature. Altar supplies and gifts, too.... *Tel 415/776-7877. 1710 Octavia St. between Bush and Pine Sts., near Japantown, 38 MUNI bus. Closed weekends.* **(see p. 156)**

Buffalo Exchange. Come here for stylish used clothing in new condition—hip street fashions at very good prices.... *Tel 415/431-7733, 1555 Haight St., 7 MUNI bus; Tel 415/346-5726, 1800 Polk St.* **(see p. 150)**

Burberry's. The famous Burberry plaid, inside raincoats and all over clothing, luggage, and other wearables.... *Tel 415/392-2200. 225 Post St., Union Square, Powell St. BART station.* **(see p. 147)**

The California Gentleman by Astanboos. This custom clothier makes dress and casual shirts and suits for men and women.... *Tel 415/781-8989 or 800/697-4478. 490 Post St. Rm. 336, Union Square; Powell St. BART station. Closed weekends.* **(see p. 149)**

Carol Doda's Champagne and Lace Lingerie Boutique. San Francisco's No. 1 stripper sells some of the sexiest women's and men's underthings in town.... *Tel 415/776-6900. 1850 Union St. #1, the Courtyard, 45 MUNI bus.* **(see p. 153)**

Cartier. Exclusive timepieces and fine jewelry.... *Tel 415/397-3180. 231 Post St., Union Square, Powell St. BART station. Closed Sun.* **(see p. 147)**

Citizen. The racks here are full of urban contemporary clothing

THE INDEX | SHOPPING

for men—pricey, but worth it.... *Tel 415/558-9429. 536 Castro St., Castro St. MUNI Metro station.* **(see p. 149)**

City Lights Bookstore. The legendary beatnik hangout and bookstore.... *Tel 415/362-8193. 261 Columbus Ave., North Beach, 15, 30 MUNI buses. Open 10am–11:45pm daily.* **(see p. 155)**

Clothes Contact. Used clothing is sold here for $8 per pound. Lots of leather jackets.... *Tel 415/621-3212. 473 Valencia St., Mission District, 16th St. BART station.* **(see p. 150)**

Community Thrift Store. It's sort of junky, but there's a great book and record section here.... *Tel 415/861-4910. 623 Valencia St., Mission District, 16th St. BART station.* **(see p. 150)**

Courtoué. Beautiful Italian designer clothing for men, classic to avant-garde.... *Tel 415/775-2900. 459 Geary Blvd., Union Square, Powell St. BART station. Closed Sun.* **(see p. 149)**

Cronan Artefact. This showroom is the home of Walking Man clothing by designer Michael Cronan.... *Tel 415/241-9111. 543 Eighth St., Powell St. BART station or 15, 30, 45 MUNI buses. Sat. by appointment only.* **(see p. 149)**

Crystal Way. Thousands of beautiful natural crystals and New Age books are sold here.... *Tel 415/861-6511. 2335 Market St. near Castro St., Castro St. MUNI Metro station.* **(see p. 151)**

D & M Wine and Liquor Co. Simply the best selection of champagne in the country, and discount prices to boot.... *Tel 415/346-1325. 2200 Fillmore St. at Sacramento St., 6 blocks from 38 MUNI bus.* **(see p. 155)**

Daljeets. These two stores, across the street from each other, sell super-hip men's clothing at not-totally-expensive prices.... *Tel 415/752-5610, 1744 Haight St.; Tel 415/668-8500, 1773 Haight St., 7 MUNI bus.* **(see p. 149)**

Danilo Bakery. Wonderful breads and *panettone.... Tel 415/ 989-1806. 516 Green St., North Beach, 15, 30 MUNI buses.* **(see p. 154)**

David Stephen. Featuring European clothing for men, this store has an experienced staff and offers same-day tailoring.... *Tel 415/982-1611. 50 Maiden Lane, Union Square, Powell St. and Montgomery St. BART stations. Open daily, Sun by appointment only.* **(see p. 149)**

Dianda's Italian American Pastry. Prize-winning Italian cakes have made this store's reputation.... *Tel 415/ 647–5469. 2883 Mission St., 24th St. BART station.* **(see p. 154)**

Dinostore. Alternative clothing and clubwear for men.... *Tel 415/861-3933. 1553 Haight St., 7 MUNI bus.* **(see p. 149)**

Discolandia. The selection of Latin music is enormous, so it helps to have an idea of what you're looking for.... *Tel 415/826-9446. 2964 24th St., Mission District, 24th St. BART station.* **(see p. 156)**

Dog Eared Books. A fun place for browsing and buying.... *Tel 415/282-1901. 900 Valencia St., Mission District, 24th St. BART station.* **(see p. 156)**

Dottie Doolittle. Look here for designer clothes for infants, toddlers, girls 7–14 and boys 4–7.... *Tel 415/563-3244. 3680 Sacramento St. between Spruce and Locust Sts., 1, 3, 4 MUNI bus.* **(see p. 155)**

Dreamweaver. A huge selection of handwoven clothing makes this spot a local fave.... *Tel 415/981-2040. 171 Maiden Lane, Union Square, Powell St. BART station.* **(see p. 148)**

East West Leather. The specialty here is cowboy boots plus jackets and clothing.... *Tel 415/397-2886. 1400 Upper Grant Ave., North Beach, 15, 30 MUNI buses.* **(see p. 148)**

Esprit Outlet Store. The place to buy Esprit outfits at dis-

SHOPPING | THE INDEX

count prices.... *Tel 415/957-2550. 499 Illinois St., 15 MUNI bus.* **(see p. 150)**

FAO Schwarz. Outpost of the world-class toy store.... *Tel 415/394-8700. 48 Stockton St., Union Square, Powell St. BART station.* **(see p. 155)**

First Step. Comfortable footwear: Nike, Reebok, Rockport, etc. Great shoes, great prices, great location.... *Tel 415/989-9989. 939 Market St., Powell St. BART station.* **(see p. 148)**

560 Hayes. Upscale vintage clothing and original works by local artists. Staff is helpful but not pushy.... *Tel 415/861-7993. 560 Hayes St., Hayes Valley, Civic Center BART station.* **(see p. 150)**

Forever After Books. Here you'll find used books on many esoteric and mainstream subjects.... *Tel 415/431-8299. 1475 Haight St., 7 MUNI bus.* **(see p. 156)**

Gargoyle Beads. This store sells zillions of beads and offers ear piercing and jewelry-making classes.... *Tel 415/552-4274. 1310 Haight St., 7 MUNI bus.* **(see p. 151)**

General Bead. The biggest bead store anywhere.... *Tel 415/621-8187. 637 Minna St., Montgomery St. BART station; 15, 39, 45 MUNI bus. Closed Mon.* **(see p. 151)**

Gimme Shoes. An eclectic, chic mix of footwear merchandise.... *Tel 415/864-0691. 416 Hayes St., Hayes Valley, Civic Center BART station.* **(see p. 148)**

Global Exchange. Hand-crafted items from international artisans are sold at this Fair Trade Network store.... *Tel 415/648-8068. 4018 24th St. near Sanchez St., J Church MUNI Metro.* **(see p. 150)**

Globetrotter. The largest U.S. source for Tin Tin and Asterix fans.... *Tel 415/434-1120. 418 Sutter St., Union Square, Powell St. BART station.* **(see p. 153)**

Good Vibrations. This is a comfortable, clean, airy, healthy place to shop for sex toys, sex books, and videos.... *Tel*

*415/974-8980. 1210 Valencia St., Mission District, 24th
St. BART station.* **(see p. 153)**

Goodwill Stores. Hit-or-miss secondhand shopping, but when
you hit, the price is definitely right.... *Tel 415/575-2101.
820 Clement St.; 3801 Third St.; 1700 Fillmore St.;
1580 Mission St.; 2279 Mission St.; 822 Geary Blvd.;
1700 Haight St.; 61 West Portal.* **(see p. 150)**

Groove Yard. If you're into jazz, blues, and soul, you'll be
thrilled with this store, where they buy, sell, and trade
new, used, and rare records and CDs.... *Tel 510/655-
8400. 4770 Telegraph Ave. (at 48th St.), Oakland; Ashby
BART station.* **(see p. 156)**

Gump's. What used to be a grand San Francisco department
store; now scaled down, but still a local classic. Orientalia
is a particular specialty.... *Tel 415/9820-1616. 135 Post
St., Union Square, Powell St. BART station. Closed Sun.*
(see p. 147)

Guys and Dolls. This vintage-clothing store for men and
women specializes in tuxedos and formal accessories from
the '30s to the '50s. Hats, ties, jewelry.... *Tel 415/285-
7174. 3789 24th St., J Church MUNI Metro.*
(see p. 150)

House of Cashmere. Cashmere, wool, and angora sweaters
are the specialties of this men's and women's clothing
store.... *Tel 415/441-6925. 2764 Octavia St., off Union
St., 45 MUNI bus. Closed Sun.* **(see p. 148)**

Irish Castle Shop. Expect everything Irish, from claddagh
rings to fishermen's sweaters.... *Tel 415/474-7432. 537
Geary St., Union Square, Powell St. BART station.*
(see p. 148)

Italian French Baking Co. Don't miss the delectable breads
baked in brick ovens and the hand-rolled bread sticks....
*Tel 415/421-3796. 1501 Grant Ave., North Beach, 15,
30 MUNI buses.* **(see p. 154)**

Jacqueline Perfumery. The best selection of perfumes in the
city.... *Tel 415/981-0858. 103 Geary Blvd., Union*

Square, Powell St. BART station. Closed Sun.
(see p. 154)

Jeffrey's Toys. Along with toys of all kinds, you can buy books and antique toys here.... *Tel 415/546-6551. 7 Third St., near Market St., Montgomery St. BART station.*
(see p. 155)

Joseph Schmidt Confections. A local treasure, this shop sells the most beautiful edible sculptures you'll ever see or taste.... *Tel 415/861-8682. 3489 16th St., near Church St., J Church MUNI Metro line. Closed Sun.*
(see p. 154)

Just Desserts. This mini-chain is famous for its decadent desserts.... *Tel 415/626-5774, 248 Church St.; Tel 415/421-1609, 3 Embarcadero Center; Tel 415/922-8675, 3735 Buchanan; Tel 415/369-6137, Sony Metreon, 101 Fourth St. at Mission St.* **(see p. 154)**

Kenneth Cole. Footwear for the fashion-conscious.... *Tel 415/227-4536. 865 Market St., San Francisco Shopping Centre, Powell St. BART station; 2078 Union St., 45 MUNI bus.* **(see p. 148)**

Lady Luck Candle Shop. Your basic Latino Catholic-voodoo-ritual botanica.... *Tel 415/621-0358. 311 Valencia St., Mission District, 16th St. BART station.* **(see p. 151)**

Let It Be. If there is a heaven for Beatlemaniacs, this may be where you buy your tickets to get there. Besides rare and out-of-print records, it has a variety of memorabilia.... *Tel 415/681-2113. 2434 Judah St., N. Judah MUNI Metro station. Closed Sun and Mon.* **(see p. 156)**

Louis Vuitton. This is the place to get that fancy luggage with the monogram that opens doors around the world.... *Tel 415/391-6200. 230 Post St., Union Square, Powell St. BART station.* **(see p. 147)**

Lucca Ravioli Co. Seemingly out-of-place in this Latino neighborhood, this wonderful Italian deli is always full of locals.... *Tel 415/647-5581. 1100 Valencia St., Mission District, 24th St. BART station. Closed Sun.* **(see p. 155)**

Macy's. This huge store occupies two full buildings and has always been a reliable favorite for locals and visitors alike.... *Tel 415/397-3333. 170 O'Farrell St. at Stockton St., Union Square, Powell St. BART station.* **(see p. 148)**

McB's Shoes. The specialty here is hard-to-find shoe sizes for women (or men who like to wear women's shoes).... *Tel 510/546-9444. 1701 Telegraph Ave., Oakland, 19th St. BART station. Closed Sun.* **(see p. 148)**

McDonald's Bookshop. More than a million used books in stock.... *Tel 415/673-2235. 48 Turk St., Powell St. BART station. Closed Sun.* **(see p. 156)**

Medium Rare Records. This is the place to find those old vinyl LPs you haven't heard for ages, as well as all the great jazz and Latin vocalists.... *Tel 415/255-7273. 2310 Market St., Castro St. MUNI Metro station. (K,L,M)* **(see p. 156)**

Minis By Profili. Local designer Christina Profili left the GAP to open her own business here. All the racks feature coordinating kids' sportswear separates.... *Tel 415/567-9537. 2042 Union St., 45 MUNI bus.* **(see p. 155)**

Mod Lang. This English modern-rock music store caters to serious collectors, as well as curious onlookers. It's got a 24-hour fax line (510/486-1860).... *Tel 510/486-1850. 2136 University Ave. at Shattuck Ave., Berkeley, Berkeley BART station.* **(see p. 156)**

Molinari's. The traditional North Beach deli.... *Tel 415/421-2337. 373 Columbus Ave., North Beach, 15, 30 MUNI buses. Closed Sun.* **(see p. 154)**

Neiman Marcus. This branch of the Texas-based luxury-goods store offers a high-class shopping experience. The cafe on the top floor is a real hoot.... *Tel 415/362-3900. 150 Stockton St., Union Square, Powell St. BART station.* **(see p. 148)**

Nordstrom. Get pampered with attentive, personal service on all five floors. Don't forget the store's eateries and full-service European spa.... *Tel 415/243-8500. San Fran-*

SHOPPING | THE INDEX

cisco Shopping Centre, 865 Market St., Powell St. BART station. (see pp. 147, 148)

North Beach Leather. This store sells the latest fashions—some custom-made—at prices to match.... *Tel 415/362-8300. 224 Grant St., Union Square, 15 or 30 MUNI bus.* (see p. 153)

North Face Factory Outlet. Quality outdoor gear at discount prices.... *Tel 415/626-6444. 1325 Howard St., South of Market, 42 MUNI bus.* (see p. 150)

Open Mind Music. New and used records and CDs, in addition to assorted esoterica and an in-store vintage-clothing shop.... *Tel 415/621-2244. 342 Divisadero St. at Oak St., 7 MUNI bus.* (see p. 156)

Pacitas Bakery. One of dozens of bakeries in the Mission District, this is in the newly Bohemian part.... *Tel 415/452-8442. 10 Persia St. near Mission St., Mission District, 16th St. BART station.* (see p. 154)

Patrick James. This store refers to itself as a "Purveyor to Gentlemen," if that gives you any idea.... *Tel 415/986-1043. 216 Montgomery St., Financial District, Montgomery St. BART station. Closed Sun.* (see p. 149)

Paxton Gate. Truly a bizarre bazaar, this natural science/garden store is best known for its stuffed mice dressed in costumes.... *Tel 415/824-1872. 824 Valencia St., 16th St. BART station.* (see p. 152)

Piedmont Boutique. Absolutely outrageous women's garments and accessories—sold mostly to men. If in your heart of hearts you've ever coveted any of the gaudy get-ups you've seen on drag queens, this is the place to find them.... *Tel 415/864-8075. 1452 Haight St., 7 MUNI bus.* (see p. 149)

PlaNetweavers Treasures Store. The official UNICEF store is full of international trinkets and works of art.... *Tel 415/864-4415. 1573 Haight St., 7 MUNI bus.* (see p. 151)

The Polo Store/Ralph Lauren. For folks who affect the

country-squire look. Tallyho.... *Tel 415/788-7656. 90 Post St., Union Square, Powell St. BART station.*

(see p. 147)

Quantity Postcards. Here's a place where you can spend less than a dollar and come out with one of the best souvenirs of your trip. A true goofatorium.... *Tel 415/788-4455. 507 Columbus Ave., North Beach, 15, 30 MUNI buses. Open 7am–10pm.* **(see p. 152)**

The Record Finder. More than 100,000 titles in stock. Good staff, too.... *Tel 415/431-4443. 258 Noe St., Castro St. MUNI Metro station.* **(see p. 156)**

Ria's. Birkenstocks, Timberland, Rockports, etc.... *Tel 415/ 398-0895, 437 Sutter St.; Tel 415/834-1420, 301 Grant Ave.* **(see p. 148)**

Rolo SF. These four stores sell clothes for the modern urban guy, at modern urban prices (big). The one at 545 Castro—Undercover by Rolo—is a super-trendy designer store.... *Tel 415/626-7171, 450 Castro St.; Tel 415/861-1999, 1301 Howard St.; Tel 415/431-4545, 2351 Market St.; Tel 415/864-0505, 545 Castro St.*

(see p. 149)

Saks Fifth Avenue. Not as glitzy as Neiman Marcus or as fun as Nordstrom's.... *Tel 415/986-4300. 384 Post St., Union Square, Powell St. BART station.*

(see pp. 147, 148)

Sanrio at Union Square. Two floors of international toys.... *Tel 415/981-5568. 39 Stockton St., Union Square, Powell St. BART station.* **(see p. 155)**

Saturn Records. An eclectic collection of records, tapes, CDs, and 45s makes this music store a really fun place to stop.... *Tel 510/654-0335. 5488 College Ave., Oakland, Rockridge BART station.* **(see p. 156)**

Stella Pastry & Caffe. The specialty at Stella's is Franco's *La Sacripantina*, a puffy slice of confectionery heaven.... *Tel 415/986-2914. 446 Columbus Ave., North Beach, 15, 30 MUNI buses.* **(see p. 154)**

Stephane Kelian. Très chic. One of the biggest French names in shoes.... *Tel 415/989-1412. Crocker Galleria, 50 Post St., Montgomery BART station. Closed Sun.*
(see p. 148)

Stormy Leather. Kinky leather goods.... *Tel 415/626-1672. 1158 Howard St., South of Market, Civic Center BART station.* **(see p. 153)**

Streetlight Records. A major source for new and used vinyl, CDs, tapes, videos, and laserdiscs.... *Tel 415/282-3550, 3979 24th St.; Tel 415/282-8000, 2350 Market St., both near Castro St. MUNI Metro station.* **(see p. 156)**

Therapy. A little retail indulgence can do more for your mood than months of analysis, so step inside for retro-contemporary knickknacks, home accessories, clothing, and new and used furniture.... *Tel 415/861-6213. 545 Valencia St., 16th St. BART station.* **(see p. 152)**

Thrift Town. The unique thing about this thrift store is its grab-bag section in the rear, with items stuffed into sealed plastic bags to be sold for a dollar or two..... *Tel 415/861-1132. 2101 Mission St. at 17th St., Mission District, 16th St. BART station.* **(see p. 150)**

Tiffany and Co. Jewelry and gifts, classic and very, very expensive.... *Tel 415/781-7000. 350 Post St., Union Square, Powell St. BART station. Closed Sun.*
(see p. 147)

Tse Cashmere. This stuff is soft—really soft. Great colors, too.... *Tel 415/391-1112. 60 Maiden Lane, Union Square, Powell St. BART station. Closed Sun.*
(see p. 148)

Uncle Mame. Toys for regressing grownups.... *Tel 415/626-1953. 2241 Market St., between Sanchez and Noe Sts., J Church MUNI Metro line.* **(see p. 152)**

Wasteland. Trendy secondhand clothing, for sure, but sometimes it's a little bit, you know, expensive. Especially, like, the denim, you know?... *Tel 415/863-3150. 1660 Haight St., 7 MUNI bus.* **(see p. 150)**

Wilkes-Bashford. The ultimate classic men's store. The local designers are literally top drawer.... *Tel 415/986-4380. 375 Sutter St., Union Square; Powell St. BART station. Closed Sun.* **(see p. 148)**

Worldware. Eco-elegant housewares and personal items.... *Tel 415/487-9030. 336 Hayes St., Hayes Valley, Civic Center BART station.* **(see p. 150)**

Yone of San Francisco. They call themselves a beehive of beads. Locals love 'em, but they're only open a few hours a week.... *Tel 415/986-1424. 478 Union St., North Beach, 15, 30 MUNI buses. Open noon–5pm, closed Sun and Wed.* **(see p. 152)**

SHOPPING | THE INDEX

nigh

6

tlife

San Francisco is
an exotic cocktail
of world cultures,
stirred with a
liberal splash of
wild-West flavor
that dates to the

Gold Rush. State laws and politically correct teetotalers and antismoking fanatics have toned things down a bit since the notorious Barbary Coast days, but nothing can ever keep this city from being an exciting place to roam when its fabled sunsets are long extinguished.

The biggest problem a visiting roamer might encounter is actually finding the party. Movable clubs that host theme parties—gay, lesbian, techno, salsa, rave, you name it—are a huge part of the night scene in San Francisco, and both the addresses and the crowds can change. What doesn't change is that the club scene in San Francisco always has been dominated by three things: neighborhoods, music, and people in their twenties who have the stamina and cash to buy lots of drinks. Every neighborhood has its own bar scene, and some are so packed with worthy joints that you can usually bar-hop on foot. Though several old-standby clubs have closed or are up for sale in the **South of Market** neighborhood near 10th and Folsom streets, you'll still find a pack of blues, rock, and contemporary music haunts as well as the "Miracle Mile" of gay sex clubs; stop off at 16th and Valencia streets in the **Mission District** for the city's hippest bar-hopping scene; head to Castro and Market streets to enter the **Castro,** gay capital of the world; the Haight is divided into two worlds—the **Upper Haight** (between Masonic and Stanyan streets), a hippie holdout with a stale bar scene that appeals mostly to neighborhood bands and their friends, and the **Lower Haight** (between Pierce and Divisadero streets), second only to the Mission District for hip bars and dance clubs; Broadway and

Fine music and fast women
*In New York, blues singer Billie Holiday had to fight to perform at uppity Carnegie Hall. That never would have happened in San Francisco, where the closest thing to Carnegie Hall is an ornate, turn-of-the-century concert hall that spent its first 30 years as a bordello and gambling hall. After the **Great American Music Hall** was taken over by a fan-dancer in the '30s, it had many lives—a swank dance hall, a jazz club, a Moose Lodge. Saved from a wrecking ball in 1972, it was impeccably restored and has thrived as a concert hall/night club ever since, hosting jazz greats from Duke Ellington to Count Basie, rock legends from the Grateful Dead to Van Morrison, and comedians from Robin Williams to Rosanne Arnold. Visit the hall's website at www.music hallsf.com for concert schedule, directions, and ordering information.*

Columbus streets form the axis from which **North Beach** jazz clubs, late-night cafes, and strip joints flow. Acid jazz is dead, but raves are still in evidence, and rock music will never go away, no matter how old or young the barflies are. What has gone away is the cocktail fad. Cosmopolitans and other party-girl cocktails went the way of the hula hoop several years ago. Then it was mandatory to drink nothing but the classics: martinis, scotch and soda, gin and tonic. That died too. Now you can drink whatever you want as long as you can pay for it, and considering how many dot-com high rollers are now living on unemployment checks, beer is more popular than ever. Also dead: the horrid cigar mania. California's strict ban on smoking in all public places killed the cigar bars that left smokers of both sexes smelling as though they just emerged from the toilet of a seedy off-track betting room.

Liquor and Smoking Laws

The drinking age is 21 in California, and bartenders can ask for a valid photo ID, no matter how old you look. Some clubs demand identification cards at the door, so it's a good idea to carry one at all times. Once you get through the door, however, forget about cigarettes. On January 1, 1998, smoking was officially banned in all California bars. The law is generally enforced and though San Francisco's police department has not made bar raids a priority, people caught smoking in bars can be—and occasionally are—ticketed and fined. Music clubs strictly enforce the law and will ask you to leave if you light up. There are mandatory "No Smoking" signs everywhere and no ashtrays anywhere; bartenders are required to tell anyone who asks that smoking is strictly forbidden. If you must smoke, do it outside. Meanwhile, the dreaded last call for alcohol usually rings out at around 1:30am, since state laws prohibit the sale of alcohol from 2 to 6 every morning. Don't be surprised to see crowded clubs empty just before the witching hour, as the revelers rush to buy enough six-packs to fuel themselves during the after-hours festivities, when some clubs stay open but stop serving alcohol. A very important word of warning: Driving under the influence of alcohol is a serious crime in California, with jail time for the first offense. You are likely to be legally intoxicated (0.08 percent blood alcohol) if you have had as little as one alcoholic drink an hour. Just don't do it. Take a taxi, as the locals do.

NIGHTLIFE | INTRODUCTION

The Lowdown

It's only rock 'n' roll... Rock, in its various forms, still dominates the live music scene in San Francisco. Any night of the week you can hit a number of clubs and hear garage bands, ska, post-punk, rockabilly, thrash, metal—in other words, just about every rock style except that acidy Jefferson Airplane/Grateful Dead thing they once called the San Francisco sound. One of the most popular spots in town is **Bottom of the Hill** (South of Market), where most of the acts are locals who have landed recording contracts, but touring bands perform as well. Musicians like the cozy atmosphere and great acoustics; when U2 is in town, they hang out there. **Slim's** is the house that Boz built. In the '80s, Boz Scaggs put South of Market on the map with his first-class music club, voted best nightclub in America by *Pollstar* magazine and best in the city by *Chronicle* readers. It originally leaned heavily toward blues but now features top names and new local faces in all popular genres, from Jimmy Vaughan and Eek-A-Mouse to the Breeders and the Paperboys. Actor Danny Glover stops by here to see his favorite blues bands, but when the joint is jammed—as it often is—he has to stand in the crowd with everyone else. The **Paradise Lounge** (South of Market) is less a club and more a rock saloon, where four separate performance rooms feature two or three acts playing simultaneously. Modern rock is the main attraction, but rockabilly, funk, acid jazz, gospel, and the spoken word are also on the bill. The **Fillmore Auditorium** has been synonymous with San Francisco's rock scene since Bill Graham put on his first psychedelic concert there in 1965. Shuttered up for years, the Fillmore reopened in the early '90s, to immense popularity with both fans and musicians. Tom Petty wanted to play there so badly that he appeared every night for a couple of weeks in order to make enough money to pay his band (which usually plays only in huge arenas for massive amounts of money). Though it's technically a concert hall, the **Great American Music Hall** is similar to the Fillmore in terms of popularity, intimacy, and the feeling of being in a club rather than an auditorium. It will never get too old to be hip. Ditto **Bimbo's 365** (North Beach), where acts like Sparklehorse, Tommy

Castro, the Cheeseballs, and Gregg Allman have replaced the swanky dinner shows and swing dancing that have made the club famous since the days when Rita Hayworth was part of the chorus line. The lineup is eclectic, so check the schedule in advance, but don't miss a chance to hang out in this lush San Francisco classic.

All that jazz... The best jazz club in the Bay Area, if not the entire West Coast, is across the bay. **Yoshi's** outgrew its former home in a small sushi restaurant near the Claremont Hotel and moved to Oakland's Jack London Square, but the setting is still so intimate that club owners insist you can be stuck in the back row and still see McCoy Tyner's fingers playing the piano. Some of the top jazz musicians in the world play at Yoshi's, which welcomes children and presents special shows and clinics for kids. Otherwise, jazz gigs are spread around town, but there's always something going on in North Beach, for free. **Enrico's Sidewalk Cafe** has live jazz seven nights a week with no cover, and **Jazz at Pearl's** consistently presents such good music that players head over there to jam after their paying gigs are over. The indomitable Pearl opened her first jazz club in a China-town basement some 25 years ago, and usually gets the best of the local talent at her current address in North Beach. The fashionable **Black Cat and Blue Bar** is a French restaurant upstairs (the Black Cat) with a very popular jazz club (the Blue Bar) in the basement. Sometimes it's live jazz and sometimes DJs, but it's always packed and definitely worth a visit. If you're near the

Even Cowgirls Hit the Booze

Country music is far from hip in San Francisco, but nevertheless there are plenty of cowgirls—of both genders—who still like to put on their silver spurs and really kick it every once in a while. The best place in town—the only place, actually—is the Sundance Saloon (www.sundancesaloon.org, 174 King St., near 3rd St.). You can get lessons (6-7:30pm) and then dance your little pea-pickin' heart out until 11pm every Sunday night. Where else but in a fabulous lesbian-and-gay gender-blender dance hall could you learn line dances like the Tush Push, Backstreet Attitude, Circle Jerk, and Dog Bone Boogie? On a good night, you might just hook up with a cowpoke wearing nothing but chaps. Yee-haw!

NIGHTLIFE | THE LOWDOWN

Haight, cross the Panhandle to Fulton Street and check out **Storyville**, owned by jazz musician Don Pender. Storyville was the original Creole name of New Orleans' French Quarter, where jazz was born, but far from being a sort of Preservation Hall, Storyville welcomes contemporary as well as classic jazz sounds. In the Mission District, **Bruno's** has two bars, one that screams '60s retro and another that looks a bit like a Greenwich Village jazz basement. Both feature live jazz, sometimes switching off during the same night. The crowd is half neighborhood hipsters and half everybody else, but they all love the music. It's amazingly unpretentious for such a happening scene. **Butterfly** is another reason many locals never want to leave the Mission District. The stage features some of the best local and touring jazz artists in the country— as well as cool DJs—and the kitchen's pan-Pacific cuisine has won national as well as local and regional awards. Remarkably, though, the place has retained a neighborhood feel and is packed with local artists and music fans.

Blues joints... Until a few years ago, all of the real blues joints were in Oakland. Then clubs started to appear in San Francisco, and though some purists might argue that these are a bit too sanitized to qualify as "joints," they do book topnotch talent and you don't need a bodyguard to get to the door. One of the most popular spots is the **Boom Boom Room** (Fillmore District), opened by blues legend John Lee Hooker, "the boogieman," who died June 21, 2001. With his credentials, he could've served nothing but tap water and it would've been a bona fide blues joint. But acts like John Cleary and the Ten Ton Chicken (two separate entities) keep this down-home juke joint hopping seven nights a week. Everybody who loves the blues loves this place, which the management proudly calls "the hippest, low-light, straight-up funky club on the West Coast." They won't get any argument from us. **Biscuits and Blues** is a nationally recognized venue, despite its unlikely location in touristy Union Square. The down-home food is delicious and the headliners are the best in the business, from venerable stars like James Cotton to local hotshots like Paris Slim. North Beach has two dives—**The Saloon** and **Grant and Green**—that have survived more than two decades and have produced a signature house-band sound dubbed "North Beach blues," most often identified with the hard-rocking, rowdy, Southern-style blues played by Johnny Nitro and the Doorslammers.

Move with the groove... Some of the best clubs in the city are actually hosts to a number of parties—sort of sub-clubs with distinct names and crowds—on different nights (for the latest listings, check out www.sfstation.com/clubs or www.sfclubs.com). **The EndUp,** a San Francisco institution immortalized in "Tales of the City," is a prime example. It's a giddy, stylish dance party known as Kit-Kat on Thursdays; a total cruise scene on Fag Fridays; the best-known rockin' lesbian scene in the city as The G-Spot on Saturdays; and a deep-house dance party (T-House) that has become such a part of club life on Sundays that many locals simply call it "church." **Club Townsend** is known for great house and techno music and for the wild decor that changes every week at Club Universe (Saturdays). On Sundays, the place is packed with a more mixed crowd—including the bridge-and-tunnel contingent—at Pleasuredome, and one Friday a month Club Q is a hot lesbian dance-a-thon. **Big Heart City** is a huge dance space that hosts a number of parties, but few are on a regular schedule. One of the regulars, Remedy, is a basic R&B dance party that describes itself as "giving you pure I.V. joy on the funky tip," whatever that means. The crowd at **330 Ritch** varies by the night, from chic SoMa types to serious salsa freaks to hard-core hip-hoppers. Every Saturday is a new theme party. **111 Minna,** which changes almost every night, has a reputation for being truly "underground," free of parties sponsored by slick promoters. Walk through the doors and you could find a live band, performance art, a movie, or a hip-hop DJ. **715 Harrison** is a popular 18-and-over hangout; Roderick's Chamber (Tuesdays) is a hard-core gothic scene that is said to "make Death Guild look like American Bandstand." All of these clubs have one thing in common—they don't really start to groove until at least 11, if not midnight. To find out about other clubs and parties, call Clubline (tel 415/339-8686).

NIGHTLIFE | THE LOWDOWN

Disco infernal... There's no longer a huge '70s-style disco scene in San Francisco—the theme parties mentioned above seem to satisfy most serious dance cravings. **Sound Factory** is one old standby that still attracts high-energy Gen-X crowds to its massive dance floors with elevated go-go cages and voyeur verandas: a glassed-in "Sky-Lounge" overlooking the club below and a catwalk that surrounds the entire building. If you're looking for a little less flash or a different crowd altogether, hop over to the outer reaches of North Beach, where **Bien Bien** is a magnet for hip, high-tech Pacific Rim partying types who love the combination of disco and karaoke in the club's numerous rooms. Or cab out to 30th and Mission streets—beyond the reach of the gentrification district—and squeeze onto the dance floor at **Club Malibu,** where the largely Hispanic crowd grooves to terrific live salsa bands and DJs spinning Latin rhythms.

Cool cocktail lounges... The lounge scene in the Mission District has made it one of the hippest neighborhoods in America, according to the *Utne Reader*, a national magazine that ranked only New Orleans' Lower Garden District ahead on the hip-o-meter. The six-block stretch between 16th and 22nd streets is door-to-door cocktail world, on Valencia Street and almost every cross-street that connects Valencia with Mission Street. At ground zero (16th and Valencia streets), step into the **Casanova Lounge** and mingle with the young and the restless while you ponder the source of the poly-resin grapes that serve as hanging light fixtures over the bar. Don't stay too long there—remember, the Mission scene is all about bar-hopping—or you could get too comfy in the living-room furniture to move on. Resist that temptation, and head up 16th Street to **Dalva,** a narrow drinking hole next to the Roxie Theatre. A neighborhood favorite, perhaps because everybody looks so fabulous in the rosy candlelight, Dalva offers a delicious Sangria along with the usual menu of cocktails. Try one, then cross the street and check out **Kilowatt,** an old fire station that has been reincarnated as many bars over the years. Have a beer, shoot some pool, dance a bit, then turn around and head back down to Valencia Street. If you don't mind a slight detour, continue down 16th Street just past Capp Street and be on the lookout for an almost-hidden sign at **Liquid,** a warm, friendly, popular bar that is remarkably unpretentious for being such a hip hot spot. Now retrace your steps back up 16th Street to Valencia—don't continue down 16th toward Mission Street. (Mission between 15th and 19th is one of the most dangerous areas in the city; you're safe in the rest of the neighborhood, but that particular four-block stretch is definitely to be avoided.) When you get back up to Valencia Street, walk left past the Casanova Lounge and take your pick of the many bars and cafes along the next few blocks. Shake-shake-shake your booty at **Amnesia,** a dance club between 19th and 20th streets that hosts nightly parties with names like Forget About It, Bubble & Squeak, Soulful Strut, and Hella Tight. They also specialize in tasty Belgian beers. Or stop in at **Oxygen,** a sleek dance club that serves hits of oh-two and exotic herbal elixirs instead of booze—seriously. Down a double shot of SuperNova (an energy blast with gobs of ginseng), then move right along to 22nd Street. Hang a left and you'll see two neighborhood favorites: the **Latin American Club** and the **Make-Out Room.** Both are crowded, hip, friendly, funky, eclectic, and always fun. These are essential stops if you want to hang with locals. Head farther down 22nd to Mission Street (this part is safe, don't worry) and you'll see a big neon sign for **Doc's Clock Cocktail Time.** With its blend of neighborhood hipsters and Latin émigrés, Doc's was an instant success from the day it opened a few years ago. R.E.M.'s Michael Stipe has been known to hang out here when he's in town. The really cool thing about all these Mission District bars is that you can truly "hop" between them on foot—everybody does. But you really do need to watch your step outside of the hip zone or you could find yourself on the very wrong side of the barrio. The two BART stations at either end of the neighborhood—16th and 24th streets—are totally convenient during the day, but can be serious danger zones at night. Don't even think about it; just take a cab.

Hangin' in the Haight... When the terminally hip Mission scene gets old, do as the locals do: Escape to the Lower Haight, where you don't have to walk more than a block in any direction from the corner of Haight and Fillmore streets to find a great little bar. Start with

Nickie's (between Webster and Fillmore), a super-friendly, unpretentious dance club that was started in the late eighties by an ex-hooker who sold barbecue during the week and had rockin' DJs on the weekends. Nickie died in 1990; while the current owners no longer sell half a chicken and a Bud for two bucks, they do maintain a hopping down-home atmosphere with a great crowd that is rarely ready to take it down a notch, even when last call rings out. And just to keep the place really, truly San Francisco, every Monday night is nothing but the Dead, with an extensive collection that includes tunes directly from the Grateful Dead's soundboard. Then check out these three great neighborhood bars tucked in the block between Fillmore and Steiner streets. **Mad Dog in the Fog** is a British-style pub that's almost always packed, especially during any televised soccer game. Though it's definitely a beloved neighborhood haunt, it also attracts young, successful jockish types who live in Pacific Heights or the Marina but somehow can't find a decent place to get sloshed near their own fancy apartments. For selection alone, the **Toronado Pub** is the best beer bar in town, hands down. It has dozens of imported beers and microbrews on tap, and it's in a lot of tourist guidebooks, so don't be surprised to find it packed with out-of-towners who pour in on Friday nights to suck up brewskies and take home souvenir T-shirts. **Noc-Noc** is more like a cozy Irish snug than a bar. The best seats in the house are the cushiony benches that line the wall, but you have to get there early to snag one. The happy hour is really popular and lasts later than any other bar in the neighborhood. They serve beer and sake—no hard stuff—and customers who are lucky enough to get a seat tend to burrow in for the night.

Kiss me, I'm Irish... Aside from O'Greenberg's, a former Fisherman's Wharf watering hole where the logo was Moshe Dayan with a shamrock for an eye-patch, San Francisco's Irish pubs for years have been clustered in the Clement Street neighborhood within a three-block radius of Third Avenue. The **Abbey Tavern** (Fifth Avenue and Geary Boulevard) is not as grungy or consistently lively as it was in the 1970s, when puddles of spilt beer and cigarette butts covered the floor and patrons stood three-deep around the huge bar, but it is still earthy enough to draw a flock of Irish regulars. Soccer posters are plastered on the walls alongside announcements of fundraising benefits for Irish political prisoners, and the bathroom stalls are covered with partisan graffiti. It's a bit too authentic to appeal to Americans who saw *Riverdance* and are now dying to share a pint with a "real" Irish person. (Not recommended for conservative Brits.) A Yankee-fied version of the Abbey is just up the block at **Pat O'Shea's Mad Hatter**. It is a mad house on weekends, when it's packed to the rafters with students from the University of San Francisco (a good Catholic college, mind you, and forget any nasty rumors you may have heard about scandals involving the erstwhile basketball team). With four satellites, 13 televisions, and a kitchen full of excellent pub food, Pat O'Shea's is also a magnet for local sports fans and out-of-towners who want to catch their team on the telly. **The Plough and the Stars**, around the corner, is a good middle-of-the-road bet for Celtophiles who love traditional Irish music but would prefer to steer clear of football hooligans or political arguments. There's live music on weekends for a minimal cover charge (usually $3), but get there early to nab a good seat.

Just your basic, friendly neighborhood bar...

When you get sick of looking for a scene or a theme or a fancy cocktail, what you need is a good old neighborhood tavern, where the bartender will strike up a conversation and welcome you to the fold. **Gino & Carlo** has been serving cocktails to North Beach natives for as long as anyone can remember. Just pay your money, drink up, and get ready to hear some good stories from the local barflies. The **Edinburgh Castle** is a special treat, a Scottish dive in the no-man's land between Civic Center and the Tenderloin. Grab a pint of John Courage, then drop a few quarters in the jukebox and get blasted by bagpipes. The crowd ranges from sodden old lushes to luscious young barhoppers. If that place is too crowded, try the best new addition to the neighborhood, **Hemlock Tavern.** The owners of the popular Casanova Lounge transformed a defunct gay dance club (the Giraffe Lounge) into a hip-yet-comfy Mission District-style neighborhood bar with lots of dark wood, warm colors, and a back room that sometimes features live music. The crowd is a bit younger than the Edinburgh Castle crew, but there's a similar mix of locals, hipsters, musicians, and visitors who would never think of themselves as tourists. The jukebox is great, and you can chow down on warm peanuts (toss the shells on the floor) and wash 'em down with a really good selection of beers. For a study in Chinatown culture, it's tough to beat **Buddha Bar.** Most tourists shy away from what appears to be a solemn atmosphere there, but if you listen closely (and you speak Chinese), you'll find that it's really just a neighborhood bar like any other. Be brave. Step inside, order a drink, and pretend you're in a Charlie Chan movie.

Three babes and a bus... Get a taste of the different ingredients of San Francisco's nightlife with **Three Babes and a Bus**. About 80 percent of the bar-hoppers who take this tour are local residents, lured, perhaps, by the chauffeured ride, the pre-paid cover charges, the priority entry (no waiting in line), and, of course, the three fun-loving women who run the business. The bus will scoop you up at a downtown bar and chauffeur you to three or four more lively nightspots. Along the way, the babes introduce their passengers to one another and lay down a few house rules, the most important of which is "Never let the Three Babes buy their own drinks." Aside from that, the total cost of this party-on-wheels is $35, which includes the clubs' cover charges.

Bustling brew pubs... The backlash against micro-breweries was in full force a few years ago. Even **Gordon Biersch**, the king of the city's microbreweries, put up a billboard that complained about wheat beers and apple beers, asking: "How about beer-flavored beer?" Now the city has settled into a comfortable old friendship with its many brew pubs, and you just don't hear the word "microbrew" anymore. Gordon Biersch's loud, yuppie-infested brew pub is generally avoided by non-upwardly-mobile locals, but the beers are exquisite and it can be a lot of fun if you don't mind yelling to be heard by the person next to you. **Twenty Tank Brewery** is more like an English pub— friendly but not deafening. Try the Red-Top Ale or Polly-Want-a-Porter. **Thirsty Bear Brewing Company** was named after an escaped circus bear who in

1991 bit the hand of a Ukrainian pub patron and ran off with his beer, or at least that's the story. This popular brew pub near the Museum of Modern Art is famous for its tapas and paella as well as the ales and beers brewed on the premises. Try the Lorca Ruby Ale, named after Spanish poet and playwright Federico García Lorca. All three brew pubs mentioned here are located South of Market.

Snazzy supper clubs... There are supper clubs *per se*, where the meal is as important as the entertainment (see our Dining chapter), and there are supper clubs *perchance*, where the crowd often arrives long after dinner, and the only thing that makes it a supper club is that it looks like the ones in old movies. The swing thing is basically dead, but some of the clubs are still fun to go to. Among those are **Cafe du Nord** (Upper Market), a former speakeasy that features live dance music and still looks enough like a bordello to bring out the party spirit in its eclectic clientele, and **Harry Denton's Starlight Room** (atop the Sir Francis Drake Hotel), where a slightly older crowd gets tanked on premium scotch and kicks up its heels on the dance floor. **Bimbo's 365** (North Beach), a swanky, landmark nightclub, is no longer a supper club, but it is a very popular rock venue (see "It's only rock 'n' roll").

Drag bars... Drag clubs did not survive the city's skyrocketing rent increases, so the drag scene shifted primarily to the long-standing neighborhood drag bars. The one exception is the hugely popular **asia sf,** where gorgeous "gender illusionists" serve some of the best Cal-Asian food in town and perform continuously. A local critic described the South of Market restaurant/club as "somewhere between Stepford and Wigstock." One of the most interesting neighborhood drag bars is **Esta Noche**, a small, Latino-oriented club in the Mission District where the drag queens are more likely to be at the bar or on the dance floor than on stage. (Esta Noche does host drag shows, but not on a regular basis.) The disk jockeys play mostly salsa music—with some disco thrown in—and the dance floor is always jammed. The bartenders are friendly, as are most of the customers, but this is definitely a gay club and not recommended for curious heteros wondering

NIGHTLIFE | THE LOWDOWN

what drag queens do in their spare time. It is also in a kind of seedy section of 16th Street, where there have been a few isolated gay-bashing incidents in the past, so take a cab to the door.

Gender blenders... You don't have to be totally gay to enjoy the free-spirited atmosphere of a primarily gay bar. San Francisco has a long tradition of gender-blender bars, where gay, straight, male, and female revelers mix it up on the dance floor, at the bar, and wherever else they choose. These places are not for peepers who want to see what queers look like up close; they're for fun-loving, non-judgmental partiers looking to get down with their bad selves. When it's karaoke time at **The Mint** (see "Where the boys are"), no one knows or cares what your gender or sexual preferences are, as long as you clap really loud for anyone who has the guts to get up on stage. It may just be the most fun karaoke crowd in the universe. And who could resist a piano bar called **Martuni's** (Valencia at Market Street)? It has everything you want and expect: a neon martini glass on the sign, a huge bar in the front room, and a cozy little piano bar in the back room, where you can sing along or listen in awe as I-coulda-been-a-star types belt out every show tune known to man.

Where the boys are... In practically any San Francisco neighborhood, there are too many gay bars to name, so we'll just mention a few "musts." If you are a gay man, you must go to **Twin Peaks** (Castro at Market Street), simply because it is the gateway to the **Castro** and is the first thing you see when you get out of the Castro Street MUNI/Metro station. The huge picture windows, the wonderful old burgundy-colored sign that beckons from a block away, and the antique wooden bar make it feel like a neighborhood cafe. Much of the crowd is over 40—it's not the top cruising spot in town—but it is a wonderful place to stop by for an afternoon pick-me-up, whether you are male or female. Around the corner is another historic Castro bar, **Harvey's** (Castro at 18th Street), where in 1979 police stormed in, dragged out gay men, and beat them. The bar won a famous lawsuit against the police department, and has been a landmark in gay history ever since. It is cozy and candlelit—a great place for a date for gay men and lesbians alike. **The Pendulum** (around the corner on 18th Street) is frequented primarily by African American men and those who can't resist them. Weekends are totally jammed—and jammin'. **The Mint** (upper Market Street near Guerrero) is one of the oldest gay bars in the city— open since World War II—and can be quite a hot spot during karaoke hours (9–2, Sun 4–2). If you think you may be Bette Midler trapped in a shy man's body, this is the place for you. The crowd applauds everyone who gives it a try, especially if it knows it's your first time at the mike. For a full rundown on the gay scene in the city, stop by **A Different Light** (tel 415/431–0891, 489 Castro St.), where you can pick up any number of free gay publications that include entertainment listings. Recommended: *Bay Times*, *Odyssey*, and *The Sentinel*.

Where the girls are... Until the late '80s, the Bay Area's homosexual population was pretty much divided into two territories—gay men in San Francisco and lesbians in Oakland. Now there is a much more active lesbian community in San Francisco—particularly in the Mission District and nearby Bernal Heights—and there are a lot of fun lesbian hangouts, including a number of gay bars with special nights for women. The longest-running Saturday night lesbian dance party in the city is The Girl Spot (at The EndUp, South of Market, Sixth and Harrison streets), commonly known as **the G-Spot.** It is extremely popular among a wide variety of women, and when the dance floor gets crowded and sweaty, there's a big outside patio where you and whoever you've got your eye on can go get a little fresh air. They've also got go-go dancers. The G-Spot is a must, but go before 10pm to get in for a reduced cover charge (usually less than $5). But the place to be on *any* night is the **Lexington Club,** just off Valencia Street (at 19th). It has everything a girl could want: cheap drinks, a pool table, loads of lesbians, and a killer jukebox with everything from the Replacements to Edith Piaf. This bar is really fun, and friendly to men and straight women as well. Our favorite semi-lesbian bar is **El Rio** (Mission District, Mission and Army streets), with a mixed crowd and most definitely a mixed motif. It's predominantly Latin, but it also has a big backyard that would give it that Doris Day/Rock Hudson patio party kind of feel if it weren't for the bigger-than-life Carmen Miranda paper doll out there. The music schedule varies, but there is often good live salsa. Sunday afternoons are the best. Go kind of late and stay for the transition from a mellow afternoon to a wild night.

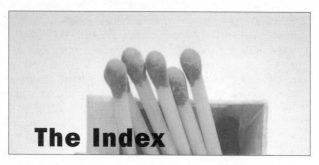

The Index

Abbey Tavern. This low-profile corner tavern near Clement Street is San Francisco's most unadulterated Irish pub.... *Tel 415/221-7767. 4100 Geary Blvd. (at Fifth Ave.), 38 MUNI bus. Open nightly.* **(see p. 180)**

Amnesia. Chill DJs set the tone on the dance floor, but side-liners can sit back and enjoy a variety of Belgian beers.... *Tel 415/970-8336. 853 Valencia St. (between 19th & 20th Sts.), take a cab. Open nightly.* **(see p. 179)**

asia sf. "Gender illusionists" serve pan-Asian food and perform hourly at this very hot new South of Market club.... *Tel 415/255-2742. 201 9th St. (at Howard St.). Open nightly. Entertainment lasts from 10pm till the party's over, Thurs–Sat. Check listings.* **(see p. 183)**

Bien Bien. A downstairs disco changes themes Friday and Saturday nights while the karaoke rooms upstairs groove.... *Tel 415/399-9555. 383 Bay St. (between Powell and Mason streets), Powell-Mason cable car; 15, 32, 39, or 42 MUNI bus. Open nightly.* **(see p. 178)**

Big Heart City. A huge balcony and high ceilings allow breathing room in this crowded, downtown ambient hangout.... *Tel 415/777-0666. 836 Mission St. (at 5th St.), Powell St. BART/MUNI Metro station; 14, 30, or 45 MUNI bus. Check listings.* **(see p. 177)**

Bimbo's 365. Plush booths, a spacious dance floor, big-name headliners, and a diverse crowd dressed to the nines.... *Tel 415/474-0365. 1025 Columbus Ave., North Beach, 15 MUNI bus. Check listings.* **(see pp. 174, 183)**

Biscuits and Blues. A congenial atmosphere and delicious Southern-style food make this popular blues club.... *Tel 415/292-BLUE. 401 Mason St., Powell-Mason or Powell-Hyde cable-car line; Powell St. BART/MUNI Metro station, 38 MUNI bus. Open nightly. Cover varies.* **(see p. 176)**

Black Cat and Blue Bar. One of the best things about this popular jazz haunt is that you can order from the full menu of the upstairs French bistro until 2am.... *Tel 415/981-2233. 501 Broadway (at Kearny), North Beach, 15 or 30 MUNI bus. Open nightly except Sun.* **(see p. 175)**

Boom Boom Room. John Lee Hooker's Fillmore blues joint.... *Tel 415/673-8000. 1601 Fillmore St. (near Geary Blvd.), 38 MUNI bus.* **(see p. 176)**

Bottom of the Hill. This Potrero Hill club is way off the beaten path, but worth the effort.... *Tel 415/626-4455. 1233 17th St., take a cab. Open nightly. Cover $5–15.* **(see p. 174)**

Bruno's. You may get squished on the tiny dance floor at this ever-so-hip Mission District spot, but the music is great.... *Tel 415/648-7701. 2389 Mission St., 24th St. BART station. Live music Mon-Sat. Cover varies.* **(see p. 176)**

Buddha Bar. It's dark. It's quiet. Not many people are speaking English. This heart-of-Chinatown bar is a great glimpse into neighborhood culture.... *Tel 415/362-1792. 901 Grant Ave., Chinatown, 1, 15, 30, or 45 MUNI bus. Open Mon–Sat.* **(see p. 182)**

Butterfly. Another huge hit in the Mission District, this pan-Asian restaurant and jazz lounge stays welcoming and casual while serving up very sophisticated food and music till the wee hours.... *Tel 415/864-5575. 1710 Mission St. (at Duboce), take a cab. Open Tues-Sat 5pm-2am.* **(see p. 176)**

Cafe du Nord. One of the hippest clubs in town, located in a dark, ornate, former basement speakeasy. An artistic crowd

NIGHTLIFE | THE INDEX

comes for acid jazz, jive, salsa, and cabaret.... *Tel 415/861-5016. 2170 Market St., Church St. MUNI/Metro station. Open nightly. Cover $3–7.* **(see p. 183)**

Casanova Lounge. Be sure to check out the high-kitsch retro light fixtures in this cozy, crowded Mission District cocktail lounge.... *Tel 415/863-9328. 527 Valencia St., 16th St. BART station. Open nightly.* **(see p. 178)**

Club Malibu. Don't go to this disco unless you love to dance to hot Latin grooves, because it is definitely too crowded to find a place to sit.... *Tel 415/821-7395. 3395 Mission St. (between 29th and 30th streets). Check listings.*
(see p. 178)

Club Townsend. An industrial-style South of Market space for floating dance parties.... *Tel 415/974-6020. 177 Townsend St., 42 MUNI bus. Hours vary; usually includes after-hours. Cover $5–20.* **(see p. 177)**

Dalva. Cozy into this narrow, smoke-filled (ssssh!) bar and sip delicious Sangria with the locals. Great jukebox.... *Tel 415/252-7740. 3121 16th St. (at Valencia), 16th St. BART/MUNI Metro station. Open nightly.* **(see p. 178)**

Doc's Clock Clocktail Time. Two former bartenders from the Latin American club opened their own Mission District bar, and it was an immediate hit. Celebrities mix freely with the neighborhood crowd.... *Tel 415/824-3627. 2575 Mission St. (between 21st and 22nd streets), 16th or 24th St. BART/MUNI Metro station. Open nightly.* **(see p. 179)**

Edinburgh Castle. Soak up the friendly atmosphere along with British Isles ale at this snug Civic Center/Tenderloin bar.... *Tel 415/885-4074. 950 Geary at Polk. 38 MUNI bus.*
(see p. 181)

El Rio. This eccentric Mission District dive is supposedly a Latina lesbian haunt, but it is also a friendly neighborhood bar, comfortable for all.... *Tel 415/282-3325. 3158 Mission St. (at Army St.), 24th St. BART station.* **(see p. 185)**

The EndUp. John Waters, Grace Jones, Naomi Campbell, and Kate Moss "ended up" here—you should too. Check out Kit Kat and Club Dread during the week; Friday nights are a major gay cruise scene.... *Tel 415/357-0827. 401 6th St., South of Market, 12, 27, or 42 MUNI bus. Check listings.* **(see p. 177)**

Enrico's Sidewalk Cafe. (See also Dining) A North Beach sidewalk cafe with great food and great jazz.... *Tel 415/982-6223. 504 Broadway; 15 or 30 Muni bus. Open nightly. No cover.* **(see p. 175)**

Esta Noche. This Mission District bar is a friendly neighborhood hangout for drag queens, with occassional preplanned shows.... *Tel 415/861-5757. 3079 16th St. (at Valencia St.), 16th St. BART station. Cover $3–7.* **(see p. 183)**

Fillmore Auditorium. The infamous concert hall that made psychedelic music a household staple during the sixties is going strong again.... *Tel 415/346-6000 (show information). 1805 Geary Blvd., 38 MUNI bus.* **(see p. 174)**

Gino & Carlo. North Beach locals have been drinking here for longer than most of them can remember.... *Tel 415/421-0896. 548 Green St., 15 MUNI bus.* **(see p. 181)**

Gordon Biersch. Probably the best microbrew in the city, but the South of Market pub is unbearably loud.... *Tel 415/243-8246. 2 Harrison St. (at the Embarcadero), 42 MUNI bus.* **(see p. 182)**

Grant and Green. Crowded North Beach blues dive.... *Tel 415/693-9565. 1371 Grant St., 15 MUNI bus. Open nightly. Cover for live music varies.* **(see p. 177)**

Great American Music Hall. Formerly a grand bordello, the Great American is now the city's grande dame of nightclubs, a wonderfully lush and civilized live music venue where you can get down wit' yo bad self in a place that looks like a scaled-down opera house. Plus there's a modern kitchen that serves really good food during all shows.... *Tel 415/885-0750, box office fax 415/885-5075. 859 O'Farrell St. (between Ellis and Geary), Civic Center BART/Muni Metro station, 38 MUNI bus.* **(see p. 174)**

The G-Spot. Lesbian dance party held every third Saturday night at a South of Market bar called The EndUp.... *Tel 415/337-4962. 401 Sixth St., at Harrison, 42 MUNI bus (cab recommended).* **(see p. 185)**

Harry Denton's Starlight Room. Big-band sound, elegant surroundings, and amazing views.... *Tel 415/392-7755. 450 Powell St., Powell St. BART/MUNI Metro station; Powell-Hyde or Powell-Mason cable car. Open nightly. Cover $5–10.* **(see p. 183)**

Harvey's. Made famous the night of the "White Night Riots" in 1979, this Castro bar is now a gay landmark. It's a quiet, romantic spot.... *Tel 415/431-4278. 500 Castro St. (at 18th St.), Castro St. MUNI Metro station.* **(see p. 184)**

Hemlock Tavern. This friendly neighborhood bar is a lot like the hip haunts in the Mission District—comfy, stylish, but totally down to earth.... *Tel 415/923-0923. 1131 Polk St. (at Hemlock), 38 MUNI bus.* **(see p. 181)**

Jazz at Pearl's. Straightforward jazz in an old-style jazz club in North Beach. Pearl greets most patrons herself.... *Tel 415/291-8255. 256 Columbus Ave., 15 or 30 Muni bus. Closed Sun. No cover; 2-drink minimum.* **(see p. 175)**

Kilowatt. The latest watering hole to inhabit this former firehouse is pretty much like the last few: pool table, beer, a little bit of cruising, the usual.... *Tel 415/861-2595. 3160 16th St. (at Valencia St.), 16th St. BART station. Open nightly.* **(see p. 178)**

Latin American Club. You don't have to be a fashion model to feel comfortable at this Mission District neighborhood bar.... *Tel 415/647-2732. 3286 22nd St. (at Valencia St.), 24th St. BART station. Open nightly.* **(see p. 179)**

Lexington Club. This is one of the first lesbian clubs that isn't just a theme night at another club, and it's so much fun that the crowd includes a considerable share of straight women and men of all persuasions.... *Tel 415/863-2052. 3464 19th St. (between Valencia and Mission Sts.), 16th St. BART station. Open nightly.* **(see p. 185)**

Liquid. A low-key and very friendly alternative to some of the unbearably hip Mission District bars up the street. It's tough to spot the tiny sign, but there's usually a bouncer outside.... *Tel 415/431-8889. 2925 16th St. (between Mission St. and South Van Ness Ave.), 16th St. BART station. Closed Sun.* **(see p. 179)**

Mad Dog in the Fog. This funky British-style pub is a favorite hangout for Lower Haight locals.... *Tel 415/626-7279. 530 Haight St. (between Fillmore and Steiner Sts.), 6, 7, 66, or 71 MUNI bus.* **(see p. 180)**

Make-Out Room. Yes, some people do. But this isn't a pick-up scene—any more than any other bar—just a pleasant, funky, casual neighborhood spot. Try it.... *Tel 415/647-2888. 3225 22nd St. (between Mission and Valencia Sts.), 16th or 24th St. BART station. Open nightly.* **(see p. 179)**

Martuni's. Admit it, you've always wanted to walk right into a piano bar and sing show tunes until you're hoarse.... *Tel 415/241-0205. 4 Valencia St. (at Market St.), Castro St. Muni metro station.* **(see p. 184)**

The Mint. If you haven't been to a gay karaoke bar, you haven't lived.... *Tel 415/626-4726. 1942 Market St., near Guerrero St., Church St. MUNI metro station.* **(see pp. 184, 185)**

Nickie's. Originally opened by an ex-hooker with the heart of a chef, this down-home barbecue joint/dance club remains a perennial favorite.... *Tel 415/621-6508. 460 Haight St. (between Webster and Fillmore Sts.), 6, 7, 66, or 71 MUNI bus.* **(see p. 180)**

Noc-Noc. Everybody loves quirky little Noc-Noc, with its cushy seating along the walls, zebra prints all over the place, and a lengthy happy hour.... *Tel 415/861-5811. 557 Haight St. (between Webster and Fillmore Sts.), 6, 7, 66, or 71 MUNI bus.* **(see p. 180)**

111 Minna. A back-alley art gallery that doubles as a dance club, this informal spot changes every night with live bands, movies, performance art, and DJs.... *Tel 415/974-1719. 111 Minna St. (at 2nd St.), 14 or 15 MUNI bus. Check listings.* **(see p. 177)**

Oxygen. There's no booze at this popular Mission District dance club, but partiers fuel up on hits of oxygen—yes, oh-two— and herbal elixirs.... *Tel 415/255-2102. 795 Valencia St. (between 19th and 20th Sts.), take a cab.* **(see p. 179)**

Paradise Lounge. Up to five bands play in this unusual South of Market club every night, where modern rock, blues, funk,

NIGHTLIFE | THE INDEX

poetry, and occasionally even a lounge-lizard act can be heard. The crowd is unpretentious and diverse.... *Tel 415/861-6906. 308 11th St. (near Folsom), 42 MUNI bus. Open nightly. Cover free–$12.* **(see p. 174)**

Pat O'Shea's Mad Hatter. This large tavern is more of a college sports bar than an authentic Irish pub, but the soccer on the satellite TVs does attract a lot of visiting Celts.... *Tel 415/752-3148. 3848 Geary Blvd. (at Third Ave.), 38 MUNI bus. Open nightly.* **(see p. 181)**

The Pendulum. This is the city's only predominantly African American gay bar, and it is absolutely packed on weekends.... *Tel 415/863-4441. 4146 18th St. (at Collingwood St.), Castro St. MUNI Metro station.* **(see p. 185)**

The Plough and the Stars. The traditonal Irish music played here can be heavenly, as long as you don't mind the Birkenstock crowd.... *Tel 415/751-1122. 116 Clement St. (at Second Ave.), 38 MUNI bus. $3 cover Fri and Sat nights.* **(see p. 181)**

The Saloon. This rowdy North Beach blues dive has live music seven nights a week. It's usually loud, local, and not well known.... *Tel 415/989-7666. 1232 Grant Ave., (near Columbus), 15 MUNI bus. Cover varies.* **(see p. 177)**

715 Harrison. A high-tech dance club with an outrageous sound system. The floating parties at this South of Market space are for a very young crowd.... *Tel 415/339-8686. 715 Harrison St., 42 MUNI bus. Hours vary. Cover $10–15.* **(see p. 177)**

Slim's. Get your tickets in advance for most shows at this South of Market music club. Go early or you'll be stuck in the suffocating crowd on the dance floor.... *Tel 415/522-0333. 333 11th St. (near Folsom), 42 MUNI bus (best to take a taxi). Cover varies.* **(see p. 174)**

Sound Factory. The biggest dance club in San Francisco, with six different rooms. The music is techno, with some funk, hip-hop, and disco thrown in. No athletic attire allowed.... *Tel 415/339-8686. 525 Harrison St., 42 MUNI bus. Open Sat. Cover $10.* **(see p. 178)**

Storyville. Don Pender's classic jazz club features live jazz on Saturdays plus hip-hop and reggae parties other nights.... *Tel 415/441-1751. 1751 Fulton St. (near Masonic Ave.), 5 MUNI bus. Cover varies.* **(see p. 176)**

Thirsty Bear Brewing Company. Close to the Museum of Modern Art, this is the best of the South of Market brew pubs.... *Tel 415/974-0905. 661 Howard St. (near Third St.), 15, 30, or 45 MUNI bus.* **(see p. 182)**

Three Babes and a Bus. These club tours happen Saturdays unless you can get enough people together for a special party on other days.... *Tel 800/414-0158 or check out www.threebabes.com for details and reservations.* **(see p. 182)**

330 Ritch. A cool, cool crowd gathers nightly in this industrial building, located on a little South of Market alleyway, for changing theme parties.... *Tel 415/541-9574. 330 Ritch St., 15, 30, or 45 MUNI bus. Food 5–11 or midnight, happy hour 5–8 Tue–Fri, music in two sets: 6:30–8 & 9–1:30. Closed Mon. Cover free–$10.* **(see p. 177)**

Toronado Pub. You'll have to go early to get a seat at the bar on a Friday night, because this excellent beer bar (best on-tap variety in the city) is a hit with locals and tourists alike.... *Tel 415/863-2276, 547 Haight St. (at Steiner), 6, 7, 66, or 71 MUNI bus.* **(see p. 180)**

Twenty Tank Brewery. This microbrewery is more like an English ale house than a San Francisco brew pub.... *Tel 415/255-9455. 316 11th St. (at Folsom St.), 42 MUNI bus.* **(see p. 182)**

Twin Peaks. The crowd at this old-fashioned, picture-windowed bar is usually relatively quiet and 40-plus.... *Tel 415/864-9470. 401 Castro St., Castro St. MUNI Metro station.* **(see p. 184)**

Yoshi's. This is definitely the top jazz venue on the West Coast. Take the ferry or drive across the bridge to Jack London Square (Oakland).... *Tel 510/238-9200. 510 Embarcadero West, Oakland.* **(see p. 175)**

NIGHTLIFE | THE INDEX

enterta

7

inment

San Francisco
sells more theater
tickets per capita
than any major
city in America.
Most people
would be shocked

to hear that little trivia gem, given the fact that so many of the high-profile productions in town are recycled Broadway musicals that appeal mostly to out-of-towners. Sure, you can spend your money on tickets to *The Phantom of the Opera* (yawn), but your hard-earned entertainment dollar would be more wisely spent on some of the most innovative, dynamic stage productions in the country—written, produced, directed, and performed by top local talent.

San Francisco leaves the monumental cost of producing mainstream shows to New York, concentrating its own money and effort on unconventional creations. The city's dozens of unusual options include the **Lorraine Hansberry Theater**, a small space in the downtown theater district that focuses on new and experimental works by established African American playwrights; **Theater Rhinoceros** in the Mission District, the oldest gay/lesbian theater group in the country; **The Marsh**, another Mission District venue for avant-garde theater and dance; and **Josie's Juice Joint and Cabaret**, a Castro District vegetarian cafe that stages informal productions in its back room. And by all means, don't leave town without going to North Beach to see San Francisco's trademark show, *Beach Blanket Babylon*, the longest-running musical revue in history.

Here's another surprising bit of trivia—the first ballet company in the United States was the **San Francisco Ballet**. And its glory is not at all in the past: the *New York Times* proclaimed the current troupe, led by artistic director Helgi Tomasson (formerly a principal dancer with the New York City Ballet), "one of the country's finest." If you're looking for more unorthodox dance performances, there are plenty of troupes to see, from the mid-size companies that perform at **Theater Artaud** (Potrero Hill) to the small, cutting-edge shows in the Mission District's **Footwork Dance Studio** and **Third Wave Dance House**.

The **San Francisco Opera** performs in the opulent 1932 War Memorial Opera House, which reopened in September 1997 after extensive renovations. The refurbished auditorium has all the requisite high-tech improvements—state-of-the-art lighting and computerized scenery-rigging equipment—plus new gold leaf and bigger bathrooms for women. (We're not sure what amenities the men got.) The **San Francisco Symphony** has its own digs—Davies Symphony Hall—and a new maestro, Michael Tilson Thomas, who left the London Symphony to become the toast of the Bay Area. Most other music—jazz, blues, folk, and rock—is performed primarily at the clubs you'll find in the Nightlife chapter.

Getting a bit too highbrow here? Not to worry. There are enough spectator sports in the Bay Area to balance out the whole culture bit—two major-league baseball teams, two NFL football teams, an NBA basketball team, an NHL hockey team, and two major horse-racing tracks. There are even two professional roller-hockey teams. Oakland fans were deliriously happy when the **Oakland Raiders** became their home team again in 1995, but lately ticket sales have been weak, and so has the team. At least the owner hasn't been sent off to court on gambling charges, like the **San Francisco 49ers'** Ed De Bartolo. Not yet, anyway.

Sources

For theater and music listings, the best mainstream source is the "Datebook" tabloid in the Sunday *Chronicle*, known to locals as "the pink section" because it's printed on pink newsprint. The *Bay Guardian* and *SF Weekly*, free alternative weeklies that can be found almost anywhere you look, are recommended for listings of more offbeat or intimate happenings. Radio stations that offer diverse programming and information on local performances and concerts include KPOO 89.5 FM, KQED 88.5 FM, and KPFA 94.1 FM.

Getting Tickets

San Franciscans are an odd lot when it comes to performing arts—they adore the opera and ballet, and snap up season

In Search of Tony Bennett's Heart

Did you ever wonder exactly where Tony Bennett left his heart? We knew his heart called to him from a spot "where little cable cars climb halfway to the stars," but we never guessed the spot was the Visitors Information Center at Hallidie Plaza, even though it's right next to the Powell Street cable-car turnaround. Take the escalator from the turnaround down toward the BART entrance and go into the center, where you'll find the "I Left My Heart in San Francisco" gold record, the original song manuscript, and an earlier draft (be sure to read it—some of the lyrics really stink). While you're there, pick up free walking-tour leaflets and ask the multilingual staff for any information you need (tel 415/283–0177). There's also a 24-hour telephone hotline—in five languages—that lists daily events and activities (English: tel 415/283–0176, Spanish: tel 415/283–0175, French: tel 415/283–0172, German: tel 415/283–0173, Italian: tel 415/283–0171, and Japanese: tel 415/283–0174).

ENTERTAINMENT — INTRODUCTION

tickets so fast you barely have time to read through the season's program if you hope to get a good seat, yet the major blockbuster shows that seem to be a priority to out-of-towners are not that big of a draw for locals. (They also dine before the theater, not afterward.) Here's the moral of that story: If you want to go to an opera, symphony, or ballet performance, make arrangements before you get to town. You can call Tickets.com (see below) for one-stop ticket shopping, but if you aren't familiar with the concert halls, you may prefer to deal directly with each company's box office, where ticket representatives tend to have much more information about the best seats. If you want to see a major Broadway-type show, mention it to your hotel concierge when you secure your room reservation, or call Tickets.com. Tickets for smaller venues and more avant-garde productions are usually available on relatively short notice, but you should check out the *Bay Guardian* and *SF Weekly* as soon as you get to town to find out what's going on and to reserve your seats.

For half-price, day-of-performance tickets to major theater, dance, and music events at selected venues, go to the **TIX** booth on the Stockton Street side of Union Square (cash or traveler's checks only, Tue–Thur 11–6, Fri–Sat 11–7; tel 415/433–7827; www.theatrebayarea.org). Even fairly popular shows sometimes need to fill seats with the steep discount. TIX also sells full-price advance tickets (credit cards accepted). **Tickets.com** is the primary advance-sales outlet for all major Bay Area events, including sports, and you can purchase tickets by telephone (tel 415/478–BASS, 510/762–BASS, 800/225–BASS outside California). In every big city, there are scalpers on the street at sold-out events—even though the practice is against the law—but if you are not familiar with the seating chart, you can easily plunk down a bundle of cash for a "great seat" behind a pillar or up in nosebleed territory. Counterfeit tickets are also a common scam, and they are very difficult to detect—unless the nefarious scalper has neglected to wash the printer's ink off his hands. If you're willing to pay more than face value for a good seat or a sold-out event, it's probably better to go through a ticket broker. They will charge a steep price for a premium ticket, but they usually have choice seats and impossible-to-get tickets. The toughest ticket to get is one to a Golden State Warriors basketball game—all of their home games are sold out to season-ticket holders—but **Mr. Ticket** might be able to help. Mr. T is the biggest ticket broker in the Bay Area, specializing in premium seating—at premium prices (tel 415/775–3031, 800/424–7328, 2065 Van Ness Ave.). You can also check the Yellow Pages—there are more than two dozen agencies listed under "Ticket Sales."

The Lowdown

The play's the thing... San Francisco's "theater district" is just west of picture-pretty Union Square, but like its New York counterpart, it brushes up against a less cultivated neighborhood—in this case, the Tenderloin. There is no particular danger during performance times, but you might want to take a cab at night, especially if you're dressed up and look like you might have a purse or wallet worth snatching. All of the theaters that specialize in Broadway and Broadway-bound shows are within a few blocks of each other—if Andrew Lloyd Webber turned the O.J. Simpson trial into a musical, it would eventually end up at the **Curran**, the **Golden Gate**, or the **Orpheum** theater. The Curran has been playing *The Phantom of the Opera* for what seems like eons; the run is open-ended, but call in advance to be sure it's still playing. The grand old Golden Gate Theater is located a little deeper into the Tenderloin than some overdressed theatergoers would prefer, but it stages lots of Broadway favorites and revivals—in 1995, Tommy Tune's new production of the fifties rock-and-roll musical, *Grease*, was a big favorite (the only thing missing was a young John Travolta). The Orpheum's meticulously restored Spanish baroque building is every bit as glamorous as the productions it hosts; when Carol Channing came to town with the revival of *Hello Dolly!*, she came to the Orpheum. But the theater district is not limited to Broadway blockbusters. One of the less-publicized casualties of the 1989 Loma Prieta earthquake, the Geary Theater—home of the **American Conservatory Theater (ACT)**, one of the most highly regarded repertory groups in the country—has reopened. ACT continues to be a company with great range, presenting modern classics such as *A Streetcar Named Desire* alongside weighty Shakespearean epics. The **Marine's Memorial Theater** presents both local and off-Broadway productions; it was the San Francisco home of Tony Kushner's *Angels in America*. The ornate **Alcazar Theater** often stages long runs of its plays; you won't see anything out of the ordinary, but classics like *The Lion in Winter* please drama lovers who can't stand the idea of another tap-dancing chorus line. The **Stage Door Theater** presents a mixed bag of top-quality local comedy productions in an intimate space.

On the fringes... Predictably, San Francisco concentrates a great deal of its theatrical resources on gay and lesbian, multicultural, and avant-garde productions. Many of the most experimental companies are housed in or near San Francisco's "New Bohemia"—the Mission District—but non-mainstream theater can be found throughout the city. The current *ne plus ultra* avant-garde venue is **The Marsh**, a Mission District performance space where you pay your money (usually $7 to $17) and take your chances, and often see remarkably talented artists right before they become trendy and famous. Aspiring actors, dancers, playwrights, and performance artists, take note: The Marsh is also the best place in town to network. Its predecessor—still among the most respected progressive art centers in the city—is another Mission District space called **Intersection for the Arts**, where Sam Shepard and Whoopi Goldberg tried out their acts before they got their 15 light-years of fame. The not-yet-discovered performers here are generally cutting-edge. Downtown, amid all the Broadway musicals and other big-money productions, the cozy little **Exit Theater** serves beer and wine and stages avant-garde "classics," from one-act comedies set in cafes to absurdist murder mysteries. You don't have to be a sullen existentialist to be experimental—this is a place to be a tad eccentric and have fun at the same time. It's always a pleasure to see a dance, theater, or multimedia production at **Theater Artaud** (Mission District), because the space itself is so well-run; this medium-sized mainstay of the experimental-theater scene has been around long enough to know how to give impeccably professional stagings of the most avant-garde works. **Climate Theater** (South of

Market) is so tiny that it makes the audience feel almost intimate with the performers. Expect all kinds of experimental works here, including individual readings and performance art. The **Lorraine Hansberry Theater** (downtown) provides a showcase for some of the top African American playwrights and artists in the country, presenting both experimental and well-known works. The **Mission Cultural Center for Latino Arts** (Mission District) emphasizes works written and produced by multinational Latino artists, much of it political in nature and aimed at the neighborhood's Mexican, Central American, and Chicano populations (many of the productions are in Spanish). **Theater Rhinoceros** (Mission District) was the first theater group in the United States to focus strictly on contemporary gay and lesbian issues; its productions range from bizarre, avant-garde performance pieces to traditional plays that feature gay characters. There's often a line stretching down the block in front of **Josie's Juice Joint and Cabaret**, a Castro District vegetarian cafe/cabaret combo where local gay performers will have you in a belly-laugh frenzy. Both gays and straights love this place, which will be obvious to you the moment you see the line full of every possible combination of couples waiting to get in. New works by local playwrights and artists are staged at the **Magic Theater** (Fort Mason)—some are stars and some are starving, but all are very, very good. The progressive **Phoenix II Theater,** which has moved from its South of Market digs to a new location in the Geary Street theater district, also features the work of local playwrights; the productions are often mounted on a shoestring budget, but they can be powerful.

Such a drag... It was a very sad day for San Francisco when Steve Silver, the mastermind behind *Beach Blanket Babylon*, died in 1995, but he left a legacy that promises to keep people laughing for years to come—the longest-running, wackiest musical revue in history. Watch reasonable facsimiles of Tina Turner, Hillary Clinton, and James Brown—all wearing huge, ridiculous headdresses—give "Snow White" advice on how to find a good man. (It sounds reasonable to us.) And you won't believe the hats—one of the more famous ones is a huge model of the San Francisco skyline. Reserve a few weeks in advance for the cabaret-style performances in North Beach's cozy Club Fugazi (to be admitted you must be at least 21 years old, with photo identification, except for Sunday matinees). There are many small bars in town where drag queens congregate and strut their stuff (see Nightlife), but the Queen Mother of all of them was Finocchio, a family-owned North Beach cabaret that had been presenting glitzy female-impersonator revues since 1936. San Francisco grieved again when its favorite drag club was forced to close its doors in 1999 because of an exorbitant—and unmeetable—rent increase.

Mostly Mozart... Under the innovative direction of maestro Michael Tilson Thomas, who left the London Symphony to become the toast of the Bay Area, the **San Francisco Symphony** grabbed national attention by winning both the 1997 Grammy award for Best Orchestral Performance and the American Society of Composers and Songwriters (ASCAP) award for Strongest Commitment to New American Music that same year. Davies Symphony Hall has had a slightly less direct route to public relations heaven. A huge, modern concert hall with what seems like acres of concrete and glass, it had a number of embarrassing acoustical glitches (echoes in the balcony, for example) when it opened in 1980. Since then it has undergone a complete renovation and is now considered one of the finest modern concert venues in the world, with amenities that include the Ruffatti Organ, the largest concert hall organ in North America (eight divisions of 163 ranks and 9,235 pipes).

Men in tights... One of the city's cultural treasures, the world-class **San Francisco Ballet** normally shares its home with the opera, performing regularly at the War Memorial Opera House. Artistic director Helgi Tomasson is a darling of dance critics, especially in New York, where he was considered a premiere danseur, and worked closely with Balanchine. His production of *Romeo and Juliet* was hailed as one of the most inventive ever staged. The ballet's primary seasons are spring and fall, but special Christmas performances include *The Nutcracker*. If you're inclined to take BART across the bay, you can see the **Oakland Ballet** perform at the gorgeous Paramount Theater, a perfectly restored landmark art-deco movie palace that alone is worth the trip. This exuberant, multiracial company is not as developed as its San Francisco counterpart, but some of the pieces are actually more interesting, in part because they feature a number of brilliant, enthusiastic young dancers. The dancing isn't always perfect, but they are a lot of fun to watch. Artistic director Ronn Guidi loves to do historical reconstructions of old ballets and present new experimental ones. In 1997 he presented Nijinsky's *Chopin Concerto* along with a world premiere of *Dim Sum*, ancient Chinese folk tales set to Chinese music.

Dancing with the avant-garde... The city's unconventional dance companies gather where the rest of the avant-garde performing artists do—in the Mission District. Small, funky groups and extreme, cutting-edge choreographers showcase their work at **Dancers Group Studio Theater**, a small Mission District studio where local choreographers are having a creative field day and neighborhood audiences are eating it up. The best part is that the "attitude factor" is minor. Some very innovative productions have been staged at **Third Wave Dance House**, with local choreographers and ethnic traditions (a natural for the Mission District). The popular company closed its doors for awhile in 1997, but reopened in 1998. It's worth checking for. A few blocks away, experimental, midsized touring and local companies perform at **Theater Artaud**.

Grand opera... The **San Francisco Opera** is an experience, not just for the thrilling performances by top international stars, but also for the little risks the company takes just because, after all, this is San Francisco. There were, for example, the nuns (played by "supernumeraries," opera's version of extras) who stripped totally naked and physically climbed the walls to illustrate their possession by the devil, and an opera composed by jazz/pop vocalist Bobby McFerrin with progressive novelist Ishmael Reed as the librettist. Then there is the audience, half of which is dressed to the nines while the other half arrives in jeans and sneakers. Boxes at the grand-old War Memorial Opera House are fabulous, with elegant brocade chairs and heavy velvet curtains. The opera season starts in September and runs through January, with a short summer season as well. Tickets are not easy to come by, so plan in advance. If you arrive without tickets, your only alternative may be standing-room tickets, available for every performance for $10. Line up at the box office at 10 that morning and hope they don't sell out before you get to the window.

Take me out to the ballgame... The Bay Area baseball scene is definitely a tale of two cities: Oakland, with four world championships and a once-terrific ballpark that has been turned into a monstrosity by the return of the Raiders, and San Francisco, with no world titles and a brand-new downtown baseball-only park that has become the hottest ticket in town. The **San Francisco Giants** opened the new millennium by playing their first regular-season game at the $300 million **Pacific Bell Park** against their archrivals, the Los Angeles Dodgers. Nearly 30,000 of Pac Bell's 42,000 seats were sold out to season-ticket holders before the stadium was even finished. Fans are thrilled to get out of windy, cavernous Candlestick Park (officially renamed **3Com Park**) with its infield mini tornadoes and freezing-cold night games. The weather at Pac Bell is sunny and bright—and a tiny bit wet when a home run sails out of the park and into the inlet of the bay now known as McCovey Cove (in honor of the team's legendary slugger, Willie McCovey). Toward the end of the 2001 season, as outfielder Barry Bonds got closer to breaking Mark McGwire's all-time single-season record of 70 home runs, the cove was gridlocked with a flotilla of yachts, small boats, kayaks, and every other imaginable water craft, all hoping to be there for the historic splashdown. Bonds not only broke the record, he managed to add a little insurance with his 73rd homer on the final home game of the season, against the Giants' archrival, the Los Angeles Dodgers. Those who can't get tickets—continuous sellouts are projected—can watch the game for free through a cyclone fence along a beautiful pedestrian pathway that separates the park from the bay. Meanwhile, over at the **Oakland Coliseum,** the red-hot 20-something **Oakland A's** are as much MTV as MLB. During the 2001 American League Division Series, when the hang-loose A's were up against the three-time world champion Yankees, *New York Times* columnist Alan Schwarz praised their youthful exuberance and nonconformity in a column headed "'A' is for Animal House." Players like pitching ace Barry Zito, who dyed his hair blue and moonlights as a guest host on a local radio talk show, have brought fans back to what used to be a small, sunny ballpark with wide-open wooden bleachers. The Raiders blitzed the bleachers and put in a huge, high-rise wall of 10,000 luxury seats—not used for regular-season baseball—and an enclosed "club" where people can sit inside, drink cocktails, and watch the game on TV. (What's the point?) The only thing left from the good old days is the beloved, old-fashioned manual scoreboard—a faint reminder that there was baseball before television. If the owners have their way, the team will get a new home—perhaps in the sunny Silicon Valley, about a half-hour down the interstate—in a couple of years. Come the end of summer, football teams start filling the stadiums—the **San Francisco 49ers**, which play on Sundays at Candlestick, and the **Oakland Raiders**. Bay Area football fans are often characterized as falling into two distinct molds: the wine-and-brie set at Candlestick and the Bud-and-burgers bunch at the Coliseum. Either way, tickets can be hard to come by, but you can usually snag one from a ticket broker.

Hockey and basketball start in October and November. The **San Jose Sharks**—whose logo of a shark devouring a hockey stick made their licensed hats and clothing into best-sellers before the team played its first game—skate at the **San Jose Arena**, about an hour south of San Francisco. The **Golden State Warriors** play at **The Arena at Oakland,** which reopened in 1997 after renovations that added 4,000 seats (it now seats 19,200). The newest pro sport in the Bay Area is roller hockey, played June through August; the **San Jose Rhinos** play at the San Jose Arena. (Frankly, we preferred roller derby.) Finally, if you like to play the ponies, you have a couple of choices for a sunny day at the races: **Bay Meadows** in San Mateo or **Golden Gate Fields** near Berkeley. Bay Meadows seems to be preferred by San Franciscans, who are loathe to cross the Bay Bridge for any reason, but Golden Gate Fields is a real salt-of-the-earth racetrack.

The Index

Alcazar Theater. A variety of top-quality, if not exactly new, plays are produced here.... *Tel 415/441-4042, 415/441-6655. 650 Geary St., 19 or 38 MUNI bus.*
(see p. 200)

American Conservatory Theater (ACT). The Geary Theater is home to the renowned repertory company.... *Tel 415/834-3200. Geary Theater, 415 Geary St., 5 MUNI bus.*
(see p. 199)

The Arena at Oakland. Some marketing genius decided to gentrify the image of the Oakland Coliseum Arena—presumably to make higher ticket prices for Warriors games more palatable—by changing its name to "The Arena at Oakland," but it didn't work. Locals still call it the Coliseum and fans haven't exactly been flocking to see the Warriors lately. Though it looks like a really cool spaceship hangar from the outside, it's just another generic NBA arena on the inside.... *Tel 510/569-2121, 7000 Coliseum Way (next to the Coliseum, where the A's and Raiders play), Oakland, Coliseum BART station.* **(see p. 205)**

Bay Meadows. This is a beautiful place for thoroughbred horse-racing, with picnic facilities and a playground for children.... *Tel 650/574-7223. 2600 S. Delaware St., San Mateo. Take CalTrain directly to Bay Meadows. To* *drive: Take Hwy. 101 South to the Hillsborough exit, head west, and follow signs to track. Seasons run Jan 21–March 29 and Sept 4–Nov 14. Post time 12:45, 7:15 on Fri.* **(see p. 206)**

Beach Blanket Babylon. It wouldn't be San Francisco without this totally wacky musical revue—and the gigantic, ridiculous headdresses that made it famous—at Club Fugazi, a cozy cabaret in North Beach. Reserve or buy well in advance.... *Tel 415/421-4222. Club Fugazi, 678 Green St., 15, 30, or 45 MUNI bus. Shows Wed, Thur at 8, Fri, Sat at 7 & 10, Sun 3 & 7.* **(see p. 201)**

Climate Theater. This South of Market theater features monologues, plays, political satires, and performance art.... *Tel 415/978-2345. 285 Ninth St. (near Folsom), 10, 12, 20, 50, 60, 70, or 80 MUNI bus.* **(see p. 200)**

Curran Theater. The Curran presents both warmed-over Broadway hits and Broadway-bound musicals.... *Tel 415/551-2000. 445 Geary St., 19 or 38 MUNI bus.* **(see p. 199)**

Dancers Group Studio Theater. Dance buffs are excited about this small Mission District studio.... *Tel 415/920-9181. 3252A 19th St., Studio B, 24th St. BART station.* **(see p. 203)**

Exit Theater. Closer to the mainstream than many neighborhood theaters, this small theater-district house is gaining a national reputation for avant-garde "classics".... *Tel 415/673-3847. 156 Eddy St., Civic Center BART/MUNI Metro station, 19 or 31 MUNI bus.* **(see p. 200)**

Golden Gate Fields. Across the bay in Albany (next to Berkeley), Golden Gate Fields offers thoroughbred horse racing and a view of the bay—but not at the same time: The track faces Interstate 80.... *Tel 510/526-3020. Seasons run Nov–Jan and April–June. Take shuttle or cab from N. Berkeley BART station. AC Transit (Tel 800/559-4636) runs buses direct from Transbay Terminal. To drive: cross Oakland–San Francisco Bay Bridge and take Interstate 80 east to Gilman St. exit; turn left to get to track.* **(see p. 206)**

ENTERTAINMENT | THE INDEX

Golden Gate Theater. This grand-old theater offers Broadway touring shows and revivals.... *Tel 415/551-2000. 1 Taylor St. (near Sixth and Market Sts.), Powell St. BART/MUNI Metro station, 6, 7, 8, 9, 21, or 66 MUNI bus.* **(see p. 199)**

Golden State Warriors. See The Arena at Oakland.
(see p. 205)

Intersection for the Arts. The oldest experimental arts center in the city features plays, visual arts, jazz, and readings.... *Tel 415/626-2787. 446 Valencia St., 16th St. BART/MUNI Metro station, 26 MUNI bus.*
(see p. 200)

Josie's Juice Joint and Cabaret. Local gay performers wow an eclectic crowd at this Castro District cabaret. There's virtually no parking, so take public transportation. Reservations are recommended, but get there early, because there's always a line to fill in for last-minute no-shows.... *Tel 415/861-7933. 3583 16th St. near Market, Castro St. MUNI Metro station.* **(see p. 201)**

Lorraine Hansberry Theater. Some of the most prominent African American playwrights and performers are featured at this downtown theater, which focuses on new approaches or pieces with social significance.... *Tel 415/474-8800. 620 Sutter St., Powell-Mason cable car; 2, 3, 4, or 76 MUNI bus.* **(see p. 201)**

Magic Theater. New plays by American playwrights are the main attraction at this Fort Mason theater.... *Tel 415/441-8822. Building D, Fort Mason, Marina Blvd. at Buchanan St., 28 MUNI bus.* **(see p. 201)**

Marine's Memorial Theater. Theater district home to serious drama.... *Tel 877/771-6900, 415/441-7444. 609 Sutter St., 2, 3, 4, or 76 MUNI bus.*
(see p. 200)

The Marsh. *The* place to see the latest avant-garde productions, it's hip, it's fun, it's good, and it's reasonable.... *Tel 415/641-0235. 1062 Valencia St., 24th St. BART/MUNI Metro station, 26 MUNI bus.* **(see p. 200)**

Mission Cultural Center for Latino Arts. Latino artists from many different cultures are featured at this Mission District showcase.... *Tel 415/821-1155. 2868 Mission St., 24th St. BART station.* **(see p. 201)**

Oakland A's. See Oakland Coliseum. **(see p. 205)**

Oakland Ballet. This lively young company is made up of brilliant dancers. Their performance hall, the landmark art deco Paramount Theater, is breathtaking.... *Tel 510/465-6400. 2025 Broadway, Oakland, 19th St. BART station (3 stops from San Francisco's Embarcadero station).* **(see p. 203)**

Oakland Coliseum. The Oakland A's and Oakland Raiders play here.... *For tickets to A's games, call Tickets.com (tel 415/478-BASS, 510/762-BASS, 800/225-BASS outside California); for Raiders tickets, call a ticket broker. Coliseum BART station.* **(see p. 205)**

Oakland Raiders. See Oakland Coliseum. **(see p. 205)**

Orpheum Theater. Fans of big Broadway musicals love this restored Spanish baroque theater in the theater district.... *Tel 415/551-2000. 1192 Market St., Civic Center BART/MUNI Metro station.* **(see p. 199)**

Pacific Bell Park. Most seats in the Giants' new downtown ballpark have already been sold to season-ticket holders, but general admission on seats is often available, or you can stroll along the Embarcadero and watch through the "peepholes" for free.... *For tickets to Giants games, call BASS (Tel 415/478-BASS). N. Judah (Embarcadero) trolley.* **(see p. 204)**

Phoenix II Theater. A progressive South of Market theater now located in the theater district downtown, the Phoenix presents works by local as well as world-famous playwrights.... *Tel 415/567-3005. 655 Geary St., Union Square, Powell-Mason, or Powell-Hyde cable car, 38 MUNI bus.* **(see p. 201)**

San Francisco Ballet. The city's premier classical ballet troupe performs at the Opera House. Some balcony seats are available for most performances, even without advance purchase.... *Tel 415/865-2000. 301 Van Ness Ave., Civic Center BART/MUNI Metro station.*

(see p. 202)

San Francisco 49ers. See 3Com Park. (see p. 205)

San Francisco Giants. See Pacific Bell Park. (see p. 204)

San Francisco Opera. San Franciscans have had an unconditional love affair with opera since the gold rush. You can go in a tuxedo or in blue jeans—nobody cares. The season runs from September through January and during June. Get tickets far in advance.... *Tel 415/864-3330. War Memorial Opera House, 301 Van Ness Ave., Civic Center BART/MUNI Metro station.* (see p. 203)

San Francisco Symphony. Buy tickets before you get to town, or give your hotel concierge a generous tip to do it for you as soon as you arrive. If you can't get into a regular performance, though, try to get into a dress rehearsal (cheap, casual, and intimate) and take advantage of the free tours of Davies Hall, Mon (except holidays) and Sat by appointment ($5 general admission, $3 seniors and students).... *Tel 415/864-6000, 415/552-8338. 201 Van Ness Ave., Civic Center BART/MUNI Metro station.* (see p. 202)

San Jose Arena. The Sharks haven't brought home a Stanley Cup yet, but their fans don't care. About an hour south of San Francisco.... *For tickets call Tickets.com (Tel 415/478-BASS, 510/762-BASS, 800/225-BASS outside CA); for other information, call the arena (Tel 408/287-4275). Take CalTrain from Fourth St. & Townsend St. depot to 65 Cahill station; free shuttle from station to arena. To drive: Take Hwy. 101 S. to Guadalupe Pkwy.; exit at Julian St.; take right. Follow Julian St. to Burns Ave. S., then turn left and follow signs to stadium. Free shuttle from parking lot.* (see p. 205)

San Jose Rhinos. See San Jose Arena. (see p. 205)

San Jose Sharks. See San Jose Arena. (see p. 205)

Stage Door Theater. Downtown theater specializing in come-dies, with local casts.... *No listing. 420 Mason St., Powell St. BART/MUNI Metro station.* **(see p. 200)**

Theater Artaud. Dance, theater, and multimedia productions appear at this well-run Mission District experimental the-ater.... *Tel 415/621-7797. 450 Florida St. (between 17th and Mariposa Sts.), 16th St. BART/MUNI Metro station, 12 or 33 MUNI bus.* **(see pp. 200, 203)**

Theater Rhinoceros. This Mission District company focuses in on gay and lesbian issues.... *Tel 415/861-5079. 2926 16th St., 16th St. BART/MUNI Metro station.*
(see p. 201)

Third Wave Dance House. This Mission District dance studio showcases local choreographers and ethnic tradi-tions.... *Tel 415/970-0222. 1275 Connecticut St. (at Army St.), 19 MUNI bus (cab recommended).*
(see p. 203)

3Com Park. Home to the 49ers, it's wonderfully balmy throughout the football season.... *For tickets, call Tickets.com (Tel 415/478-BASS, 510/762-BASS, 800/225-BASS outside CA) or a ticket broker. Express bus service available through MUNI (tel 415/673-MUNI). If you must drive (not recommended), take Hwy. 101 S. to sta-dium exit.* **(see p. 204)**

hotlines & other basics

Airports... Two major airports serve the city—**San Francisco International Airport (SFO)** (tel 650/876-7809; www.aiportsintl.com/sfo) and **Oakland International Airport (OAK)** (tel 510/577-4000; www.oaklandairport.com). Most travelers will use SFO, which is served by 46 major airlines and is located 15 miles south of downtown San Francisco (Highway 101 or 280). Fares to either airport are usually identical, so if a flight to SFO is sold out, there may still be available seats on flights to the lesser-known stepsister, OAK, situated within a few minutes of the Coliseum BART stop (four stops from San Francisco's Financial District).

Airport transportation to the city... Super-cheap public transport is available from the airport to downtown via **SamTrans** (tel 800/660-4287; www.samtrans.com); from the International terminal on the upper level or the United Airlines terminal, catch the KX express bus for just $3 (you are allowed only one carry-on bag) or the 292 bus for $1.10 into the city, $2.20 outbound (bring as much baggage as you like). The KX express takes about 30 minutes; the 292 takes about an hour. A taxi ride to the city center costs about $30 including tip and usually takes about 20–30 minutes, depending on traffic. Shuttle vans that carry up to six passengers offer door-to-door service for around $10 to most hotels and take 20–30 minutes; they're easy to catch at the airport, but reservations are recommended for your return trip from the city to the airport. Some of the most popular shuttles are **American Airporter Shuttle** (tel 415/546-6689); **Bay Shuttle** (tel 415/564-3400); **Door-to-Door Airport Express** (tel 415/775-5121); **Lorrie's Airport Shuttle** (tel 415/334-9000); **Quake City Shuttle** (tel 415/255-4899); **Super Shuttle** (tel 415/558-8500, 650/558-8500, or 800/BLUEVAN, www.supershuttle.com); and **Yellow Airport Shuttle** (tel 415/282-7433). The **SFO Airporter** (tel 415/641-3100) is an express bus that offers door-to-door service to most major hotels for $12; no reservations are required.

All-night pharmacies... Got that itchy, sneezy, whatever-else-it-is, can't-sleep thing happening? Worse yet, did you just drop your last estrogen pill down the drain? Not to worry. **Walgreens 24-Hour Prescription Service** (tel 415/861-3136, 498 Castro St.; tel 415/931-6417, 3201 Divisadero St.) is there to help.

Babysitters... First ask the concierge if your hotel offers child-care service. Otherwise, try an agency that is a member of the San Francisco Convention and Visitors Bureau, such as **American Childcare Service** (tel 415/285-2300), which offers private in-room service at your hotel, excursions arranged for children 12 and older, and is fully licensed, bonded, and insured.

BART... Bay Area Rapid Transit (BART) is essentially a commuter railway that links neighboring communities with San Francisco. There are eight stations in the city itself. Fares depend on the distance of the ride, but for a special $4.05 excursion fare, you can ride the entire system as far as you want, in any direction you want, as long as you exit the system at the same station you entered. All tickets are dispensed from machines at the stations. Contact its website at www.bart.gov.

Buses... San Francisco Municipal Railway (MUNI) buses are marked on the front with the number of the line and the destination. Fare is $1 for adults, 35¢ for children and seniors. To find out which bus to take to get where you want to go, call 415/673-MUNI (www.sfmuni.com). Official MUNI route maps are available throughout the city at newsstands and many other stores for $2.

Cable cars... There are three cable-car routes: The Powell-Hyde line begins at Powell and Market streets and ends at Victorian Park near the Maritime Museum and Aquatic Park; the Powell-Mason line also begins at Powell and Market streets, but it ends at Bay and Taylor streets near Fisherman's Wharf; the California Street line starts at California and Market streets and ends at Van Ness Avenue. Fare is $2.

Car rentals... Suit yourself—pick up a tiny little bread box on wheels from Enterprise Rent-A-Car at the airport for less than $20 a day, with unlimited free mileage; or cruise through your vacation in a Jaguar XK8 or Corvette convertible from Sunbelt Sports Cars for $250 a day. Or settle for something in between—economy cars with unlimited mileage tend to rent for around $30–$40 a day, while a zippy convertible like a Mazda Miata will set you back about $80 a day. Here are several San Francisco rental companies (most have more than one location): **Alamo Rent-A-Car** (tel 415/882-9440, 687 Folsom St.); **Avis Rent-A-Car** (tel 800/331-1212 or 415/885-5011, 675 Post St.); **Bay Area Rentals, Cars, Trucks and Vans** (tel 415/621-8989, 229 Seventh St.); **Budget Rent-A-Car** (tel. 800/601-5385 or 415/292-8400, 321 Mason St.); **Dollar Rent-A-Car** (tel 800/800-4000, 1831 Bayshore Hwy., Burlingame, San Francisco International Airport); **Enterprise Rent-A-Car** (tel 800/RENTACAR or 415/441-3369, 1133 Van Ness Ave.); **Hertz Rent-A-Car** (tel 800/654-3131 or 415/771-2200, 433 Mason St.); **Reliable Rent-A-Car** (tel 415/928-4414, 349 Mason St.); **Thrifty Car Rental** (tel 800/367-2277 or 415/788-8111, 520 Mason St.).

Cash advances, check cashing, and ATM cards... If you aren't having any luck at automated teller machines and want to ask a human teller for a cash advance against your credit card, try calling **Bank of America** (tel 415/622-2452). **American Express** has a downtown office with full financial services, including personal-check cashing: (tel 415/536-2600, 455 Market St.). To find the nearest ATM that will accept your **Cirrus Network** card, call 800/424-7787; for **Plus System**, call 800/843-7587.

Chauffeurs... Can't resist a man in uniform? Sometimes you've just got to lounge in the back of a long, black limousine with a chauffeur at the wheel. If the need arises while you're in San Francisco, call **WeDriveU, Inc.** (tel 800/773-7483). The company name may be a bit tacky, but what do you want for borrowed luxury?

Climate... Everybody knows that Mark Twain supposedly said the coldest winter he ever spent was summer in San Francisco. It's true that July can be downright chilly, but the truth is that the city is rarely—if ever— what a New England Yankee would call cold, or what a New Orleans belle would call hot. In fact, the weather is predictably unpredictable. A sunny morning can turn into a chilly afternoon, just as a thick morning fog often gives way to a gorgeous sun-drenched day. The standard pitch is that temperatures don't drop below 40°F (5°C) or rise above 70°F (21°C), but don't believe it. Every year there are many 80° days that are sworn to be the exception; there's just no predicting when they might occur. In general, September and October are the warmest months, and May through September are the driest. No matter when you visit, be sure to dress in layers. Whatever you expect the weather to be, it will almost certainly be otherwise— at least part of the time.

Concierges... If you're not staying at a hotel that offers the services of a resident concierge and you want personalized travel planning, shopping excursions, entertainment, ticket purchasing, or any other special arrangements, enlist your own private concierge— after you arrive or while you're still planning your vacation. Try **Ideas Unlimited/Unlimited Ideas** (tel 800/900-4884 or 415/668-7089), **Instead of You, Inc.** (tel 800/446-7832), or **Leisure Resources** (tel 800/758-5479).

Convention center... The elegant—and extremely popular—**Moscone Center** (tel 415/974-4000, 747 Howard St.) was named in memory of San Francisco's well-liked mayor who was slain—along with the city's first openly gay elected official, Harvey Milk—by a man who convinced a jury he could not be held responsible because he had eaten too many Twinkies and it made him insane. It was a bitter tragedy for San Franciscans, but the Moscone Center is a fitting tribute in its unparalleled success—it is one of the most popular convention sites in the country, despite all the bad press about the city's earthquakes and frigid summer weather.

Dentists... The San Francisco Convention and Visitors Bureau recommends **San Francisco Dental Office** for 24-hour emergency service (tel 415/777-5115, 131 Steuart St., Suite 323, between Mission and Howard Sts.; Non-emergency hours: Mon, Tues, and Fri 8–4:30; Wed–Thur 10:30–7; closed Sat and Sun).

Doctors... If you have a serious emergency, you should go directly to a hospital emergency room, but for other medical needs, try **Traveler Medical Group** (tel 415/981-1102), a 24-hour, multilingual medical staff of internal-medicine physicians who will make "house calls" to your hotel. No appointments are necessary at **Physician Access Medical Center** (tel 415/397-2881, 26 California St.). Same-day appointments can be made at **Downtown Medical** (tel 415/362-7177, 450 Sutter St., Suite 1723), whose doctors are familiar with all travel-related medical conditions.

Driving around... Lots of people drive in the city, and as a rule they're much more courteous than in New York City or Paris or Rome. The city is compact, but can be a bit confusing, so if you're going to drive be sure to get a map. Your driver's license from any other state (and most Western nations) is valid in California for a year, but there are a few things you should know about local safety precautions and laws. Remember, San Francisco is a city of hills (43, to be exact), and since you probably don't want your car to roll down one while you're not in it, there's only one sure bet: **Curb your wheels**. Turn the front tires toward the street when you're parked facing uphill and toward the curb when you're parked facing downhill. This is not just a good idea, it's the law in San Francisco. **Know what the curb colors mean: Red** means no stopping or parking; **yellow** means all commercial vehicles may stop for up to a half-hour; **yellow-and-black** means only commercial trucks may stop for up to a half-hour; **green-yellow-and-black** is a taxi zone; **blue** is for cars with California disabled placards; **green** means all vehicles may stop for up to 10 minutes; **white** means all vehicles are limited to a 5-minute stop while the adjacent business is still open. **Towaway zones**: Nobody loves to tow cars more than San Francisco's Finest. It's big money for the city (almost 30% of all parking tickets issued in the state are issued in San Francisco), and the odds are always against you if you park illegally. You'll shell out a minimum of $20 for the most minor parking violation, plus another $100 for towing, plus storage fees. If you park in a disabled zone, the violation alone will cost $250 to $275, not to mention the towing fees and hassle of getting the car back.

Emergencies... Like anywhere else, **call 911**, but don't be surprised if you get put on hold. It's always best to try to stay out of dangerous areas and situations to begin with. Other emergency/information numbers: **Ambulance** (tel 415/931-3900); **Poison Control Center** (tel 415/502-6000, 800/876-4766); and **Suicide Prevention** (tel 415/781-0500).

Events hotline... Call the **Visitor Information Center** 24 hours a day for a recorded message listing San Francisco's events and activities in five different languages: English (tel 415/283-0176); French (tel 415/283-0172); Italian (tel 415/283-0171); Spanish (tel 415/283-0175); Japanese (tel 415/283-0174); and German (tel 415/283-0173).

Ferries... Several ferries connect San Francisco with communities around the bay. Be sure to call for schedule information. The **Blue & Gold Fleet** (tel 415/705-5555) provides daily round-trip service from the Ferry Building and Pier 39 to Oakland, Alameda, and Vallejo. Fare to Oakland or Alameda is $5, $2.25 for children, $3 for seniors; to Vallejo, $9.50, $4.50 for children and seniors. **Golden Gate Ferries** (tel 415/923-2000, TDD 415/257-4554) serve Sausalito and Larkspur from the Ferry Building. Fare is $5.30, $4 for children, $2.65 for seniors; weekdays to Larkspur, $3.10, $2.05 for children, $1.35 for seniors. **Harbor Bay Maritime Ferry** (tel 510/769-5500) goes to Harbor Bay Island in Alameda from the Ferry Building. Fare is $4, $2 for children, $3 for seniors. The **Red & White Fleet** (tel 415/673-2900, 887/855-5506) offers bay cruises and land tours. One-hour Golden Gate Bay cruises cost $18, $14 for ages 12–18, $10 for children 5–11 and seniors; the price includes audio narration from a selection of six languages. Motorcoach tours of San Francisco, Muir Woods, the Napa/Sonoma wine country, Monterey/Carmel, and Yosemite depart daily.

Festivals and special events... From the crowning of Japantown's Cherry Blossom Queen and the Gay Pride Parade of self-styled queens to Chinese New Year and *Dia de los Muertos* (Day of the Dead), San Francisco's extraordinary diversity is celebrated year-round in one festival after another. A complete monthly listing is published in the *Bay City Guide*, free at information racks in the airports and at most hotels. Here is a brief sample of some of the major events:

January: **Sports and Boat Show** (tel 415/931-2500), Cow Palace; nine days. **Tet Festival** (tel 415/885-2743), Vietnamese New Year, held at Larkin and O'Farrell streets.

February: **Chinese New Year** (tel 415/391-9680) can be in late January or early February, depending on the lunar calendar; climaxes with giant parade down Chinatown's Grant Avenue. **Russian Festival** (tel 415/921-7631), three-day celebration around Sutter and Divisadero streets.

March: **St. Patrick's Day Parade** (tel 415/731-0924) starts at Market and 2nd streets and goes past City Hall.

April: **International Film Festival**, one of the most popular film festivals in America (tel 415/931-FILM; Kabuki 8 Cinemas, Fillmore and Post Sts., www.sfift.org). **Cherry Blossom Festival** (tel 415/562-2313), held in Japantown and Golden Gate Park's Japanese Tea Garden, offering traditional arts, music, theater, and food booths.

May: **Bay to Breakers** (tel 808-5000, ext. 2222), a kooky-costume footrace across town from the Embarcadero (on the bay) to the ocean. **Black and White Ball** (tel 415/864-6000), a flashy fundraiser held in odd-numbered years to benefit the San Francisco Symphony; Civic Center is closed off for this all-night party-hop that attracts the city's biggest celebrities and those who are willing to pay $185 apiece to rub shoulders with them. **Carnaval** (tel 415/826-1401), a week-long fiesta in the Mission District, leading up to a parade that ends up on 14th Street (near Harrison Street) with a huge samba party. **Cinco de Mayo** (tel 415/826-1401), two-day fiesta; parade runs from 24th and Mission streets to Civic Center Plaza.

June: **Lesbian/Gay/Bisexual/Transgender Freedom Day Parade** (tel 415/864-3733, www.sfpride.org), a celebration of gay pride with floats and groups from the Sisters of Perpetual Indulgence to Dykes on Bikes. **Stern**

Grove Midsummer Music Festival (tel 415/252-6252, www.sterngrove.org), a series of free 2pm Sunday concerts held at 19th Avenue and Sloat Boulevard, featuring local performers, from the opera and symphony to jazz and ballet.

July: **San Francisco Chronicle Marathon** (tel 800/698-8699, www.chroniclemarathon.com), mid-month. **Jewish Film Festival** (tel 415/621-0556, held at Castro Theater and Wheeler Auditorium, Berkeley), the world's largest Jewish film festival; three weeks.

September: **San Francisco Shakespeare Festival** (tel 415/422-2222), free performances in Golden Gate Park run through October. **Blues Festival** (schedule, tel 415/979-5588; www.sfblues.com), outdoors at Fort Mason; two days. **Opera in the Park** (tel 415/861-4008), a free opera in Golden Gate Park kicks off the San Francisco Opera's fall season.

November: *Dia de los Muertos* **(Day of the Dead)**, a Mexican fiesta and parade in the Mission District designed to honor the dead and to be so much fun it entices their spirits to return for the party. *The Nutcracker* (tel 415/865-2000, 415/776-1999, San Francisco Ballet box office) and **Sing-It-Yourself Messiah** (tel 415/864-6000, Louise M. Davies Symphony Hall box office) are extremely popular holiday traditions that are sold out far in advance.

Gay and lesbian resources... The lesbian and gay communities in the Bay Area are very well organized and have countless resources at their disposal. The *Bay Area Reporter* is the best-known gay publication, with complete listings of organizations and events (www.ebar.com). Some useful websites include the **Lavender Pages** (www.lavenderpages.com), **Amazon Online** (www.amazon.org), Q San Francisco (www.qsanfrancisco.com), and **Frontiers** (www.frontiersweb.com/sfcurrent). All are distributed at bars, bookstores, cafes, and stores around the city. The **Pacific Center for Human Growth** (tel 510/548-8283) is in Berkeley. **Electric City Network** is a gay television show on cable channel 53, Fri 10:30pm. **Lavender Lounge** is a gay variety show, Tues 10pm, cable channel 47. **Fruit Punch** is a long-running gay radio show (since 1973), Wed 7pm, KPFA 94.1 FM and KPFB 89.3 FM; **Hibernia Beach** is a gay radio talk show, Sun 7am,

KITS 105.3 FM. The **Deaf Gay and Lesbian Center** (tel 800/735-2922 for Cal Relay voice callers) provides news and updates on community events. The **Names Project** (tel 415/882-5500) AIDS memorial quilt consists of more than 26,000 panels.

Liquor laws... Packaged alcoholic beverages are sold at liquor, grocery, and some drugstores 6am–2pm daily. Most bars and restaurants are licensed to sell all alcoholic beverages during those same hours, but some have only beer-and-wine licenses. No alcohol may be sold 2am–6am. Legal drinking age is 21; proof of age is required.

MUNI Metro streetcars... There are five streetcar lines that operate underground downtown and on the streets in the neighborhoods. Fares are the same as for buses— $1 adults, 35¢ for children and senior citizens.

Newspapers... There are more than 30 foreign-language publications in the Bay Area, not to mention the sex tabloids, business and professional journals, entertainment publications, and dozens of others. The two major English-language dailies are the *Chronicle* (www.sfgate.com) and the *Examiner* (www.examiner.com), which combine for a single paper on Sunday. Local weekly newspapers, such as the *Bay Guardian* (www.sfbayguardian.com) and *SF Weekly* are free, and have better entertainment listings than the dailies.

Parking garages... You can spend a fortune to leave your car for a half-hour or a pittance to park it overnight, depending upon the garage. City-run garages tend to be cheaper than those privately owned, but you should call in advance to check rates and availability, if possible. The best deals in town used to be the **Sutter-Stockton and Ellis-O'Farrell garages**, where you could leave your car overnight for just $3, but now that'll cost you a cool $25. Other garages: **Chinatown** (tel 415/956-8106, 651 California St.; tel 415/982-6353, 733 Kearny St.); **Civic Center** (tel 415/863-1537, 355 McAllister St.; tel 415/626-4484, 370 Grove St.); **Downtown** (tel 415/982-8522, 833 Mission St.; tel 415/771-1400 ask for garage, Mason and Ellis Sts.; tel 415/986-4800, Ellis-O'Farrell, 123 O'Farrell St.; tel 415/982-8370, Sutter-Stockton; tel 415/397-0631, 333 Post St.); **Embarcadero Center** (tel 415/433-4722, 250 Clay St.); **Fisherman's Wharf** (tel

415/673-5197, 655 Beach St., at Hyde St.); **Japan Center** (tel 415/567-4573, 1660 Geary Blvd.); **Mission District** (tel 415/567-7357, 90 Bartlett St., near 21st St.); **Moscone Center/Yerba Buena Gardens** (tel 415/777-2782, 255 3rd St.; tel 415/543-4533, Museum Parc, Third and Folsom Sts.); **North Beach** (tel 415/558-9147, 766 Vallejo St.); **Union Street** (tel 415/563-9820, 1910 Laguna St.; tel 415/495-3772, 2055 Lombard St.); **Van Ness** (tel 415/567-9147, 1230 Polk St.).

Phone facts... The area code for San Francisco is 415. As is the case with most big metropolitan areas, though, the number of area codes in San Francisco is expanding with the population and use of the Internet and other digital services. For now, dial 1-510 before numbers in Berkeley, Oakland, Richmond, and most of Alameda County; dial 1-925 for numbers in Walnut Creek, Concord, and most of Contra Costa County; dial 1-650 for numbers on the Peninsula; and dial 1-408 for numbers in San Jose and Santa Cruz. When in doubt, dial the operator. Local calls are free on private phones, 35¢ in a pay phone. For directory assistance, dial 411. **TDD users**: California Relay Service relays calls between a TDD caller and any other phone in the United States and allows people without TDD to call TDD users. It is a free, 24-hour service, 365 days a year. All calls placed through California Relay are billed at discounted Sprint rates. To use the service, call 800/735-2929 if you have a TDD, or 800/735-2922 if you don't have a TDD.

Taxis... It's fairly easy to hail a cab on major thoroughfares, especially in tourist areas, but if you're on a tight schedule, it's best to phone in advance for door-to-door service (the wait is usually 5–15 minutes during the day, occasionally up to a half-hour during rush hour or on busy weekend nights). There are more than 40 taxi companies listed in the Yellow Pages, but the most commonly used are: **Yellow Cab** (tel 415/626-2345); **De Soto** (tel 415/970-1300); **Luxor** (tel 415/282-4141); and **Veteran's** (tel 415/552-1300). The fare is the same in every cab (regulated by the city): $2.50 plus 40 cents for every $\frac{1}{6}$ mile. Since the city is no more than 7 miles in any given direction, most cab rides are around $5 to $10 plus tip (15 percent is customary).

Time... For the correct time, call 767-8900 from the 415, 510, 650, or 925 area codes.

Tipping... Gratuities are not included in restaurant or bar checks. Most guides suggest 15 percent of the total amount as a decent tip, but 20 percent has become more commonly accepted at restaurants. Taxi drivers should be tipped around 15 percent; skycaps and bellpersons should get at least $1 per bag each time they carry it.

Visitor information center... The **San Francisco Visitor Information Center** (tel 415/283-0177, TDD 415/392-0328; open 9–5, Sat, Sun and holidays until 3) is located at Benjamin Swig Pavilion on the lower level of Hallidie Plaza at Market and Powell streets. The center's neighborhood-walking-tour leaflets are really unbeatable. When you arrive, it's definitely worth a stop here to help plan your adventures.